10 0136578 1

D0708115

THE MUSICIAN'S HANDBOOK

Edited by Trevor Ford

Third Edition

(with index)

RHINEGOLD PUBLISHING LIMITED
241 SHAFTESBURY AVENUE
LONDON WC2H 8EH
TELEPHONE 0171 333 1721
FAX 0171 333 1769

First published 1996 in Great Britain by
Rhinegold Publishing Ltd, 241 Shaftesbury Avenue,
London WC2H 8EH, Great Britain.

British Library Cataloguing in Publication Data. A catalogue record for this book
is available from the British Library.

Rhinegold Publishing Ltd has used its best efforts in collecting and preparing material
for inclusion in *The Musician's Handbook*. It does not assume, and hereby disclaims
any liability to any party for loss or damage caused by errors or omissions in *The
Musician's Handbook*, whether such errors and omissions result from negligence,
accident or any other cause.

ISBN 0-946890-67-6

Printed in Great Britain by Biddles Ltd, Guildford, Surrey.

1001365781

CONTENTS

SECTION 3 – SAFEGUARDING YOUR FUTURE

SECTION 4 – THE LEGAL SIDE

SECTION 5 – A BUYER'S GUIDE TO FINANCIAL SERVICES

Christine Norman

EDITOR'S PREFACE

In the ten years since the appearance of its first edition, **The Musician's Handbook** has established itself as the one essential source of advice for professional musicians. No other single publication covers such a broad range of subjects, and few reference books can boast such a star-studded cast of contributors. Whether you are a first-year music student or a seasoned professional, there is so much valuable information within the pages of this book that you may well wonder how you ever managed without it.

The first edition of **The Musician's Handbook** offered its readers a generous twenty-seven chapters: the third edition comprises forty-one. This rapid expansion does not imply that there were omissions in the first edition, but rather emphasises the fact that the range of opportunities available to the professional musician has grown considerably over the past decade. In addition, it must be said that success within an ever more competitive profession requires a wider range of skills, and the Handbook offers advice in areas which might well not have been considered relevant ten years ago.

Readers needing guidance on career options will find four new chapters in the first section of this book. Gone are the days of the all-powerful and petulant maestro, and aspiring conductors (and even some of their well-established colleagues) will find a cornucopia of common-sense advice in Colin Metters' chapter. David Nevens unravels the complex structure of the education system, and Helen Tyler's excellent chapter on music therapy may well tempt readers to consider becoming involved in this immensely rewarding work. Lieutenant-Colonel C.J. Ross, the Army's Principal Director of Music, explodes a number of myths about life in the Services, and emphasises the versatility required of today's military musicians. We also welcome as new contributors to this section Dominic McGonigal, Geraldine Allen and John Ludlow, who breathe new life into old subjects.

In a profession as unstructured as ours, few musicians can progress very far without some advice on how best to present themselves to those who hold the keys to success. The nine chapters of the Handbook's second section guide the reader through the various stages involved in building a career, and include a valuable new contribution on audition technique from Anthony Legge, Head of Music at English National Opera and author of *The Art of Auditioning*. Anne Rushton of Collins Classics and John Bickley of Magenta Music International have written new chapters on record companies and artists' managers, and Julia Seddon gives excellent advice to those faced with the daunting task of investing in an expensive instrument.

In these days, when state support for the arts is woefully lacking, casualties are inevitable. Fortunately, a number of organisations exist to provide support for musicians, and the third section of **The Musician's Handbook** explains what some of them can offer. A new chapter by Maggie Gibb, Secretary of the Royal Society of Musicians of Great Britain, provides information about charities for professional musicians, and it is reassuring to know that, for those who fall on hard times, help is always available. Self-help is, of course, equally essential, and all readers would do well to read the chapters on health and insurance, updated from the second edition by their respective (and respected) authors. Finally in this section, for those faced with a premature end to their careers, a chapter on the legal rights of musicians who are threatened with dismissal, made redundant, or who find themselves unemployed, is required reading.

Many readers will find the fourth section of the Handbook the most useful – after all, almost all musicians will have an interest in income tax and national insurance legislation, even if they are subjects which do little to inspire. The law affecting other relevant topics has grown more complex, especially as attempts are made to harmonise our legal system with that of the European Community, and the chapters on VAT, the law of contract, copyright and charity legislation will be invaluable to those seeking a guide through the legal maze.

Finally, for those who have enjoyed some success and who are interested in preserving its fruits, both for themselves and for their dependants and descendants, the final section of the Handbook explores the financial marketplace and examines the products on offer. Christine Norman's new chapter on financial advisers will arm the unwary against the unsolicited caller with the once-only offer.

As in earlier editions of **The Musician's Handbook**, all our writers have, as far as possible, avoided giving information which is likely to go out of date. Readers needing comprehensive lists of addresses and telephone numbers, or current information on examination syllabuses or college entry requirements, should consult the *British and International Music Yearbook* and the *Music Education Yearbook,* which should be regarded as essential companions to this Handbook. For those who wish to keep themselves fully in touch with the music scene, *Classical Music, Music Teacher, The Singer, Classical Piano* and *Early Music Today* exist to provide regular news and comment on our ever-changing profession. All are available from Rhinegold Publishing.

My thanks go to my wife, Marianne Barton, former editor of the *British Music Yearbook,* the *British Music Education Yearbook* and *Music Teacher,* whose idea this Handbook was in the first place, and to Keith Diggle and Richard Thomas of Rhinegold Publishing, without whom the music profession would still be waiting for its publication.

Trevor Ford
May 1996

Rhinegold Publishing Ltd
241 Shaftesbury Avenue
London WC2H 8EH

FOREWORD TO THE FIRST EDITION

SIR DAVID WILLCOCKS CBE MC

There has for many years been a need for a single book, containing within its covers factual information about, and practical advice concerning, almost every aspect of the musical profession. That need has at last been met by **The Musician's Handbook**, which contains 27 chapters written by men and women of wide experience in their various fields.

To survive, let alone prosper, in an increasingly competitive world, a musician requires – in addition to talent, dedication, good health, and an element of good fortune – understanding of the many career opportunities, a thorough knowledge of the workings of the musical profession, and some business acumen. All these matters are fully discussed in lively fashion in this book.

The Musician's Handbook will, therefore, be of the greatest value to performers and teachers at all levels, to agents and concert promoters and to all those engaged in the many forms of musical administration. But it will also be of considerable interest to those who, though not in the musical profession themselves, derive enjoyment from listening to music in the concert hall, on records, or via television and radio, and who are thus the consumer of the musicians' product.

Many godparents present a bible to their godchildren at baptism or confirmation. **The Musician's Handbook** may well become the book to be presented to everyone entering the musical profession.

David Willcocks
Cambridge
May 1986

SECTION 1

OPTIONS FOR THE PROFESSIONAL MUSICIAN

A KALEIDOSCOPE OF OPPORTUNITIES

DOMINIC McGONIGAL

Dominic McGonigal is the Administrator at the Incorporated Society of Musicians responsible for performers & composers, and for marketing & public relations. In addition, he is Musical Director of Opera Spezzata, W11 Children's Opera, Cori Spezzati, Stoneleigh Choral Society and Singers of St Cecilia, and a Director of the National Federation of Music Societies. He has previously worked for festivals, local authorities and regional arts associations, promoting, marketing, researching and fundraising for music and the other arts.

'I do play the violin, but not well enough to hold a steady job – just a series of one night stands.' What hope is there for the rest of us if even Isaac Stern can't get regular employment! He illustrates two common misconceptions about the music profession: those outside it often assume that it is impossible to make a living as a musician, that musicians have 'day jobs' and simply perform or compose for amusement. Conversely, some music students believe that their education is leading inevitably to 'a place in the profession'; having spent years training to the highest level to do a job, they expect there to be a job for them to do.

Of course, neither of these views is accurate. There are many thousands of people earning a living from music: not necessarily earning vast sums of money, but devoting a considerable amount of time and energy to pursuing their chosen career. But these musicians rarely occupy positions which will automatically result in vacancies when they move on. The music profession is fluid: it grows and contracts according to demand, a demand which is often generated by the music business itself. For example, the interest in early music was spawned by a few enterprising conductors and performers who 'sold' enthusiasm for a type of music which had long been neglected.

There have always been musicians who have created their own cult followings, or who have exploited a particular trend. Recently, composers such as Tavener, Górecki and Pärt have been swept into popularity on the back of a wave of spirituality. Others have to be more responsive: as the number of film sessions fell in the 1980s, session musicians had to look to alternative sources of work. Similarly, some piano teachers, observing that fewer children want to learn their instrument, have begun to specialise in teaching adults.

The music profession is always changing, but technological and political factors are, perhaps, creating change at a greater pace than ever before. Audiences expect higher standards of performance as they are exposed to more and more music through radio, television, compact discs and, soon, the Internet. Legislation has exposed the provision of instrumental services to market forces, and pressures on subsidies have endangered the viability of orchestras and opera houses.

The ability to cope in this fluid environment is one of the hallmarks of the successful professional musician. Versatility is a valuable asset. Whatever the opportunities are now, they will be different in ten years time!

Managers and administrators in the music business have to be flexible, too. Often overstretched, with minimal resources, they have to fulfil a multitude of functions and adapt to a constantly changing environment.

One characteristic that has remained unchanged, and is likely to remain so, is that the music business is made up of individuals, often in business on their own account as freelance musicians, administrators or consultants. Even the high-profile companies are dominated by one or two individuals. These individuals operate within their own networks, overlapping and linked with all the other networks that make up the music profession.

This chapter explores the world which these individuals inhabit, and gives some indication of the options open to the many who want to become a part of it, and to others who may be contemplating a change within it. It is only an overview of the business; later chapters give more detailed advice on how to be successful within each sector.

Composers

At the beginning of the creative process are the composers. They divide roughly into three groups – the 'serious' composers, the 'media' composers, and the songwriters (and, as in every other area of the business, the groups overlap).

There are several hundred 'serious' composers trying to make their mark in the concert field. For the favoured few, commissions, often funded by the Arts Councils, Regional Arts Boards and trust funds, provide an income while the composers wait for the royalty payments to trickle in. Building up sufficient repertoire, with enough performances, broadcasts and recordings, to make a living out of royalty payments takes a long time, and few achieve it.

The 'media' composers tend to work to commission only, writing incidental music for radio, films, commercials and corporate videos. The commissions are very demanding: music is usually the last thing that a producer thinks about and, with the programme or film in the final stages of editing and due for delivery in a few weeks' (or even days') time, the composer has to write to order, adapting his material to the last millisecond to fit around the pictures. Very few composers are able to meet these technical demands.

Conversely, there are many thousands of songwriters, eagerly working on what they hope will be the next No. 1 chart success. Skill in producing something with a familiar ring, yet distinctive and fresh, is only one ingredient in the recipe for success. Luck, contacts and personality are all equally important.

Working with the composers are the arrangers and orchestrators, who may find themselves preparing the score for a new musical one day, and transcribing the latest hit tune for piano and clarinet choir the next.

Performers

Music only comes to life when it is performed. Performers are an essential part of the process of producing music, even though a single performance can be recorded and broadcast to millions by radio, and then be available on CD for as long as the recording remains in the catalogue. Fees and royalties from the use of recordings are becoming an increasingly important part of a performer's income.

Most professional instrumentalists undertake orchestral or session work. There are about twenty full-time orchestras, and a few hundred ad hoc orchestras engaging musicians on a session basis as and when they have work. Some of these ad hoc orchestras are very active. In general, the members of a full-time orchestra will be salaried employees, although a seat may remain vacant for several months while the orchestra seeks the right person to fill it. Deputies and extras are contracted on a freelance basis to fill these vacant seats, to cover for absent players, or to expand the orchestra for particular works. The extras and deputies are drawn from a pool of freelance players, based mainly in and around London. For freelance orchestral musicians, however, the most lucrative work is provided by recording sessions for commercials and film sound-tracks.

Orchestras usually appoint an orchestral manager (or fixer) to engage the freelance players. Fixers, who are often players themselves, also book musicians for shows and commercial recording sessions.

In addition to orchestral and session work, instrumentalists may perform chamber music, undertake solo engagements, or be involved in educational work. A very successful string quartet can generate enough engagements to enable its members to devote themselves entirely to chamber music, and a few musicians spend the bulk of their time presenting educational workshops and performances for children.

Soloists

It takes a number of years to build up enough contacts to work regularly as a freelance orchestral musician. Becoming established as a solo performer can take far longer, simply because so many more people need to be convinced that you have something special to offer. Emerging from college, with the ability to get your fingers around every awkward corner in your instrument's repertoire, is not enough (although it is a good start!). You must be able to engage your audience (and your fellow musicians), you have to have a musical quality which people find attractive – and you have to be able to exploit your gift. Such qualities are rare, and so are successful soloists.

For the aspiring soloist, there is the circuit of competitions, awards, and auditions for bursaries and scholarships, invariably aimed at the younger musician. If you attract enough attention on this circuit, there will be concert agents eager to sign you up as the next *wunderkind,* but agents are only interested if you are going to bring in enough work to make their commission worth their time. You will need a full, or rapidly filling, diary before you can hope to impress them.

Singers

Singers usually spend longer at a conservatoire than instrumentalists, and may work for a year or two on the choral network before being able to pick up enough solo work to earn a decent living. Because the voice takes time to mature, singers are not usually ready for operatic roles or major oratorio engagements until their late twenties or early thirties.

The singers' world revolves around opera houses, the largest employers of singers. The Royal Opera House, English National Opera, Welsh National Opera, Opera North and Scottish Opera have full-time choruses providing work for regulars, extras and deputies, as well as opportunities for outstanding singers to take minor roles and understudy. The other route into opera is by way of the growing number of smaller opera companies, which tend to engage younger singers.

Outside the opera houses, only one choir, the BBC Singers, offers a full-time contract. The handful of other professional choirs, usually specialising in early or contemporary repertoire, contract singers on a freelance basis. Like the orchestras, professional choirs and opera choruses are booked by fixers, who tend to stick to their lists of tried and trusted singers.

The oratorio circuit provides regular work for a few singers, and young singers can often obtain engagements with the smaller choral societies. There are fewer opportunities for solo recitals, simply because they attract smaller audiences. Lieder is more popular in recorded format, especially when performed by a singer who is attracting attention.

Many singers start (and sometimes continue) their careers in cathedrals, or in one of the London churches where a professional vocal quartet or octet is employed. For the more versatile vocalists, there are the West End musicals and commercial session work, lucrative but sporadic.

Music education

The largest area of employment for musicians is teaching – in schools, in conservatoires, in universities and privately. The National Curriculum requires that every child learns music between the ages of five and fourteen, and there are several thousand music teachers in secondary schools. In the primary sector, teachers train as generalists, and only a few choose music as their speciality. The music specialists will often take responsibility for overseeing the music curriculum for the rest of the school, offering support to staff with less musical ability. In some primary schools, music teaching and support is supplied by a peripatetic primary music specialist who visits a number of schools each week.

Within the state sector in England and Wales, all teachers have to obtain Qualified Teacher Status (with a BEd, PGCE, or similar qualification). In Scotland, teachers have to be recognised by the General Teaching Council.

There is a growing demand for instrumental teaching in schools, even though the service is no longer free in many parts of the country. Some Local Education Authorities still run their own instrumental services. In other areas, schools engage peripatetic teachers either directly or through a music services agency. The music services agencies have panels of teachers who teach regularly but not necessarily full time.

The ten conservatoires are mostly staffed by performers or ex-performers who may be full- or part-time. The seventy-odd university music departments are staffed by academic musicians who invariably have a second degree in music.

Private teachers fall broadly into two types – those with a full-time teaching practice, and those who take on a few pupils alongside a career as a performer. Piano is still the most popular instrument to learn, but there is an increasing demand for tuition on other instruments and in singing. Private teachers have traditionally worked on their own, in isolation from their colleagues elsewhere in the profession. However, many are now becoming involved with local schools, performing (with composing and listening) being one of the key elements in the National Music Curriculum.

Music therapy

A relatively recent application of music is as therapy for physically and mentally disabled people, and for the mentally ill. Music therapists work in hospitals, special schools, day centres, Adult Training Centres and rehabilitation centres. In many cases, music is a more powerful means of communication than speech, enabling disabled people to express themselves and to release their emotions. There is a growing demand for music therapists, as the value of their work has become recognised and as more part-time posts are created.

Arts management

Concert agents, concert halls, local authority promoters, festivals and Regional Arts Boards all fall within the broad term 'arts management'. Some organisations specialise in music; in others, music is just one art form competing with several others for time, space and money. Although most arts administrators are full-time employees, there is a fair amount of movement of staff between organisations.

Two of the most popular areas of arts management are orchestras and concert agencies. Orchestras are managed by very small teams: even the full-time orchestras employ only about fifteen staff, responsible for securing engagements, booking soloists and conductors, promoting concerts, planning the orchestra's schedule, organising tours, and handling payments for musicians and others. In some freelance orchestras, all of this is done by just one or two people.

Agencies, likewise, are small, employing only a handful of people to manage the diaries, negotiate fees, sort out contractual details, and arrange travel and accommodation for their artists. They also have to maintain an active network of contacts among promoters here and abroad to enable them to put their artists forward at every opportunity.

There are, however, many other areas of work within the broad category of arts management, including concert halls, festivals, opera and ballet companies, associations, funding agencies and local authorities. Even the largest arts organisations, such as the Royal Opera House, employ only a few hundred people. Arts administrators, therefore, need to have a wide range of skills – organisational, planning, marketing, fundraising and financial – in order to succeed.

Record companies

The record companies are driven by consumer demand, and most of their effort goes into promoting artists and repertoire which sell well. It is worth noting that the recent boom in sales of classical recordings is entirely due to a handful of very big sellers (such as the Three Tenors). The A & R (artists and repertoire) and marketing departments – small departments staffed by people who have developed a sound working knowledge of the record industry – are crucial to the commercial success of these companies. The larger record companies also have departments responsible for business affairs and royalty administration, and may contract out (sometimes to a subsidiary) the distribution and retail sales functions. The recordings themselves are usually produced and recorded by freelance producers and studio engineers.

Broadcasting

The BBC is still the major employer of musicians. The principal outlet for live music is BBC Radio, which produces many thousand hours of live music programming each year. Radios 1, 2 and 3 all have music departments employing in-house producers. Radio 3 has about thirty producers, supported by production assistants, secretaries and administrative staff.

Classic FM relies on commercial recordings for most of its output. It employs a few producers to work with the roster of freelance presenters.

Music programming accounts for a small proportion of television output. BBC TV has a Music and Arts Department, and Channel 4 employs one commissioning editor for classical music.

Publishing and collecting societies

The role of the publisher is to exploit the copyright, that invisible piece of property which is created when a musical work is composed. The principal means of exploitation are performing, broadcasting and recording. There may also be income from sales of sheet music and from the hire of scores and orchestral parts. A major publisher will, therefore, have departments (often comprising only two or three people) responsible for print production, composer promotion, marketing and royalty collection.

Print production is highly specialised, and typesetting, copy editing and proof-reading are normally contracted out. Royalty collection is essentially a clerical operation, although some knowledge of copyright law is valuable since royalty departments also have to handle sub-licences. For composer promotion and marketing, sound administrative skills and commercial sense are required.

There are two collecting societies for composers and publishers. The PRS (Performing Right Society) licenses the performance and broadcasting of copyright music, and the MCPS (Mechanical-Copyright Protection Society) licenses recordings. Each employs a few hundred people to handle licensing, distribution of royalties, the works and recordings databases, and membership services.

Other options

In addition to composing, performing and teaching, musicians find themselves in a host of related businesses – music journalism, music libraries, museums with musical collections, music retailing and instrument technology. Musical expertise is not always essential, although, in practice, most people working in these areas will have had a musical training followed by training in their particular profession. They remain loosely linked to the music business, however, and need to have some knowledge of how it works.

The musical choice

The musical world is not one for the half-hearted. It is a world of individuals in which you may have to carve your own niche rather than finding one that fits you. While every sector of the profession has its own network, each one is inextricably linked to the others. Personal contact counts. Getting to know the other people in your area of the business and developing your own network of contacts are the keys to success.

To some extent, you will always be dependent on others within the profession, but it helps if you are self-sufficient, both personally and professionally. You will need self confidence to survive the rigours of a freelance (or quasi-freelance) existence, just as the employees in the business also need to have the versatility and flexibility normally associated with freelances.

There are people and organisations who can help you, and the chapters in this Handbook offer introductions to many of them. Add them to your own network of contacts!

THE SOLOIST

GERALDINE ALLEN

Geraldine Allen specialised as a solo clarinettist before her career was interrupted as a result of a road accident in 1993. A specialist in contemporary music, she also plays wind synthesizer, and her work has encompassed cross-cultural music and music theatre. She is a music adviser to the Arts Council of England and the East Midlands Arts Board, District Councillor for the Incorporated Society of Musicians, an executive member of the Eastern Orchestral Board, and an examiner for the Guildhall School of Music and Drama. She is also a partner in the music consultancy 'Impulse'.

The art of the solo performer

The solo performer has held a special place in the cultural life of the community for as long as society has existed. As we approach the millennium, that presence is undiminished. Its form, function and value, however, has changed, and we are probably in one of the most diverse and exciting decades ever to be faced by the solo artist. Almost daily, there are technological advances which affect the scope of performance, the means of self-promotion, and the demands of potential audiences: the world of the soloist is ripe with possibility, both for developing the traditional art and also for creating the new. However much the role of the solo performer undergoes change, it is certain that talent, musicianship, dedication, imagination and a passion for performance are all essentials if this is to be your chosen career. Confident that you have these qualities, and that you will be able to develop your ability to communicate them, you must give plenty of thought to the practical matters in the structure of your career.

Stardom is the province of all, but the privilege of few, and, while it would be marvellous to be represented by a good agent, most careers are not launched into the stratosphere but require a steady build of profile, experience and performances. Desk-top technology makes available to the solo performer the means to prepare high-quality publicity material, and to fulfil many of the functions traditionally left to agents and managers; communications hardware, in the form of answering machines and faxes, means that you are always available to respond to an enquiry or invitation to perform. If you are so-minded, composing software will even facilitate musical arrangements or, particularly useful for singers, transposing music to a different key.

You are starting out, and the world *is* your oyster, but whatever fervent activity you engage in to launch your career, always have clearly in your mind why you wish to specialise as a soloist. Being a soloist is not about technique alone, it is about personality, as a musician and as an individual. Perhaps you should begin by asking yourself a couple of questions: first, do I need the company of others to enjoy rehearsing and performing, or am I happy to work alone? Whether you are embarking on a career as a soloist, or as a soloist within an ensemble, there will be a quite different mental approach and lifestyle from playing in an orchestra or singing in a chorus. Second, as a performer do I enjoy creating a sound that blends with other sounds, or am I drawn to experimenting and projecting in tone and dynamics; do I prefer to express someone else's idea of the music, or do I want to be totally involved in the interpretative process? Being a soloist is much more than playing a solo line, and I am assuming that the reader is intent on building a solo career as a full-time profession, and not something only to be dipped into when the opportunity arises.

Creating a professional identity

A professional identity comprises a number of facets, and a successful performer will be recognisable by any one of them. You don't need to think very far to be able to name an artist known for his or her 'sound', for personal style or charisma, or for a particular repertoire. No less than a composer, a performer needs to find his or her own individual voice or thumb-print: a means of instant recall, be it via recording, photograph, programme or publicity material. It goes without saying that professional identity is always underpinned by a high standard of carefully prepared performance.

Competitions
Winning a competition can be enormously helpful in launching a solo career. Competitions and creativity are not always comfortable partners, and the finest musicians are not necessarily the competition winners. However, there is much to be gleaned from entering a competition over and beyond the ultimate laurel of winning – there is the opportunity to put together, learn and perform a programme; pointers to be picked up from discerning comments made by senior colleagues in the profession; the exchange of information and ideas natural to the green room situation; the experience to be gained from playing the same programme in different acoustics and, on occasions, in major venues. If you do not win, you will nonetheless have gained some valuable experience which will help you to fashion your musical identity, and giving a creditable performance of a well-constructed programme may have got you noticed anyway.

Programming
You will probably have a good knowledge of standard repertoire, some of which will need time to ripen in musical maturity like a good claret: as musicians, we are so lucky because there is always the chance that the best is yet to come. For most soloists, there is also such a wealth of music available: new repertoire is always on the horizon waiting to be performed. When constructing programmes, try to get a balance between the familiar, the less well-known, and the new. As performers, we are not only interpreters but creators, and there needs to be a direct and personal involvement when learning new works. If you have the opportunity to play a work by a living composer, do contact him or her and talk about it. You may have questions concerning tempi, notation, interpretation, or perhaps you just want to say you like the piece. Do commu-

nicate it – I have not met a composer yet who does not like talking about his or her music, and don't forget that they rely on the performers, the executive artists, to pass on their creation to audiences. You may also learn more about the piece, and not only musically – there may be a story behind its writing which you can share with your audiences. Getting to know composers will give you an opportunity of widening your repertoire, and you may perhaps want to commission a new work as a result.

Contemporary works

It is the responsibility of the solo performer to provide a platform for the performance of new work whenever possible. I have found that it is almost always acceptable to include one contemporary piece in each programme, provided that it is interestingly introduced, and that an indication of its length is given. It is important to discuss the programme enthusiastically with the promoter first, particularly as the audience is often much more receptive to new music than the person who has the worry of selling the seats. Specialising in contemporary music opens all sorts of doors. It is well supported by the Regional Arts Boards and the Arts Councils, a proportion of whose funding is available for commissioning new works. If you can establish contact with a local composer, it may be possible to obtain funding from your Regional Arts Board for a new commission and for the first performance. If you have works written for you by established composers, opportunities for broadcasting and recording may follow.

Specialisation

Not all performers will have an interest in, or affinity with, new music, but it is useful to find a specialist area for which you have a particular passion. What will identify you from the many other highly-talented musicians of your generation? It may be that you are drawn to early instruments, or that you have researched manuscripts of little-known music composed in the last century, or that, through a distant relative, you have been able to obtain music which has never before been performed in this country. The most important thing is that it is music which you would like to share with others, prepared, presented and performed to a high standard, and that it represents the sort of repertoire for which you would like to be particularly known.

Personal image

Your identity as a performer is determined not only by the individuality of your musicianship, but also by your visual presence. I take the word 'visual' in the broadest sense, meaning not just the way you look and dress, but the identity projected by your promotional material, whether in photographs, brochures, posters, programmes or letters. The solo performer is larger than life, and by this I do not mean that each performer has to perform with exaggerated gestures! It is a fact that, for whatever length of time your performance lasts, you will be the centre of attention. It may well be that your playing, concentration and involvement in the job in hand is more than enough to hold the attention of every single person in the hall. Fine, but be aware of that. To be a successful soloist, you will need something which enables you to stand out. Consider what this is, and look at some of the great soloists: often, it is only a presence, a charisma, a twinkle in the eye, but, above all, it will be the ability and desire to communicate this wonderful art of music. What you wear is important; it need not be extravagant, unless that is how you see yourself, but it should be carefully considered by everyone: men, women, singers and instrumentalists alike! Be aware of how you deport yourself on stage, how you walk on and off the platform, how you receive the acclamation of your public, and how you look when you are not playing. You should not detract from the music, either by upstaging it, or by denying it the respect it deserves. In the age of the screen, the visual is important: ignore it at your peril!

Presentation

In one of my early Radio 3 recordings, a presenter was invited into the studio to announce each work before it was performed – to the studio crew! The producer wanted to maintain the feeling of a live performance, and it helped me to feel more relaxed. The on-stage verbal presentation of programmes can be an enormously powerful tool for drawing audiences into the 'world of performance'. Some people will find talking a good way of forming a relationship with the audience, others will not be so comfortable with this approach but will find other ways of involving the audience – for example, with the use of personal notes in the programme. To have a stage presence which is open and draws the audience into the performance is a natural gift, and it may not be necessary to add anything more. A carefully-judged combination of all these elements is ideal from an audience point of view – they are as diverse as listeners as we are as performers. Classical music must serve not just a minority of musically-educated people, as important as they are. It is expanding its horizons into areas where it competes in venues with drama, dance and pop music to an audience who may have little or no experience of classical music – witness Vanessa Mae!

Interaction is perhaps the buzz-word of the nineties, and this is having its impact throughout the arts. Involving the audience as part of the production is not new to contemporary theatre, and exhibitions of modern art can embrace the viewer through contemporary media as a three-dimensional, living and evolving part of the creation. The role of the audience continues to change, and we as performers need to be aware of that.

Self-promotion

If being computer literate has not been part of your training to date, then you should make sure that it is now. Time taken to learn how to create promotional material, mail merge, and even how to use e-mail and the Internet, will enable you to communicate with promoters, producers, venues and potential audiences. If you really cannot do it yourself, then find a friend who can, or at worst pay for someone to do it for you. What you must do from the very beginning is to support the development of your identity as a performer with the style of your publicity, and that means being involved in its creation. With a computer, promotional material can be continually updated, refined and expanded. Correspondence is kept on file, and mailing lists can be compiled and updated. It will also give a very professional look to all your correspondence, and can be extended to graphics and printing your own programmes, should you get really adventurous.

Photographs

A good-quality photograph is an essential part of your presentation package. This can take many different forms, depending on the image that you want to convey to your audience – you may want a traditional chin-in-hand classical pose, an outdoor effect, or even to throw yourself across a piano. The type of photograph will be determined by your personality, style of performance, instrument and repertoire. Photographs should be professional-quality black and white. The most useful sizes are 10 x 8 and 6 x 4. Try to ensure that the pose you choose from the contact sheets has some area around the image for cropping. This makes it cheaper for the promoter responsible for the programme, who may otherwise decide to leave out your photograph because of the cost of making a reduction.

Demonstration recordings

As soon as you are financially able, it is a good idea to have a demonstration recording available. Never be persuaded by a promoter or agent that anything will do, because it will not! The expectation of professional sound quality is increasing all the time, and if your recording is poorly balanced or distorted it will only do you a disservice; do not send it! Sometimes it is possible to make a good domestic recording of a live concert, provided the microphones are high quality. Better still, go into a studio, or use a mobile recording company which records in a venue with a good acoustic. Look for advertisements in classical music magazines or in the *British Music Yearbook*. Send off for several quotations, and ask for names of other people who have recorded with them. Try to get a quotation for a complete package. If not, remember to check the costs of the master tapes as well as cassettes, and allow time for editing, which can significantly increase the price. When you make a recording, have as clear an idea as possible as to the type of sound and balance you would like, and always insist on listening to the first part of the recording to make sure that the engineers are reproducing the sound quality that you want.

You can begin by having a good quality sixty-minute cassette, along with a short demo of excerpts lasting no longer than ten minutes. Promoters often do not want, or do not have the time, to listen to an hour's worth of music, and you can choose extracts demonstrating what you consider to be the most significant aspects of your playing. You can always offer the full version if they become sufficiently interested. The recording will almost certainly be edited on to DAT, and you should ask for a copy of the master to make available to broadcasters.

At a later date, you may even wish to produce your own CD, if a recording company has not offered to do it for you. There are companies now which offer the complete service of recording, photography and packaging CDs for a fixed price. These can then be sold after performances, and, with drive and energy, you can even sell them through high street retail outlets, if you are prepared to charm the managers – but don't order too many for your first batch until you see how they sell!

Marketing

This is a very important aspect of building a solo career. In the early stages, you will need to be able to sell yourself with tact, persistence and enthusiasm. For more important performances, it will be worth investing in a publicist. Eventually, you may be represented by agents and recording companies who will provide the necessary hype. Meanwhile, it is down to you.

Publications
It is important that you read music magazines and publications to keep up with what is happening in the profession, and for news about performing opportunities. There is an abundance of very useful information now available to the solo performer, which you have already discovered in part as you are reading this book! Within certain publications, there are free listings for you as a performer, and also for news of your recent activities. Make use of networking opportunities, such as the alumni (past students) magazine of the college where you trained, and the journal of any professional organisation you may join.

Mailings
Contact lists are available from many different sources, but try to be selective in your mailing by targeting areas which have a particular significance. For instance, do you or the music you are playing have a specific connection with a particular area of the country? Look for addresses in the *British Music Yearbook*, and contact the Regional Arts Board, which should be able to provide you with a comprehensive list of venues, promoters and local councils. Write a letter which gives the promoter a clear and concise idea of what you are offering. Along with your brochure, attach one or two specimen programmes, as well as the offer of a demonstration cassette if one is available. The promoter needs to visualise you as being part of his or her plans for the season, and a sample programme will facilitate that. I have also found it helpful to give an idea of the fee. This should be negotiable and, in the first instance, will probably be exclusive of expenses. It is often a good idea to follow the mailing with a telephone call. When approaching promoters, there are three questions you should be asking yourself: Who are my audience? What do they require? How can I fulfil those requirements and surpass expectations?

Regional Arts Boards
You will need to build your own lists of contacts, and the Regional Arts Boards are a very good place to begin. RABs have lists of venues within their area, often with details of the types of programmes they promote. Keep the Music Officer of the RAB area in which you live informed about your performances. It is sensible, also, to contact the other RABs by sending them your publicity pack. The RABs all work differently, and so you should get to know their

individual music policies. They know the community they are serving; some may have a rural touring policy which sends performers into the most unlikely places to provide live music for people who otherwise may not have the opportunity to hear any. Do you have the versatility to adapt to these types of performances? If so, it is worth while letting the Arts Boards know.

Diversification
Are you able to perform programmes without a piano, or would a good-quality electric piano be acceptable? Can you provide your own equipment? Do you have educational concerts or workshops available, which you could offer to promoters along with your standard programmes? Are you able to share your music with people with special needs or learning difficulties? The wider the scope of the performances that you are able to offer, the more likely you are to be able to arrange a tour of the region instead of a single performance. Are you able to include lighter music in your repertoire, and would you consider using synthesized sound, and making use of the vast amount of new technology available? The answer to all of these questions may at first be 'no', but try not to close your mind to exploring areas which may provide you with work, and which may even surprise you by their musical potential and stimulus. You could just be the one person who is taking a lively interest in the music of the region at the right time.

Engagements

There is no doubt that the music club circuit no longer exists in the way that it did in the 1950s, 60s and even 70s, and neither do the choral societies and amateur orchestras. Funding is also far less specifically aimed at classical music. The Regional Arts Boards are serving a broad-based community in which classical music plays a small and comparatively expensive part. Combine this with dwindling audiences and far less press coverage for live performance, and the picture could look pretty black – but it need not be as daunting as it sounds. There is still work, funding and publicity available for the soloist, but it may take a different form than in the past, and it may need a more imaginative and individual approach to secure it.

Contracts
When you are successful in obtaining an engagement, send an artist's contract. This makes the conditions clear for both parties. Be prepared to send photographs, posters, leaflets and programme details. Some venues will print their own posters, but to others you can send your master leaflet, designed on your computer, which they can photocopy. For some venues, offering to help with the publicity in this way may encourage them to choose you instead of another performer. Always approach local radio if you have a recording. Either ask the venue to do this for you, as well as to contact the local paper, or make the contacts yourself. Invoice the venue on the day of the concert or in advance. Your terms for payment will have been stipulated on the contract. Finally, do write and thank the promoter, who has often gone to a lot of trouble to make

your performance a success. They may even invite you back!

Fees

Never perform for less than a reasonable fee. It is better to perform for nothing than to be poorly paid – it does nothing to help your reputation as a soloist, and it sets a bad precedent for other performers. I am not suggesting that you turn down work, but just make it perfectly clear what your normal fee is, and then, if you particularly want to accept the engagement, you can negotiate a concessionary rate. Fee guidelines for solo performers are published by the Incorporated Society of Musicians.

Professional bodies

As well as providing guidelines on fees, the ISM produces an excellent contract. Joining the ISM keeps you in contact with other soloists and ensembles, and provides professional advice and public liability insurance cover. For many solo instrumentalists, there are also bodies which take a special interest in their promotion and sphere of activity, such as the British Flute Society, the Clarinet and Saxophone Society, and so on. There is also the Musicians' Union, and singers may, of course, find it beneficial to join the actors' union, Equity.

Broadcasts

If it is appropriate, try to find a pianist with whom you can work regularly. A strong duo partnership can contribute effectively to musical identity, which will be very important as your career takes you to national and international venues, as well as into broadcasting. BBC Radio 3 audition procedures fall into two categories. For post-graduate performers, including recital (but not opera) singers, there is the Young Artists' Forum. Auditions take place throughout the country, and these are advertised in *Classical Music* and other publications. Successful artists take part in a shared recital, which is recorded and broadcast, with interviews with the artists. More experienced performers can audition to become a Radio 3 artist. This involves a 'blind' audition, adjudicated by a panel of three or four people, one of whom will be an expert from outside the BBC. Successful auditionees will be offered a debut recital, and will be admitted to the Radio 3 register. They may then be booked by any BBC producer throughout the country. There are other opportunities for broadcast performances with independent radio stations, such as Classic FM and some of the larger stations in the regions. Independent radio can also be a good outlet for DAT recordings or CDs.

Back-up and review

There is undoubtedly a great deal that you can do to promote your own career, but it can become a lonely undertaking. Unless it suits your particular temperament, don't allow yourself to become isolated. There is plenty of support and back-up through the contacts and organisations already referred to both in this chapter and more widely throughout this book. Every so often, it is useful to review the breadth of your interests, the relevance of your publicity material, and the scope of your marketing efforts. Weed out the activities that are not cost effective, or that are not bearing the right fruit in terms of artistic or financial rewards: there is no point continuing in a particular direction just because that is what you have always done. Try to find ways of introducing new ideas into your musical environment: no artist can maintain a high level of output without a degree of quality input.

Performing experience is the fundamental of the soloist's development, and it is at first difficult to get the balance right between performing, practising, promoting and earning a living. Indeed, earning a living entirely from performing will not happen straight away, but always leave enough time to do the job properly, or you will be successful at nothing. An audition for Live Music Now!, the Council for Music in Hospitals, and similar organisations, can provide you with opportunities to perform and to communicate directly with many different types of audience, as well as giving you scope to broaden your repertoire.

Musicians are in a unique position: they have a special talent which, if nurtured and trained, can be a true gift to society. To cultivate a solo career requires continual questioning and a constant search for new ideas, always stemming from the desire to share the love of music with the audience. If you are a solo performer who can combine energy, vision and a fresh outlook with the enjoyment of music-making, then the time is ripe for you!

THE CONDUCTOR

COLIN METTERS

Colin Metters' conducting career has taken him to many parts of Europe, Australasia, Poland, Russia and the Far East. He has recorded for the BBC on a number of occasions for both radio and television, conducted many of the leading symphony orchestras in the United Kingdom, and worked extensively with orchestras abroad. He has given conducting seminars at a number of European conservatoires and is regarded as one of the foremost teachers of conducting. Since 1983, he has been Professor of Conducting and Director of Conducting Studies at the Royal Academy of Music.

Musicians of all generations and from all areas of the profession at some point aspire to conduct – or so it seems! Whether it comes from genuine talent, a frustrated sense of 'I could do it better', a state of boredom with the current routine, or perhaps a combination of all three, this fascination with conducting can strike at any time. For the young aspirant, one cautionary word right at the start: don't be misled by the apparent glamour, fame and fortune that you may associate with the lifestyle of the professional conductor. True, a certain number of conductors do appear – constantly – on the front covers of glossy magazines, but, compared with the many hundreds of conductors who have successful careers all over the world, only a very few achieve the sort of recognition that makes them household names. The majority, many of them very fine musicians, are known only to a relatively small circle. The life of any performing artist is a tough one, often with disappointments and frustrations. Conducting is no exception, and it is not the profession to enter with false hopes and unrealistic dreams. Aspiration and ambition – not to mention ability – along with resilience, determination and commitment will be needed in full measure. For anyone seriously considering conducting as a career, however, I hope this chapter will, in some small degree, help along the way.

A proper training

Hermann Scherchen, in his excellent *Handbook for Conductors,* wrote: 'The force of personality and artistic potency cannot be learnt or acquired; that much is nature's gift. But professional training is of a technical order, and the technique of conducting can be learnt as any other.' In the words of the great violin pedagogue, Ivan Galamian: 'Technique is to have total control over the realisation and execution of a musical idea.'

There will continue to be those who like to think that 'conductors are born, not made', believing that the only qualification needed to be a famous conductor is to have been born. If you share this belief, I am afraid that you will find little of interest in what follows. It is perfectly true that the art of conducting remains intangible, and that elements of it cannot be taught. There is much, however, that demands our serious attention and study.

'Force of personality' and the ability to communicate are indeed important, but the conductor must first and foremost be a sound musician. The background and foundation for all future aspirations must, therefore, be a full and comprehensive music course, with all the attendant disciplines and the necessary instrumental accomplishment. This can be complemented by an accompanying study of conducting at undergraduate level, through private tuition or summer schools. Following the completion of undergraduate training, the young conductor will more than likely be looking for a period of concentrated study at postgraduate level. All the major UK conservatoires offer some form of postgraduate tuition for young conductors. There is, however, no consistent level of what is available, and there are widely different perspectives on technique, philosophy and the pedagogic approach. Indeed, not all have a fully-structured course of study. It is essential for any serious student to look carefully at what is actually on offer, and not simply at the literature and brochures, which can be as impressive as they are misleading. Take the trouble to speak with members of staff and the course directors. Talking to former students is an invaluable way of discovering the strengths and weaknesses of the various courses and of helping you to choose the one most suited to your needs.

This advice is also broadly applicable to summer schools and courses abroad. Take care before making any major commitment, both in terms of time or money. I have known students who have thought that being located in Vienna, Berlin or the USA must, by definition, be better than being in the UK. They have returned, having found little of value, and with constructive help and tuition virtually non-existent. There are many excellent conducting courses in this country and abroad, but always seek advice, and try to speak to someone who has been on the course you are considering.

The organised course of study must, at some point, come to an end. What then for the young conductor?

The early years

The biggest difficulty faced by all young conductors is in finding opportunities to learn and practise their craft. However much assiduous study is undertaken, a conductor cannot gain real experience without an orchestra, and orchestras (understandably) are not enthusiastic about engaging conductors without experience. The aspiring conductor should adopt two maxims coined from the world of home improvement: for conducting, 'Do It All,' and for promotion, 'Do It Yourself'!

For those conductors who are now established, it is obviously possible to trace a career path back to their student days. This can be misleading and not always a useful indicator, since their opportunities often came from specific and personal circumstances. The one lesson that can and must be learnt from this, however, is that there is no established and easy career path – there is no 'career structure' for conductors. This is, perhaps, a hard truth, and sometimes conductors fight against it for years with some bitterness. However, if this can be understood and accepted from the outset, then your music-making and the development of your career will be a more positive and constructive journey.

Be patient – be prepared to take time to listen and to learn. However successful your training, for the conductor learning never stops. You need to study a vast amount of repertoire, to consolidate an effective and efficient technique that is your own, to develop an understanding of the corporate personality of the orchestra (realising that each group and every orchestra is different), and to acquire the experience and sensitivity to enable you to handle difficult situations – all this and more, whilst constantly striving to become a better musician. One lifetime is hardly long enough!

Don't be too hasty in turning down opportunities which may appear on the surface to offer little. Never underestimate the possibility of making new contacts and increasing your sphere of influence from what might seem to be very meagre means and limited resources. The time will come, of course, to move on and be more selective in what you accept, but don't forget the very many hours you ultimately need to spend in front of musicians, directing ensembles of all shapes and sizes, listening and learning, keeping an open mind and building on the advice and help that can be offered from the more experienced and worldly wise. It is very important, in the early stages, to adopt a philosophy that allows you to take on almost anything and everything that is available – 'the sublime to the ridiculous' should be the young conductor's maxim. Finding opportunities to broaden and extend your experience and to learn the trade should be your central objective. There are few circumstances for the young conductor that are entirely devoid of a learning opportunity.

A small number of conductors will, of course, get an early break through a competition or from a lucky coincidence of being 'spotted', but this cannot be the rule or be looked on as a career path. Even if an unexpected opportunity does arise, it should not be accepted without serious consideration, and the possible ramifications thought through. While it is true that a competition winner will become instantly 'engageable', going from 'Mr Who?' to 'Mr BBC Feature Interview' overnight, both will tend to have one thing in common – limited experience. After the initial euphoria, the lack of sufficient experience and repertoire can sometimes present problems, and the opportunity may turn out not to have been the blessing it first appeared to be. If this way does not open up for you, and, more importantly, if it does for some of your contemporaries, don't be disillusioned or discouraged. Although there are a number of conductors who have made their names in this way, this is not the only route to success, and it is worth remembering that there are far more equally well-established conductors who have never won any competitions.

It is encouraging that a number of regional orchestras in the UK are now offering attachment schemes for young conductors. What each offers will be different, but they all give an invaluable opportunity to work in a professional environment with professional expertise on hand to give help and advice. There is no centralised information on these schemes, and details need to be obtained from each orchestra independently. In the present economic climate, continual funding for such schemes cannot be guaranteed, so what is available from one year to another may change, but don't hesitate to get in touch with the orchestral managements.

Starting late

For musicians who choose to take up conducting later in their careers, a full-time course may not be a practical option. Private lessons, summer schools, talking with playing colleagues and other conductors, may be the only ways to gain help and advice. There are, of course, numerous text books on the market, some of which offer valuable and essential information covering the vast amount of background knowledge and scholarship so necessary for the conductor. As far as the physical basis of conducting technique is concerned, this does not lend itself to a 'Teach Yourself Conducting' booklet, and, whilst there will undoubtedly be points of interest that may be useful, you can no more truly learn to conduct from a book than you could gain your pilot's licence from reading a flying manual.

For those who may be considering changing careers, a cautionary word: Many musicians, particularly instrumentalists, decide to take up conducting because they get annoyed and frustrated playing for conductors who, they feel, do not know their business, convinced that they could do better themselves. That is fair enough, and, in certain cases at least, they are probably right. If you are one of those, think carefully about what it was that frustrated you in those conductors you did not respect – and make sure that you don't simply repeat the cycle! The orchestra will know immediately whether you have taken the responsibility of your new role seriously – in terms of score learning, the study of technique, and your philosophy and attitude to the players you now wish to conduct – or whether you see this as a rather easy option, with no further qualifications needed other than being musical. However well-liked and re-spected you were before, having left the relative security of your seat in the orchestra remember you will then be alone, this time *facing* the orchestra, with eighty pairs of eyes looking at *you*, thinking that *they* could do it better!

Some practical advice

This is not the place to attempt any sort of *Conductor's Handbook*, but perhaps a few guidelines for readers with limited experience might be useful.

Apart from the obvious academic study – score learning, transpositions, historical background, performance practice – you should give serious thought to the orchestra itself. Apart from your musicianship, your knowledge of the score, and so on, your manner in front of the orchestra is very important. It is a complex and highly-sophisticated musical instrument, and its make-up – sociological, psychological and emotional – has a strong corporate persona, as well as containing a myriad of individual ideas. Hermann Scherchen wrote: 'The conductor is playing upon a live instrument, and he must understand not only the laws of his art, but also the idiosyncrasies of this instrument.'

Your rehearsal technique will develop gradually, along with your own conducting style, but it is important to remember that every orchestra is different in the way it works and responds. No 'one way' will be right for all orchestras or in all circumstances, and you must be sensitive to the changing dynamic from one day to another. Be aware, also, that, particularly in the early years, you will be performing repertoire which is new to you, but which may be very well known to the orchestra.

Players will expect you to be organised in your use of rehearsal time. It is your responsibility to watch the clock, not theirs, and players will not thank you for wasting their time. Whenever possible, schedule repertoire to avoid a player having to sit for five-and-a-half hours in the band room, waiting for you to decide when you are going to rehearse the only work in the programme that involves the piccolo. Equally, don't call the full orchestra for Prokofiev's Symphony No. 5 at 10 am and then decide to begin with Elgar's Serenade for Strings. 'All too obvious!', I hear you cry, but all too often forgotten. Of course, it is sometimes impossible to avoid players having to wait, but your consideration will be noticed and appreciated.

Your vocal communication is important, and it is far better to speak in such a way that the whole orchestra can hear, even if your comments are primarily directed at the cello section. Not everyone will listen, of course, but it does give a continuity to the rehearsal and maintains the sense of involvement for the whole orchestra. By the same token, avoid indulging in private discussions with the front desk strings. This habit is intensely annoying to players further back, for whom the discussion is obviously relevant, but who can't hear a thing. I have seen this situation produce some very vocal demonstrations of frustration on more than one occasion (although not in my own rehearsals, of course!).

Having mentioned vocal communication, you should constantly remind yourself that your aim and intention is to speak as little as possible, and to show everything through your conducting. To simply indicate when to play means little in itself unless it incorporates a broader musical understanding. The 'how' to play is ultimately more important, and your goal should be to develop a clarity in your technique which enables you to convey the essence of the music, so that the musical intention is unambiguous and of immediate meaning for the orchestra.

Even with all the difficulties, tensions and disagreements, the relationship between conductor and orchestra is a partnership – albeit occasionally a problematic one. Remember that, at all levels, development for the conductor is very much 'empirical learning': you apply what you have learned, and what experience has taught you, and, with that as a foundation, you have to experiment, take risks, try things in different ways. Never be afraid to admit to a musical error of judgement over something you intended but failed to achieve (or even basic mistakes – occasionally!), and don't be defensive about acknowledging your fallibility. Players may not always be outspoken in support of those things that we do well, but they see through us in an instant when we try to cover up something that is quite obviously our mistake. Don't do what a well-known conductor once did with regard to tuning: 'Trumpets, you're sharp.

Play it again.' 'You're still sharp. Play it again.' 'Trumpets, you're playing even sharper!' At which point, the leader intervened and asked for a quiet word with the Maestro down by the leader's chair. A few words were spoken, and then the conductor asked the trumpets to play again. 'That's an amazing thing,' he said. 'From up there on the rostrum you're sharp, from down here you're flat!' Think about it. Not the sort of psychology to impress ...

Self-promotion, marketing and representation

You may feel that what you have to offer, musically and in every other way, is going to change the world, and that your talent is all you need. You may well be right. On the other hand, and at a more practical level, you cannot afford to ignore 'the market'.

It is unlikely that you will find professional representation immediately. Until you have a track record, and can offer something concrete to agents, it can be difficult to persuade them of your unproven brilliance whilst sitting on opposite sides of a desk. Representation and promotion remain your responsibility until such time as you persuade someone to do it for you.

Within the profession, there are mixed feelings about the effectiveness of sending glossy brochures to managements. It may well be true that their next port of call after the letter box will be the waste paper basket, but it is equally true that other people's awareness of your existence will not be increased by doing nothing. You should also remember that videos are now a basic prerequisite for virtually every competition application worldwide.

Another aspect of self-promotion involves what I can only describe as 'attitude'.Whatever may have been the case in the past, there is a growing disinclination to accept histrionics and indulgent displays of artistic temperament from conductors. There should be no limit to the intensity and commitment you bring to your work, and you should fight vociferously for those things in which you believe, but no longer will simple bad behaviour be accepted (and certainly not expected), just because you consider yourself to be 'the maestro'. Your manner, attitude, professionalism and ability to work with colleagues are all of major importance. In all your dealings, be they with players, agents or managements, your attitude will be noticed. The impression you make is important at all levels and in all circumstances.

It is absolutely understandable that, as a student, even at postgraduate level, you may have enjoyed the student environment and lifestyle. As you move away from this way of life, you must move on. This is not simplistic or patronising: I have seen young conductors who have found it difficult to shed the student mantle, and how this has affected the way they are perceived by professional colleagues. Being 'professional' is not just an attitude of mind, it must become a way of life. In all aspects of the music profession, there are those who are professional and those who are not, and this has nothing to do with how much they are paid! You cannot begin too early to understand what this really means.

Recording studios

If the chance arises, take the opportunity of sitting in on recording sessions to learn how the recording studio works. I don't just mean the mainstream EMI 402nd Complete Beethoven Cycle, but also the world of film scores, TV theme tunes and jingles. The demands and techniques are very different from the workings of the symphony orchestra and the concert hall. The conductor will be expected to deal with up to twenty or thirty very short 'cues', with all the musicians, including the conductor, wearing headphones and working with a 'click track'. One thing, however, you would recognise immediately: the composer, arranger, musicians and technicians are true professionals – and you would be expected to be one too. This area of work is no easy option, and is very demanding and exacting – from that comes its own satisfaction and reward.

Final thoughts

Anyone contemplating music as a career should reflect carefully on what will be involved; the profession is a hard taskmaster. For the conductor in particular, it can be a long and lonely road, with no guarantee of future success and with the recognition of talent illusive. The aspiring conductor must, therefore, ask him or herself further questions, questions both of ability and of suitability. Why do I want to conduct? What do I hope to get out of it? What can I offer? What do I intend to put into it? These questions must be honestly asked and honestly answered. The competition is increasingly intense, with the expectation of ever-higher standards.

Having said that, the life and work of the conductor can be exciting, demanding, and very rewarding, musically, personally, socially – and, sometimes, financially!

In trying to find your own career path, you will experience frustrations and disappointments, but, if your love of music and your commitment to it as a way of life still drive you forward, and if you retain that overwhelming compulsion to communicate and share it with others – then go for it!

THE SINGER

TERRY JENKINS

Terry Jenkins sang in the Westminster Abbey choir as a boy chorister and later obtained an engineering degree at London University. While studying part-time at the Guildhall School of Music, he worked for the John Lewis Partnership and, through their music society, met the director of the London Opera Centre who engaged him for Opera for All. After further study at the LOC, he worked as a freelance for many years, undertaking session work, singing in the Glyndebourne chorus and taking leading roles with the smaller opera companies.
From 1972 until 1994, he was a principal tenor with English National Opera. He made his Covent Garden debut in 1976.

Many people setting out on a career as a professional singer have been fired in their original ambition by a natural talent. This may have been evident at school, where they acquired a reputation for 'having a voice worth teaching', or later in life, through singing with local amateur societies as a hobby. But, in considering a professional career, they will be entering a much wider pool of talent where individual capabilities might not be as great as was first thought. Indeed, if anyone were to ask me if they should to take up singing as a career, I would advise the utmost caution.

Most singers enter the profession dreaming of a solo career leading to international stardom. This is quite different from instrumentalists, who generally see their careers in terms of joining an orchestra or playing in smaller groups. But every singer wants to be a soloist: indeed it is considered a sign of failure by people outside the profession (and, unfortunately, by some within it) to be anything else. A realistic appraisal will show that there are very few international singers, and that the qualities which set them apart are usually obvious. Very often, this is purely and simply the timbre of their voice; they possess a unique sound that is both instantly recognisable and is also what the public likes to hear. A Gigli or Callas can be identified by one phrase of music! If this is you, then you are indeed fortunate, for it is a quality given to very few. But there are many other ways to build a successful career and the first essential is to have a clear knowledge of your own particular talents and shortcomings. As an amateur, you can remain a large fish in a small pond; as a professional, you will never have a satisfying career if you are always yearning for the unattainable.

Obviously, the first requirement is a voice, but natural ability is not enough. Indeed, a singer who has always sung 'naturally' can experience far greater difficulties when things start going wrong than one who has always been aware of technique. Acquiring a technique takes time, and many singers, finding the process lengthy and irksome, rush into work for which their voices are ill prepared and then suffer the consequences. Nobody would expect to pick up a bassoon and play it instantly, but many a singer expects to do just this with a voice.

Your voice is an integral part of your whole metabolism, and when your body is not in perfect health this will be reflected in your singing. Actors and dancers often push themselves to the limits of endurance in a desire to perfect their performance, but this is a very dangerous way for singers to work. A good technique, which can also cope on those 'bad' days, is essential; but, as the voice is an internal organ, it is not easy to recognise and eradicate faults. A teacher is, therefore, generally necessary: someone who not only gives advice but who also listens dispassionately to the sounds you are making which, of course, are not the sounds you yourself can hear. One needs to continue working in this way throughout one's career, with a teacher who can spot the insidious faults that creep in gradually and of which one is not aware. Conductors and coaches generally listen to the music, not the voice, and may well be unaware of these faults: they probably do not have the time or expertise to correct them and should not be expected to do so.

It is debatable whether or not there is only one way to sing correctly; what is certain is that the methods used by singing teachers to achieve this end are innumerable. All teachers employ a different use of imagery to explain to their students what they should be doing, and one approach may suit one student better than another. In order to progress, you certainly have to trust the teacher you have chosen, but against this you have to balance a blind belief that the teacher is some kind of Svengali who alone knows the magic formula which you have to swallow wholesale, even though your voice is suffering in consequence. Many students get into worse difficulties through a misunderstanding of what the teacher is trying to achieve. Surely, any method of teaching should try to eradicate the stresses and strains which will eventually wear and damage the voice. Unfortunately, there are teachers who attempt to impose a quality on the voice which they like to hear, rather than allow it to develop its intrinsic individuality. Some appear to be unaware of the effect they are having. It must always be the pupil's ultimate responsibility to realise this and to make a change when necessary, although it is not always easy to recognise what is happening. Singing is a physical activity, but the effort needed has to be carefully learnt and controlled; then you may acquire the ability to sing difficult and taxing music and enjoy a long career.

It is not only vocal fitness that is important, but also physical fitness. A singing career is hard work, and you must be able to cope with the late nights and early morning rehearsals, the travel and the meals snatched at odd moments. As relatively few singers work on a continuous contract, illness can mean having to cancel work and, therefore, losing money. It can also lead to a reputation for unreliability. I have often wondered whether entertainers have bio-rhythms that peak in the evening, but recording sessions are just as likely at ten in the morning, so you must be able to cope with those as well. A factor which can limit your progress, but over which you may have little control, is physique. This is especially true in opera: gone are the days of overweight sopranos and short, fat tenors (though they do still exist!). If it is only a question of weight, then you will need to diet. Singing is not merely a matter of producing the notes: the whole manner of presentation is crucial. Two points are of equal importance: care of your body I have already mentioned, the other is personality. One sees examples of singers with good voices and no personality at all, not just on the opera stage, but in concert and recital work. No audience wants to look at a singer who feels embarrassed and ill at ease. To communicate with an audience, you need to develop a confident manner which you can use as a basis for stylistic interpretation. This will, of course, grow with age and experience, but it is a requirement very often not given due attention by the student.

And it is this inner confidence which will help you to control nervousness. If you find the mere thought of performing makes you sick and a nervous wreck, then I would question whether a career as a performer is for you. Of course singers get nervous, but it is rather the nervousness that comes from wanting to perform to the best of their ability. You have to enjoy performing, although it is never the easy satisfaction that the public believes. Even though you are doing something you like, you will always be dissatisfied with the results you achieve.

Many singers regard the ability to read music as relatively unimportant; they somehow think it is below their dignity to be bothered with such trivia. However, you do not find many instrumentalists unable to read music. At the early stages in a career you have to seize the opportunities when they arise. If you can learn quickly – and reading music is only the first stage in doing this – this could tip the balance in your favour. If, however, you are reliant on someone else even to teach you the notes, then it could well be another opportunity missed. It is often said that people who can easily read music have more trouble memorising it. I do not believe this: memorising is boring and time-consuming but necessary, and continues right through the career. The established singer reaching the end of a career will still be learning and memorising new repertoire.

Now, how do you start to find work? People will only offer you an engagement if they know your voice and capabilities. As a student, you will meet many young conductors and singers who can help you, either by directly offering you work or by telling you of opportunities. A useful way of getting known can be to enter competitions, some of which offer engagements as prizes. Whereas it appears that virtuoso pianists need to win a competition to start their careers, the same is not true of singers and there are many successful singers who have never won a competition in their lives. But at an early stage it will be necessary to do many auditions. You will find out about these by looking on notice boards or in the musical journals. Beware of choosing only very well-known arias to sing – the panel will have heard them many times before and will either be bored or hypercritical. Far better to choose something lesser known and let them concentrate on your abilities. Foreign opera houses, however, prefer to hear familiar arias, so they can immediately classify the voice and place it in the appropriate *fach*. Never be too ambitious in your choice of arias: you will have a better chance of demonstrating your potential if you sing something well within your capabilities. It is always advisable to rehearse with the accompanist before the audition. Either take your own, or arrive in sufficient time to rehearse with the accompanist provided. Most singers find auditions daunting, and draw comfort from the popular belief that people who give good auditions give bad performances. Many of the singers at English National Opera even claim to have given poor auditions when they were engaged, so never get discouraged; but there is no escaping the fact that you will have to audition many times in order to make the essential contacts.

The more people know about you, the more chances you have of finding work. The majority of people in the profession are freelance, and obtain work from many sources: job security is a very rare commodity. Although West End musicals may run for many years, this type of work is not predictable, and the only area of guaranteed continuous employment is in a chorus – either with a major opera company or with the BBC. Ours can also be a lonely profession: travelling round the country, always working with different people, leads to many acquaintances but few deep friendships. There is a ready camaraderie working in a chorus, an easing of financial worries, and still the fulfilment that comes from being involved in music-making of a high standard. For these reasons, many people find chorus work a satisfying way to make a career. Indeed, a chorister of long-standing with a wide repertoire is probably more use to an opera company than a young soloist making his debut. There are usually opportunities to sing and understudy parts as well, and there is no reason why a singer should not join a chorus for a time to gain experience and then leave. At one time, it seemed to be a virtual necessity for all operatic soloists to have sung in the Glyndebourne chorus at the start of their careers.

Nevertheless, 'chorus' can be an emotive word. 'I'm only in the chorus' is often said with an expression of regret, as if accepting second-best. But there are many operas which depend on the choral contribution for their success: *Boris Godunov* and *Aida* are examples which immediately come to mind. Alternatively, the BBC Singers require excellent musicianship to tackle the varied choral repertoire they perform, and the small professional choirs are setting standards of performance and authenticity that have never been heard before.

Many of the London churches maintain a very high standard of choral singing through the use of professional singers. The requirements vary with each church: it may involve services during the week or only on Sundays. Some, especially the cathedrals, will have their own choir schools to sing the treble line, but there are opportunities elsewhere for women as well as men.

A lot of chorus work, however, is arranged on an ad-hoc basis. This can include the need for extra choristers in the opera houses or with the BBC Singers, or session work for individual chorus masters and fixers. Most singers are not the snobs that the public, or even the critics, might expect and enjoy the versatility to be found in the musical world. Well-known, established singers will happily accept session work, whether it be commercial recording, film scores or TV jingles. Whereas, in solo work, the individual characteristics of a voice are crucial, in chorus work there is room for all. You need the ability to sight-read well and to be familiar with many different styles of music. For modern music, you will need to be able to cope with the extreme complexities of rhythm as well as pitch, although it is rare for perfect pitch to be a necessity. You will also need a telephone number where you can be easily contacted and which you can give to anyone you think may be useful. These days, it seems to be almost essential to have a mobile phone.

Before starting to look for solo work, singers must have a much clearer idea of their voice: they must know its qualities, its strengths and its weaknesses. Is it light or heavy in timbre, for example? Is it youthful sounding or dramatic; is it clear and pure in tone or does it possess a vibrato; is it flexible and good at coloratura; where are the upper and lower extremes of range, and to which styles of music is the voice best suited? In these days of small, portable tape-recorders it seems surprising that most singers only use them as an aid to learning music. Although the standard of recording thus achieved is poor and not to be compared with professional quality, it can be useful to hear yourself as others do. Sometimes it will be a salutary shock! You may have a predilection for one type of music more than another and this will be where you would hope to channel your greatest enthusiasm. However, it may well be that your voice is not suited to this style of music, and then you will have a difficult decision to make. You have to face up to the reality that your talents and ambition are irreconcilable and accept a career doing what you are best suited for, rather than what you hoped for. Five-foot soubrettes very rarely get cast as Wagner heroines!

As a soloist, the whole business of agents arises. It is always useful for a young singer to have an agent: he will have many useful contacts, know of work that is on offer and have more experience of financial affairs. But the agent does not need you as much as you need him. It serves very little purpose if the agent is only collecting clients and does no work on your behalf; you can then find yourself in the invidious position of paying commission on work which you find yourself. These days, the oratorio business is not dominated by a few agents as it once was: choral societies are just as likely to book artists through personal recommendation. They are all in financial difficulties and it is wise to be flexible in the matter of fees; it is better to accept work for a lower fee than to have no work at all.

A few years ago, there were many more small opera companies than there are now; companies which could offer a young singer the opportunity to sing leading parts in smaller theatres away from the glare of national critics. Many of today's established artists learnt their trade in this way. But again, economic pressures have altered the position. However, there are still more opportunities than one might realise. A brief list that immediately springs to mind includes English Touring Opera, Opera Factory, Pavilion Opera, university societies, groups in various towns that use an amateur chorus, and the ever-increasing number of performances given in country houses. Many of these companies advertise in the musical journals, which may also carry reviews of past performances.

The larger, full-time companies generally have a small nucleus of contract soloists, but English National Opera regularly uses over 100 different soloists in a season, and auditions are held all the time. Opera, of course, requires other talents than purely musical ones: it is necessary to be able to act, and this can add to the difficulties of the music. You may well be encumbered with a heavy, awkward costume and suspended on a wire! It is, therefore, wise to be cautious and only accept roles suitable to your stage of development: it would be dangerous, for example, for a young singer to sing Sarastro in *The Magic Flute,* as not only is the music deceptively difficult, but the whole character of the role needs qualities that only a fully mature person can bring to it. The operatic world has been a minefield for young voices, many of which take far longer to develop than their owners realise.

The BBC is probably the largest single employer of musicians in the country, offering work throughout the whole range of music. To be accepted by them, you will need to pass a rigorous series of specialist auditions (light music, for example), although personal contacts can be useful. Like the opera companies, they have departments which co-ordinate and arrange auditions. The first step, therefore, is to write and request an audition, stating the areas of work in which you are interested and telling them of your previous experience. In general, it is not necessary to make and send a demonstration tape unless you are thinking of working abroad, when it may be necessary as a first step, preparatory to going to audition in person; although there may be a delay, with perseverance they should eventually hear you as it is in their own interests to discover new talent.

Never forget self-promotion. It is soul-destroying work to write to all the music societies and local authorities listed in the *British Music Yearbook,* yet it can lead to a solo recital or, more probably, to a concert with two or three other singers based on some theme – a Victorian evening or a Viennese concert, for example.

I would, therefore, advise any young singer to gain experience wherever and whenever possible; regardless of the obscurity of the music or of the venue, regardless of the fee offered, or even for no fee at all. You never know who may hear you and where. Singing is a practical occupation and not a subject over which you can theorise. To start with, you can evade the issue by simply talking of your intentions, but eventually you have to commit yourself to a performance and be judged; even the least knowledgable member of your audience will have an opinion on your performance, and why not? We are not just here to perform to the cognoscenti, but to anyone: as a professional, you are a member of the entertainment industry.

However, opinions on the sound of a voice are always subjective, and what one person likes, another can hate. This is just as true of managements as audiences; indeed, very few managements understand voices or even listen to them as other singers do, leading to exploitation of voices that are not able to cope. This is not necessarily management's fault; singers must always preserve their own interests. After all, it is the singer who gives the performance, not the army of advisers, coaches and teachers standing in the wings. You must be aware of your limitations and ultimately take all the responsibility – and glory!

Like all artistic pursuits, there are always more people striving to make a career than there are places for them to fill. If the caution I recommended at the outset is sufficient to deter you, then you probably do not have the commitment to succeed: if my warning simply serves to strengthen your resolve, then that can only be a good thing, for much resolve and belief in your own abilities is needed. At times, all may seem to be purely a matter of luck; you may well find other people achieving early successes which, in your opinion, they do not deserve. However, in the end, genuine talent will always be recognised.

THE ORCHESTRAL MUSICIAN

JOHN LUDLOW

John Ludlow was leader of the National Youth Orchestra for its first two years, subsequently studying at the Royal College of Music with Henry Holst and Manoug Parikian. After three years with the Royal Philharmonic Orchestra under Sir Thomas Beecham, he was appointed, at the age of twenty-six, leader of the Sadlers Wells (now English National) Opera Orchestra. Four years later began a short spell with the BBC Symphony Orchestra, followed by five years as sub-leader at the Royal Opera House, Covent Garden.

In 1968, John Ludlow turned freelance, spending five years as co-leader of the London Mozart Players. He now leads a number of orchestras in and around London, and has been a professor at the Royal College of Music since 1970.

Being able to play and knowing how to belong – the two biggest elements in professional orchestral life. Of course, there are plenty of others, like being strong and healthy, being resilient, having persistence without being obstinate, being sensitive without being neurotic – and, especially, being reliable.

First steps

Your training may be nearing its end, but not your professional development: some of that is only just starting, but what you have already learnt will be your basis. Whether you have studied at a music college, at a university or privately, and whether it has been in the UK or abroad, or both – however excellent your training, there is no way at present that you can have been fully prepared for the demands of working in professional orchestras. Your first engagements will be like an old-fashioned apprenticeship – except that you'll be on full pay and expected to produce the finished article straightaway. Don't be discouraged – most musicians survive!

When you are ready, you will set about building your reputation, and that means auditions. Far from the popular belief that the scales are weighted against them, graduating students have the great advantage of being at a high point of their playing ability, with recently-studied solo works on offer, a confidence in their technical skills, and a freshness which the more experienced orchestral musician may no longer be able to match; all great assets at an audition.

The first step is to survey the market. Where are you willing to work, and where would you prefer not to? What are your preferences about the sort of work you would like to do – symphonic, opera, ballet, chamber, radio, educational, recording? (If your answer is 'a mixture', that's good, because in most orchestras that's exactly what you'll get!)

Contract or freelance?

This question is perhaps the most fundamental: you have to decide what sort of a balance you want in your professional life. Do you want time and opportunity to follow other interests, such as teaching, composing or arranging? Do you want to be able to keep a high priority for your own chamber group, rather than having to rely on leave of absence at the discretion of your orchestral management – who might have great difficulty in agreeing to your confirming a chamber date twelve months ahead, before they know the orchestra's commitments for that time.

When you've thought about these points, turn to the *British Music Yearbook*, where there are listed over 150 potential sources of performing work of one sort or another.

Making contacts

Elsewhere in this book, you will find Trevor Ford's advice on entering the freelance world. This is based on Trevor's experience of the profession from both aspects – as a player and as a manager. Much of this advice applies equally to those looking for permanent appointments.

For those opting for permanent orchestras (which, we all hope, includes the four independent London orchestras), the first contact is usually the letter and CV. A simple rule? Think what you would want to read if you were the orchestral manager: '... asking to be considered for a position (or for extra/deputy work) ...' – that goes in the covering letter; all other details will be of interest to the selection (short-listing and audition) panels, so they go into the CV:

Name, address, telephone number and diary service

Instrument – it's surprising how often it's forgotten!

Experience – professional if you have some, but outstanding items of student achievement are worth including

Where you studied, when and with whom

The names of two referees who are known and respected in the orchestral profession – and make sure you have warned them!

Anything else which presents you favourably

The clearer and simpler it is, the more effective it is.

Auditions

What do they want to hear? That is the question to ask yourself. Select pieces relevant to the orchestra to which you are applying. Most will want to hear you demonstrate tone quality, rhythm, sensitivity, agility and understanding of styles, so present a classical piece and a contrasting romantic one, including some fast passages and some expressive sostenuto playing.

Specialist groups will assume that you are interested in their repertoire, and will expect something suitable – a baroque panel might suffer an allergic reaction to Tchaikovsky!

If you are sent repertoire extracts, they will probably be regarded as almost as important as your solo pieces, possibly more so. Real sight reading is also important, although some orchestras don't now rate it as highly as they used to. You can improve your sight reading by practising it, but play each piece only once! Take any unknown piece, set a steady tempo, and *keep going*. Sight singing also helps.

If you don't get the job, it only means that someone else was considered to be more suitable: every single candidate might have been acceptable. So swallow hard and keep practising; remember – resilience.

Congratulations – you're on trial

Making the right impression is what matters. Of course, that is mostly a matter of playing well under whatever conditions, but there are other things that count:

> being early enough (but not *too* early) – there's a saying, 'if you're on time, you're late'

> fitting in musically and personally – being too conspicuous is pointless, as it suggests an obtrusive character, which is not helpful in an orchestra

> keeping a 'professional face' – not showing disapproval of anything (not even of oneself), and especially not appearing to know better

> real ability, coupled with charm and modesty – *there's* a winning formula!

These you may know as 'orchestral etiquette' or perhaps 'professionalism'. Call it what you will, it's sad to report that it has been deteriorating badly in the past few decades. But the principles behind it still hold good, and the promising young contender for an orchestral position would do well to take good note. Whatever others do, you might like to consider whether it is in your interest to discipline yourself to work by these (mostly self-imposed) rules.

More congratulations – you've got the job!

Now keep it! Listen, watch and learn – for the rest of your life. Continue the self-disciplines you developed on trial, and more. Especially:

don't stare at orchestral soloists – you'll know why when *you* have to play the 'tunes'

never practise someone else's solo (except at home) – same reason

bandroom concertos – right out; everyone's heard them before, and better, however impressive they may sound to you

train yourself not to look at anyone who's made a mistake – in the words of one eminent conductor, 'Never laugh at the car in front whose back wheel is wobbling: for all you know, your own may be about to fall off!'

At first, your playing may seem to deteriorate; with all those new notes to learn, there's little time to repair the damage which orchestral playing can inflict, especially on string players. Weak spots begin to show, and must be dealt with, apart from the eternal care over intonation and tone production. It's a matter of self-preservation as well as preparation for promotion. After two or three years, those who are not too committed financially may choose to look into the possibility of another period of full-time study, possibly lasting from six months to a year. There may be some financial support available if you search hard enough, and the benefits could improve your long-term career prospects.

Relating to colleagues

Now is the time for getting to grips with that other difficult area of the orchestral profession – getting on with your colleagues. Working in an orchestra means spending many hours a day alongside people you haven't chosen as your friends – and, in some cases, wouldn't have, given the choice! The work is emotional, and so is the personal ambience; and, to make matters worse, everyone's faults and weaknesses soon become apparent to everyone else. Sensitivity and tolerance come to the rescue, and life is peaceful, on the surface at least, for a surprising proportion of the time. But just occasionally the tension breaks, and those are the moments when real professionalism counts. The saviour is often that great asset of the profession – humour. Not only is it a lifeline in dangerous moments, it is also one of the greatest enrichments of a musician's life. Fortunately it thrives, and long may it do so.

It is often difficult for the young virtuosic player to respect an older colleague whose ability has obviously lost its freshness. Merits differ, as do deficiencies, and the loss of freshness may well be balanced by a depth of experience which is helping to hold things together, and which may be the very ingredient most needed under pressure. Perhaps in earlier years he had just as much virtuosity – possibly even more. Everyone makes his or her best contribution, and we all have to be grateful to those who fill in the gaps in ours.

Relating to conductors

This is the really tricky one! Most conductors are honest musicians, who are just as sincere about music as the rest of us, but quite a few are not as sensitive as they might be about how they try to get us to do what they want. One of the hardest things for a recent ex-student is to learn to subordinate his or her own newly acquired sense of taste and style to that of the silent (musically, anyway) conductor, whose ideas will rarely seem superior at first.

There are also a few conductors who are downright unpleasant, either by nature or as a means of establishing their superiority, and they can be dangerous if you allow their insensitive comments to undermine your belief in your own musicality. It helps to remember that they must be sad people to have to behave like that in front of skilled colleagues. Just think how their insensitivity would sound if they were playing an instrument – then remember that that is probably the very reason why they aren't! The last resort in self-defence is to imagine them sitting on the loo – it seems to take the sting out of even the most objectionable!

Looking for promotion?

If you are after a senior seat, you can prepare yourself all the time – and, of course, you may be called upon to occupy your local 'hot seat' at a moment's notice, even if you don't particularly want to. There are ways of preparing yourself:

listen and learn how other sections work

in a familiar piece, listen for things you may not have noticed before

without changing your playing, imagine how you would influence the performance if you had the chance – phrasing, balance, character, colour; string players can also indulge in their favourite fantasy of devising better bowings!

A few general suggestions

One of the problems that may arise unexpectedly is boredom – conductors don't always manage to inspire, especially at rehearsals. But boredom can be programmed out of your working hours by always demanding more of yourself than is demanded of you. That way you also make sure that you don't stagnate.

Ernest Hall, the great British trumpet player, advised students: 'when you have a quiet patch, look after your playing – that's the time to do basic repair work'.

Always speak of orchestral *musicians* instead of 'players', then discipline yourself to live up to the title.
No experience is ever wasted, however unwelcome at the time.

Professionalism is 90% preparation, 10% inspiration; you need both.

It's wiser to learn from other people's mistakes than from your own.

Never do anything which would, or could, discredit a colleague in the eyes of the public or the profession. Even major disagreements should, if possible, be sorted out in private so as not to upset the working atmosphere.

There's no such thing as being the only one who's right in an orchestra.

It's no shame as a professional to retain the dedication of the amateur; there's no point in arguing with the cynics, but don't let them influence you either. Just aim to live up to your own convictions.

However skilled you are, there will be moments when, from sheer embarrassment, you will pray for instant evaporation! It's happened to us all. There's only one thing to do – laugh at yourself; at least then you're joining everyone else, perhaps even the audience – they love a first-class mistake!

Don't expect conditions to be ideal for playing – they rarely are. A recording studio may have excellent air conditioning, but it may have to be turned off because it makes a noise in the takes. Churches are often too cold (cathedrals usually are) for comfortable playing; some halls get wretchedly hot. Light is frequently less than ideal, and many copies are too small, over-marked, or just difficult to decipher. But none of this concerns the audience – we have to leave them with their naïve belief that we are always playing under ideal conditions and in top form. Professionally, no excuse is ever offered – not even to the critics.

Finally, don't expect professional life to be 'fair' – like the rest of life, it isn't, but dwelling on the fact is negative and useless, and produces the sort of moaners who are the bane of orchestral life. Reflect on the fact that life has already treated you a lot better than average; you've had help to do what you chose to do – to learn to play your instrument; you've been given expensive opportunities to develop your skill. Others have not been so lucky, but you've been given the start in life which you showed you deserved, and you can't expect to be given any more; it's up to you now, and you've got to earn every step of your professional progress from now on. Nobody owes you anything, but you owe it to those who have supported you so far to see that you create opportunities for yourself and fulfil your own potential – which may be a lot greater than you yet realise.

FORMING AND RUNNING AN ENSEMBLE

BRYAN ALLEN

Bryan Allen and studied music at Birmingham University at both undergraduate and postgraduate levels. In 1980, he formed Fine Arts Brass Ensemble, in which he has been involved, both as manager and player, ever since. As well as an international schedule of concerts and broadcasts with the Ensemble, he has an active freelance career in a variety of fields. In 1995, Bryan Allen was appointed Head of Brass at the Royal Scottish Academy of Music and Drama.

Forming an ensemble is, in essence, a simple operation. All you need is good musicians, good organisational sense and plenty of persistence. Keeping your group going over a number of years is a different matter, however, and you will soon encounter a whole range of complex problems. There is no right or wrong way to go about it, and circumstances vary enormously from one type of ensemble to another, but a few guidelines will help you to avoid some of the common pitfalls. Most of the problems encountered can be solved along the way, and if you have don't have the necessary skills to cope with situations as they arise, then it is fairly likely you are not a suitable person to be running an ensemble.

Choosing your players

The decision to form a group may come from an individual or from a group of players, but the initial choice of players is crucial to the success of the group. Establish from the outset what type of ensemble you want to form, and pick your players accordingly, whether it be a flexible ensemble playing music for different combinations, or a fixed line-up, like a string quartet, wind or brass quintet. Although your aims may change once the group is up and running and receiving input from a number of sources, it is important to establish initial objectives and a group identity.

While you want to select the best players available, be careful to choose players who have the same desire to succeed in chamber music as you. While it is important that you 'get on' professionally (and also socially), don't choose players just because they are your friends – this could make it even more difficult if a change of personnel is felt necessary later. And remember, the best individual virtuosos are not necessarily the best players for an ensemble. An ensemble selected from the best players at music college often disbands early as one or more of the players seeks the stability of an orchestral position before your group has had time to develop and establish itself.

Forming an organisation

Having selected your players and decided you would like to 'give it a go', there are a number of procedures which are best carried out early on.

First, you have to decide on what basis the group is to be run, and there are two options. If the ensemble is the brainchild of one individual, he or she may decide to run it themselves, taking responsibility for finding engagements as well as booking players. This arrangement works best if the group is to be a flexible combination with different players for each concert. The players can be paid a set fee per engagement, regardless of the ensemble's running expenses and, while the director may make a loss on some concerts in the early years, he or she will stand to make larger profits should the group succeed.

For ensembles with a fixed line-up, it might be worth drawing up a partnership agreement (your bank will help with this). This will list the members of the partnership, and will assign joint responsibility for all assets and liabilities of the ensemble. In the event of one member leaving, the agreement provides for his share of responsibility to be passed on to the other members. This way, all the members receive an equal share of the profits, and you can expect to receive much greater commitment and loyalty from them. It is in their interests to ensure that the group is as successful as possible, and they are less likely to be tempted to take on work which clashes with one of the ensemble's dates, even if it means accepting a smaller fee in the first instance. In addition, all the players will feel part of the decision-making process, and will feel much more willing to help with administrative chores.

You may also want to look into the possibility of forming a limited company, which limits the liability of the individual members should the ensemble incur debts beyond its means. I personally don't think this is necessary, as it is not a problem you should encounter if the group is managed efficiently.

It is a good idea to agree on a rough percentage of the ensemble's earnings which are to be reinvested for promoting and marketing the group. No player is going to feel too committed if, in a month when no concerts take place, he is asked to pay back money to meet his share of a new word processor. Major purchases are best made at times when the group's earnings are high.

Some groups form a charitable trust in order to raise money to promote concerts. You will need the services of a knowledgeable solicitor, and it may not be worth the expense unless you plan to promote a large number of concerts yourselves. If this idea appeals to you, then it is best to obtain a copy of a deed of a charity with similar aims to yours from the Charity Commissioners and use this for a guide.

Administration and finance

While the artistic policy of the group may be decided by a group of people, it is important that one person establishes himself as an administrative leader. The ensemble will need a contact address and telephone number (preferably with an answering machine attached), and promoters will expect decisions on availability, fees, programmes, etc, immediately they write or phone; they will not want to wait until the next group rehearsal for a decision.

You will need a bank account in the name of the group, into which you can pay your fees, along with a cheque book to pay for expenses and players' fees. It also helps to establish a good working relationship with your bank manager, as you will often have to pay out the expenses for concerts before you receive the fee.

It is important to keep accurate financial accounts right from the beginning, although it may seem tedious at the time. In the first instance, it is likely that all the players will be earning money from other sources, and will therefore make individual income tax declarations. As each member may organise his or her tax year from a different date, it helps if you produce monthly, or at least quarterly, accounts. If the group becomes busy, then the players will want regular payments in any case, and monthly accounts will help you to calculate them. In due course, you may be asked by the Inland Revenue to submit accounts on behalf of the partnership.

VAT is not a problem you are likely to encounter for a while, but keep a careful check on your income as a group, and notify HM Customs and Excise as soon as it exceeds the VAT registration limit. It can cause serious problems if you do not register at the correct time as you can be obliged to backdate your registration. Because most of the promoters you will work for initially will not be able to claim back the VAT you charge, it is advisable to avoid registration until it is legally necessary.

A word of warning: HM Customs and Excise can classify the ensemble as a partnership, even if you haven't drawn up any agreement and want to consider yourselves as separate businesses for VAT purposes. The VAT registration limit must therefore be applied to the ensemble as a whole, and not to the members as individuals.

Marketing

There are many ways to promote your ensemble, and it is important to work out where your potential market is and to target this area. The first thing you need, apart from a word processor and a telephone/fax, is a good product to sell! You can spend hours writing and telephoning potential promoters, but when it boils down to it, your best advert is the concert itself. It is possible with good marketing to sell a bad product, but this will eventually fall flat and cannot be sustained forever. Likewise, many worthwhile groups have never got past the first hurdle because no-one has been prepared to put in the necessary donkey work.

The first task in marketing your ensemble is to produce a brochure and letterhead, along with a good quality set of black-and-white photographs. These may prove expensive, but ask around: it is quite likely that one of your friends or family will work in a printing or photography company and may be able to offer assistance. Be careful about the wording on your brochure. Don't draw attention to the fact that you've just started up, and don't mention individual concerts and events unless they are of real interest. If you mention forthcoming concerts in, for instance, Leicester, Watford and Reading, it makes it obvious that this is the sum total of your engagements. Much better to say the ensemble works extensively at concert clubs and societies throughout Britain. You needn't be embarrassed about being liberal with the facts as long as you are confident you can produce a good concert if booked. Although your means may be modest, try and make your brochure attractive, and give your group identity with a logo and co-ordinated letterheads.

Mailing lists

Top of the list of essential publications is the *British Music Yearbook,* an invaluable source of information in a variety of areas. It is possible to build up an extensive mailing list from this book alone, but other useful publications include the *National Federation of Music Societies Yearbook* and the *British Performing Arts Yearbook.* While it is possible to buy into a number of mailing lists, a much better and cheaper way is to create your own. Word processor packages are relatively cheap and, although it takes time to enter addresses into the computer, you only need to do it once!

Start with a fairly small list and expand it over a period of time, and this way you can also pinpoint your potential market. Try and work out when certain promoters will be putting together their next series and time your mailing accordingly. For instance, most music clubs will select artists for the following season (September-July), from the September of the previous season, and a mailing in November of that year will probably be too late.

Arguably the most economical way to do large mailings is to have a standard letter printed to accompany your brochure. It is best not to mention fees in the brochure as it will otherwise date very quickly, but this information must be included in the letter as you cannot expect promoters to phone you back if they have no idea what you will cost. It is always a good idea to offer reductions and packages for concerts tied together in the same area, or for repeated programmes, as the more concerts you do in the early years the better you will become. Remember, it is always easier to sell a busy group.

In due course, you may use your word processor to do the whole operation. While it may take time printing all the letters, you can spread your mailing throughout the year and alter the contents according to the recipient.

It is wise to spend the majority of your marketing budget on trying to persuade promoters to book your ensemble, rather than promoting your own concerts. This way, the promotion of the concert is not your responsibility, and even if there is only a small audience you will still receive your contracted fee.

A final word: don't be discouraged if you receive little, or no, response to your first efforts, and remember that a 1% success rate on a mailing of 1,000 letters will produce 10 concerts. If you've got something interesting to say, each mailing will usually pay for itself many times over. Don't sit by the phone as soon as you've posted your letters, as many promoters will keep your details on file and may respond several months (or years!) later.

Promoting your own concerts

Depending on the quality of work you manage to attract, there will probably be a time when you will need to promote your own concert or series of concerts in high-profile venues, such as the South Bank or Wigmore Hall. Try to put on attractive programmes that will interest critics and potential promoters. It is an expensive business promoting such concerts, so make the most of any free advertising you can get. Many papers and magazines have concert listings with free entry, and a number of papers run special offers – for instance, the *Independent* will sometimes publish an interesting photo of your group and will advertise your concert in exchange for ten pairs of tickets for their readers. Make yourselves available for local radio interviews and try to attract interest from feature writers. Above all, use every means available to secure much needed publicity to raise the ensemble's public profile.

Agents

It is a fallacy to think you cannot succeed without an agent working on your behalf. While they can be extremely valuable, and necessary, in certain markets, you will probably find it difficult to attract the interest of a good agent until you have become well established. By this time you will have learned so much about the business yourself that you may be loathe to pass on all your hard-earned contacts to an agent. Bear in mind that, however good your agent, he or she is unlikely to be able to work as hard for your group as you can yourself. If your group becomes successful, you will inevitably attract more attention from agents, and you may decide to engage one (or more) to relieve your workload, but don't sit back and expect work to flood in. Work out how much you are spending on agency fees and evaluate whether it would be more economic to employ your own administrator, perhaps on a part-time basis.

Touring

Should you wish to secure overseas engagements, you will undoubtedly need good agents working on your behalf in the countries you hope to visit, especially in the more lucrative markets, such as the USA, Japan, and some of the European countries. Often, a British agent will work in conjunction with an overseas counterpart to secure your bookings, but it takes a long time to build up contacts in all the big markets, and you have to establish a successful career here before you can expect any overseas agents to take an interest.

Recordings

The most obvious way to establish your name on the wider international stage, and to attract the interest of overseas agents, is through recordings. While it is a difficult area in which to get initial success, don't accept no for an answer. If you have a good product, someone will eventually want to record it. In general, there is not a lot of money to be made in recording, but the benefits in terms of marketing and securing other engagements are countless. If you don't have any luck obtaining a recording contract with an established label, you might consider producing your own recording – an increasingly popular practice. It is actually possible to make more money this way in the long run, but you have to be prepared to lay out a certain amount of capital to finance the recording in the first place. As you're not likely to be able to secure the worldwide distribution offered by a large company, you will rely primarily on sales from live concerts, so this is not a venture to be entered into lightly if these are infrequent.

Sponsorship

It is not advisable for a small ensemble to become dependent on sponsorship in the same way as a large arts organisation can. Most of the concerts you do will be sponsored in some way or other but, fortunately, it is the job of the promoter to raise the necessary funds for your fee. This is not to say that extra funds from sponsorship would not be useful, and there are countless projects you could doubtless undertake with more funds. Again, don't be discouraged by your first efforts. My advice would be to avoid sending out blanket mailings to a variety of companies, and to target a small number of carefully chosen companies, concentrating on a more personal approach. Telephone to find out the name of the marketing manager, and show an interest in the work of the company. Take advantage of any friends you have in local companies, no matter how small, and look out for companies who haven't sponsored the arts before but are looking for ways to increase their public profile. In this way you can take advantage of awards which exist, such as the Pairing Scheme, administered by the Association for Business Sponsorship of the Arts (ABSA).

There is no right or wrong way to form and run an ensemble, and most of the skills required will be built up over a number of years. The best way to learn is to have a go yourself, but you must believe in the group and aim for the highest possible standards. It is not easy trying to juggle with several managerial problems and also fit in your own personal practice, so be prepared for countless sacrifices and heartaches along the way. Your persistence may reap great financial rewards and offer immense job satisfaction. Good luck!

THE COMPOSER

DAVID BEDFORD

David Bedford began composing at the age of seven, subsequently studying with Lennox Berkeley at the Royal Academy of Music and with Luigi Nono in Venice. His compositions encompass a wide range of styles, from major orchestral commissions to rock arrangements, and from school operas and other innovative music involving children to orchestrations and original music for film. He is, at present, Chairman of the Association of Professional Composers.

Young composers today are likely to discover their talent, or their desire to compose, much earlier than composers of a previous generation. Composition is one of the requirements for anyone taking music at GCSE level, so young people are liable to find out whether or not they like composition when they embark on a GCSE course at the age of 13 or 14. Additionally, the problems encountered at the outset by music teachers faced with teaching and assessing student compositions, led to an explosion of composers going into schools and doing creative workshops with children to get them ready for GCSE. Composers have, therefore, been working with top junior and first-year secondary children who are getting composing experience far, far earlier. Anyone with a burning desire to compose might therefore find out as early as 11 or 12. A love of composing will have been indulged throughout the pupil's school course, and he or she will have been able to hear the results since not only GCSE, but also a lot of the A-level syllabuses, require pieces to be recorded. The only disadvantage is that pupils are obliged to write music which can be played by the instrumentalists around them, and comparatively few schools have symphony orchestras for the performance of large-scale compositions. But this is a minor cavil, and pupil composers will also have benefited from guidance from teachers, most of whom will, thanks to a lot of in-service training over the last three or four years, be quite experienced at teaching composition.

The composer at college

I shall assume that you are past the GCSE stage, and that you have definitely decided that you want to be a composer. Your next step is, therefore, to select a composition teacher with whom to study at tertiary level. It is perfectly possible to study privately with a composer, but there are few, if any, advantages in doing so. By studying at an acknowledged institution, you would be making friends amongst future instrumentalists and other composers (some of whose styles may be very different from your own), you would be able to write pieces and have them performed within a matter of weeks, you would get valuable feedback from the instrumentalists as to how well (or otherwise) you had written for their particular instrument, you would be able to make use of the recording and electronic studio facilities of the department, and you would be able to take advantage of all the various opportunities and competitions available to internal students. In fact, if you were prepared to restrict your writing to works playable by your fellow students, there is no reason why you should not be able to hear every single one of your works performed – a luxury not to be enjoyed by composers in any other sphere. The teaching of composition has never before been so practically biased; previously it could have taken composers years to find out exactly how their music sounded. Institutions also offer the academic grounding which is so useful – history of music, development of instruments, history of orchestration, and so on – all valuable stuff for the young composer but for which you would have to seek separate lessons if you chose to pursue your composition studies independently.

There are plenty of composers teaching in colleges and universities, and you should seek out the places where the composition teachers are people whom you admire, or whose style you feel is similar to your own. It probably matters little whether you choose a university, music college or college of higher education at which to study. Some institutions may have very good musical reputations, but these are general and, as a young composer, you are looking for something quite specific. Send off for the prospectuses of several institutions which look feasible, and examine what they offer: how much emphasis is placed on contemporary music, for example, as a normal, natural part of the course; what opportunities are there for the performance of contemporary music. Don't be afraid to ask for advice from an established composer as to what you should be looking for. Few of us would mind spending a little time evaluating a bunch of brochures with a student. Go and talk to one or two of the composers whom you have selected as possible teachers: you may admire their music, but they may not be the right teacher for you. Some composers believe that there is only one way to write music, which would cause problems if you wanted to forge ahead with your own particularly individual style. You must make sure that any teacher you choose has some sympathy with your style of writing, as well as you with theirs. Avoid the dogmatic approach like the plague, because you might decide that you wanted to change direction at some point, and branch out in a more popular or electronic vein, for example. Whichever way you choose, your teacher needs to be able to go with you and help you; he or she needs to be open to all styles, even if these are not reflected in his or her music.

Whilst at college or university there are certain things of which you must take advantage, besides those directly related to composition. Composing is not going to yield much of an income, certainly not in the early years, and now is the time to consider developing an additional skill which will enable you to earn enough money to live on when you leave college. Take a teaching degree if this is one of the options, or work hard enough at your instrumental technique to 'qualify' you in this respect as well as in composition. Make sure you do all the copying of your own parts for performances, because badly written scores are seldom given more than a moment's glance by selection panels when you try to get performances and commissions after leaving college, and now is the time to get the experience of writing quickly, accurately and with good musical grammar. Your instrumental colleagues will soon tell you if what you have written is illegible, or if the markings on the parts do not convey what you had intended. If you have access to a computer notation programme, make sure that you have a very secure knowledge of correct notation before you use it. Most notating programmes, even those used by professionals, have serious errors of grammar, particularly in their notation of scale passages and enharmonic notes. If you are unaware of these errors, you will let them go without correction, which will make the score look amateurish.

When one of your pieces has been performed to your satisfaction, make sure a cassette is made of it, so that you can build up a 'library' of performances to take to publishers, or people who might commission works from you, when you leave. An alternative method of acquiring 'performances' on tape would be to take advantage of any computer facilities in the department and make demo tapes using the sampled orchestral sounds available on many computer programmes. (One word of warning here. Sampled electronic instruments do not need to take a breath, nor are they limited by physical restrictions as to how fast they can play. Beware of creating a score, supposedly for 'real' players, but, in reality, impossible for human musicians to perform.) Discipline yourself to write for specific, sometimes unusual, combinations of instruments, as well as purely following your own inspiration. This will prove invaluable later on, when competitions or workshops specify works written for a certain instrumental combination only.

The composer at large

Having now been coddled for as much as ten years, getting your works performed at school, by your colleagues at college, with all the facilities of the institution at your disposal, and workshop performances to give you all the feedback you need about your work, you now have to venture out into the real world. At this point I should emphasise that this chapter is addressed to composers of 'concert music' as opposed to 'commercial music' (music for film, television or advertising jingles). There is no criticism or snobbishness behind this distinction, just an acknowledgement that two totally distinct branches of composing exist and that composers seldom manage to achieve recognition in both. The way of working is different, the aesthetic is different, and the finances are different – a reputable commercial composer can make a very good living without resorting to the kind of tactics I will be discussing here. It should be emphasised, however, that it is a very difficult world to break into. If you look at the credits of television programmes, you will notice the same few names over and over again. There is no reason, as a young composer, why you should not keep a completely open mind about the 'kind' of composer you want to be. Take every composing opportunity which comes your way, concert or commercial, and you will soon find out what you are best at and what you like doing most, regardless of how much money is involved.

The drawback of having your compositions performed so easily and frequently at school and college is that leaving these places is far more of a shock to the system: suddenly you find that nobody in the outside world is the slightest bit interested in your music. I have already mentioned the importance of pursuing options other than composition while at college: you now have to earn a living, and there are very few composers, even well-established ones, whose income derives solely from their writing. There are several 'jobs' for composers: 'composer-in-residence' schemes which are advertised from time to time in the music press, and which tend to be aimed at the younger, struggling composer partly because of the lowness of the salaries offered; also publicly advertised are the Arts Council funded 'composer-in-association' schemes with orchestras, some of which are looking for young composers, and some for the more established people. These don't run for ever – two to three years at the most – and so should only be regarded as a 'stop-gap'.

Now comes the business of sending off your scores and cassettes to the people who can further your career as a composer. Unless you have enough money (£2,000-£3,000) to invest in enough sophisticated home computer equipment to enable you to produce cassettes of the works you have composed since leaving college or university, you will soon have to rely on scores alone to make the necessary impact, since you are likely to become dissatisfied with your student works. Pay particular attention to the presentation of your scores in terms of handwriting and musical accuracy. Those of us who read scores for the Society for the Promotion of New Music (SPNM) soon get put off by poor layout and sloppy, incorrect notation; just as off-putting are scores produced by computer with grammatical mistakes. At almost every SPNM workshop criticism is made of badly prepared scores, and we have come to the conclusion that those teaching composition simply do not tell their students how important it is to pay attention to this aspect of the job. Panels will just not look at a badly laid-out score, especially if it contains grammatical notational errors. Somehow you have to learn how to get this right – it will do you no good at all to comfort yourself with the thought that the scores of some of the great composers of the past were virtually illegible. If you have disciplined yourself to write out your own parts at college you will already have discovered how to make your musical intentions clear on paper, and how not to waste rehearsal time because players cannot tell if a note is meant to be B or B flat, or because you have left them insufficient time to turn over. Doing your own copying is something which it is advisable to continue doing for the first four or five years of being a professional composer, and you should still ask for feedback from the players. There are several good books on the subject, which I will list at the end of this chapter.

Having accumulated a pile of impeccably notated scores, to whom do you send them? Top of the list must be the SPNM, which is the only organisation in the country which sifts through scores and selects those which it considers merit performance. The most it can hope to perform, out of the 350-400 scores which its reading panel peruses each year, is about 20-25, with workshop performances being offered to another 15-20. The process of selection is quite cumbersome: you have to be accepted for performance by three separate readers, so if two say 'yes' and one says 'no', the score has to go out again until there are three concurring opinions either way. At this point a programme director takes over for the final programming decisions. The SPNM also organises special workshop days with a named ensemble, for which it invites scores to be submitted. Your piece has to be written for the instrumental line-up as dictated by the ensemble's personnel, but far fewer scores get sent in for consideration for these 'special' or 'regional' days, so a far higher percentage is chosen for performance. These workshops are advertised first in the SPNM's own magazine 'new:notes', so it is well worth joining the SPNM for this reason alone, although you can submit scores even though you are not a member. The Society has special rates for students, so you can join whilst still at college and have the opportunity to have your student compositions selected. One of the main advantages of having a work accepted by the SPNM is that publishers, performers and critics attend the concerts and may well be keen to follow up a young composer whose work has impressed them. It is very hard to think of any leading composers of today who did not start their careers by sending scores to the SPNM, even if they were, at first, rejected.

After the SPNM come publishers, and here the business of the neat score crops up yet again because, nowadays, publishers are liable to print a score from the composer's own manuscript since engraving, or even the modern computer equivalent, is far too lengthy and expensive a process. Publishers may take a long while to respond, and fewer and fewer of them are now prepared to take on new composers, without prior endorsement from a body such as the SPNM.

The BBC has a similar system to the SPNM: a panel of readers who will recommend scores for a broadcast performance. The panel does not meet regularly, however, and distinguished people – composers, performers and critics – are simply co-opted from time to time to read scores which have been sent in. The BBC has three responses to a score: 'reject', 'accept', and 'accept if offered'. The first two are straightforward enough, but the third requires a little explanation. If an artist or ensemble is already on the BBC's list of accredited performers, and offers a programme which contains one of your pieces, then, if the work concerned has been 'accepted if offered' it will be broadcast as part of the programme. It is therefore worth trying to interest a well-known performer or ensemble in your work, since this can be yet another route to having your compositions publicly performed. Another way to get yourself a broadcast is via the individual programme producers. Look through the *Radio Times* for all the programmes which feature contemporary music, and find out who the producers are. There are several producers at the BBC who are very sympathetic to the cause of contemporary music, and you can send your scores direct to them. Send a well-laid-out CV as well, stating where and with whom you studied, what works you have had performed (include the more notable student performances), and any other relevant information.

However distasteful it may seem, the best way to persuade people to consider your work is often to be a pest. There are always a fair number of small- to middle-sized ensembles which specialise in contemporary music, and you should write and send cassettes to the artistic director, or even go to their concerts and introduce yourself. If butting in at the end of a concert seems unnecessarily intrusive, ask if you can make an appointment to see the ensemble's leader on a date in the future, taking scores and cassettes along with you. Alternatively, find out the most common instrumental combination for the ensemble and either look out existing scores for that combination or write a piece specially for it. This latter course carries some risks, of course: you may spend many hours on a piece with the same instrumentation as Messiaen's *Quartet for the End of Time* (which you know the ensemble performs regularly), only to find that the ensemble in question never looks at it. Being a pest sometimes elicits a rude response, but you are more likely to be taken notice of than if you remain virtually anonymous and the people whose interest you are trying to arouse never find out what you look like or what kind of a person you are. For the same reason it is important for you to go to concerts of contemporary music, both to be seen and to talk to like-minded people who are more likely to be interested in what you are doing. Don't be afraid to ask advice from any established composers you meet at such gatherings – you will find, in general, that people are very helpful.

Ballet and dance companies who specialise in, or regularly feature, contemporary dance, are also worth approaching. Find out whose job it is to select or commission the music for new ballets, and send that person a CV and a selection of cassettes. Add the names of a few chosen choreographers to the list of people whom you need to get to know.

Several composers have found their niche in their own locality, writing for local choirs and orchestras, involving themselves in schools and community centres, running workshops, composing for local occasions, and so on. This can be very satisfying, but you do need particular skills, of personality and communication, to be able to do this, especially a knack of putting your ideas across to non-musicians (teaching skills are very valuable in this kind of work). Terms like 'animateur' or 'facilitator', even 'enabler', are heard increasingly frequently, and refer to this kind of community involvement by a musician.

Whenever a performance of one of your compositions is scheduled, make sure that the critics get to hear about it, and try to persuade them to attend. Criticism, even 'bad' criticism, is useful, because your name appears in the music pages, and the fact that the critics have bothered to give you any space at all indicates that they think you are worth writing about. I had an electronic piece performed at the Aldeburgh Festival in the early 1960s, at the same time as the first performance of Benjamin Britten's *Psalm 150*. The first sentence of the criticism made the most horrible comparisons between the 'masterful compositions' of Britten and my new piece, and a couple of people telephoned me very excitedly to say 'Did you know you're in the same sentence as Benjamin Britten?'. A fairly thick skin is useful, because criticism can be wounding, but try to remember that your name has appeared in print one more time, and that can only be good. I doubt if any composer's career has been destroyed by adverse criticism – my first review said 'This composer ought to take up some other profession'.

The composer and commissions

Commissions are in the remit of the Arts Councils, the Regional Arts Boards, business sponsors and, very rarely, private people or groups. These are the people with the money, but the impetus and inspiration for the commissions comes, in the first place, from the performers – orchestras, choirs, ensembles and soloists. You cannot write to a Regional Arts Board and say 'Please will you commission me to write...?'; the request has to come from the performer, because they are the people who will receive the money.

Each year, the APC/Composers Guild and the Regional Arts Boards draw up accepted fee guidelines which are accepted by the BBC and the Arts Councils, and an ensemble applying for commission money will not, therefore have to haggle over fees. There are a number of categories, according to the scoring of the proposed composition (solo flute, string quartet, full orchestra, chamber orchestra, etc), and each category stipulates two fee-bands: one for less-established composers, and one for more-established composers. The fees are increased each year, and the only cause for argument would be if you disagreed with your classification as a 'less-established' composer when they offered you the lowest rate. Commissions for works which will be toured, performed in several venues up and down the country, or receive their first performance abroad, are awarded by the Arts Councils, whereas those concerning performances within a particular region are usually handled by the appropriate Regional Arts Board. Here another snag arises: the majority of RABs do not offer the full fee. This is not really their fault – there is simply not enough commissioning money in the kitty, and there are likely to be far more applications for commission money than there is money to go round. If a Regional Arts Board has £60,000, and 100 commissioning grants are applied for at £1,000-£2,000 each, then the sums go awry, and the guidelines state quite clearly that it is better to give small amounts of money to many applicants than large amounts to few. The way out most commonly used is for the RAB to offer 'part funding' of a commission, probably half, on the understanding that the ensemble will make up the difference by raising money from private donations or sponsorship. In practice, the ensembles very rarely manage this, so you have to accept that, if you get an RAB commission, you are likely to be working for half price.

Businesses are, of course, another source of funding. Some local businesses are very good for local commissions, because they know that they will receive a lot of publicity in their own locality, but, generally speaking, businesses want to know what will be in it for them, and if you show them the programme and tell them that there may be an audience of only 25 people, they may not be terribly keen to be involved. Businesses will sponsor concerts, but to persuade them to sponsor a commission is less easy than is sometimes made out. An exception might be if you were using a company's products, such as electronic or MIDI instruments, in which case the company might be quite willing to fund a composition which would display its equipment prominently in front of the audience for a whole evening or more. Other than this, you are better off to cultivate your relationships with the performers themselves, and let them cajole the sponsors.

Don't be fooled into thinking that you will make a lot of money from commission fees – it is not, by itself, a way to earn a living, even if you are well known.

The composer and supporting organisations

There are several organisations which composers can join. Mention has already been made of the SPNM, which carries other benefits of membership besides the possibility of workshop performances. Any composer can apply to belong to the Composers' Guild (which also has a student section), whereas the Association of Professional Composers will only, as its name suggests, admit established professional composers who must be at least associate members of the PRS (see below). This doesn't mean that you have to earn your living solely from composition, or that you compose only 'concert music' (the APC has a large number of 'commercial' composers among its members), but that you have satisfied the hierarchy that you are serious about composition, and not merely flirting with it every now and then. There are various criteria which they will accept as being proof of your 'status' – membership of the PRS, for instance. Composers can also join the Incorporated Society of Musicians (the Performers' and Composers' section) and the Musicians' Union (the British Music Writers' Council is the section of the Union dealing with composers, arrangers and copyists and has replaced the old ACCS – Arrangers' Composers' and Copyists' Section).

The PRS (Performing Right Society) is the organisation in the UK which collects and administers royalties from live performances and broadcasts on behalf of its composer, author and publisher members. You do not *have* to join the PRS, but you will not be able to collect royalties from the performances of your works unless you do. If you haven't applied before, you should at least apply when you get your first commission. There is no charge involved in being a member of the PRS, but membership depends on the number of public performances your works have received. Some student performances would probably be eligible (so do keep a record of these), and the PRS would certainly acknowledge any performances given under the umbrella of the SPNM. Both of the foregoing are dependent on the work having been performed in one of 500 or so 'significant venues' or 'significant festivals'. This is a PRS list which calls venues 'significant' if they fulfil certain criteria of seating capacity and frequency of concerts. These venues *must* send in programmes. If your work is performed anywhere else, you can make use of the Unsolicited Programmes Scheme (UPS) and send in a programme signed by the hall manager or concert promoter. The criteria for membership of the PRS are quite complex, but information and advice is available from PRS staff. Any royalties payable in respect of performances of your compositions are divided between you and your publisher, so one piece of information which is needed on your PRS application form is the name of your publisher. This does not mean that you have to persuade a publisher to take you on before you are accepted as a member; you can instead be 'self-publishing', in which case you would receive the royalties in full. A book entitled *The Composer's Guide to Music Publishing*, which will answer most of the questions you could possibly ask on this topic, is available from the APC and is free to members.

Joining one of the composer associations is a good way of keeping in touch with your colleagues, but you should keep an eye open, too, for summer schools and courses, both in the UK and abroad. Bursaries are often available towards the cost of such courses, and are not restricted to students only. Sometimes specific aspects of composing are addressed: 'writing for film', 'composing for the voice' and so on; others are more general. In January and February, magazines like *Classical Music* and *Music Teacher* have page after page of summer schools, a reasonable number of which would be of interest to composers. Course are not only useful from the point of view of learning a new skill, but they are also excellent places for meeting people and for getting works performed, officially or unofficially. Funds, usually in the form of scholarships, are also sometimes available for longer periods of study abroad, and details are normally advertised in the music press.

The composer and competitions

The *British Music Yearbook* carries two sections on competitions for composers: one for competitions in the UK, another for competitions abroad. (The *Yearbook*, incidentally, is an invaluable source of information in general. It not only contains the addresses and telephone numbers of orchestras, ensembles, the Regional Arts Councils, broadcasting organisations, choirs and competitions, but also provides an instant telephone directory of British composers, regardless of whether or not they belong to a particular organisation.) If you want to enter for a competition, write off for the prospectus which will give you up-to-date information on length of piece, specified instrumentation (if applicable), deadlines and prizes. Some competitions will accept any piece, others stipulate that the work must never before have been performed, and there are drawbacks in such cases. A submitted work may be 'tied up' for as much as a year while the competition takes its course, and any performance of that piece before the end of the competition, no matter how insignificant the venue, will disqualify it. Winning a competition would give a tremendous boost to a young composer's career, but even if you don't win, the experience, the discipline involved, the chance to have your work performed, and the chance to meet yet more people, are likely to make the exercise worth while.

Festivals, too, other than those featuring contemporary music, may have a composers competition from time to time to celebrate a particular event or anniversary.

If there is one piece of advice which I would like to emphasise more than any other, it is to urge you to remain open to any opportunity which presents itself. Whether it's music for a ballet, an art exhibition, some arranging, a piece for a local school, a solo for an up-and-coming singer or instrumentalist – the more music you can have performed, the more you will learn about the problems of translating a written score into a performance which correctly reflects your original intention. You will become more *au fait* with instrumentation, notation, dynamics, balance between instruments, time-scale within movements, and all the other things which can seem so straightforward on paper and so disconcertingly wrong when played by someone else. It is worth remembering that, although you are the creator and the performers the interpreters (giving you, morally speaking, the 'higher ground'), you are, nevertheless, entirely in their hands and you must treat them with the professional respect they deserve. Your need to create a particular texture or timbre cannot override a human need on the part of the performer to breathe, for instance. Performers are seldom shy about telling you what they think (things, sometimes, which you don't really want to know), and it is well to take note of any practical points which they may raise. Your experience and knowledge will grow with every work you have performed.

Useful books:

Norman Del Mar: *Anatomy of the Orchestra* (Faber & Faber)
Walter Piston: *Orchestration* (Gollancz)
Alfred Blatter: *Instrumentation/Orchestration* (Longman)
Gardiner Read: *Music Notation* (Gollancz)
Colin Matthews & Susan Homewood: *Essentials of Music Copying* (Music Publishers Association)
Annie Gunning: *The Composer's Guide to Music Publishing* (APC Publishing)

WORKING IN MUSIC EDUCATION

DAVID NEVENS

David Nevens is a composer who has had a parallel career in music education. He has worked most recently at the Welsh College of Music and Drama in Cardiff, where he was Director of the School of Music for nearly twelve years. His interest in the promotion of music to young and old alike has led him to work as an adjudicator, examiner and writer, and to advise aspiring musicians on courses and careers; he also inspects schools and colleges. During 1994/95, he was Warden of the Music in Education Section of the Incorporated Society of Musicians.

Opportunities, qualities and training

Perhaps the most striking aspect of working in music education today is the flexibility that it offers with regard to time, style and character. It is still possible, for example, even in these days of rapidly changing patterns of employment, to find relatively secure contracts with associated benefits, including sick pay and pension entitlement. On the other hand, there are many possibilities for part-time or occasional work, which can usually be made to fit in with other activities, such as performing, composing or private teaching.

The range of needs is also wide, from infant, junior and senior pupils in schools and colleges to specialist young musicians and further and higher education students; from adult learners, community enterprises, people with special needs, enthusiastic amateur performers and composers to the high demands of appraisal, inspection and assessment.

Except for ever-increasing flexibility, versatility and self-reliance, however, the qualities needed from the musician working in education remain relatively constant. To be involved in any field of education is a privilege that demands boundless enthusiasm and the ability to project that enthusiasm, high expectations matched by the highest of personal standards, resilience, perseverance, self-discipline, and honest self-evaluation. And beyond these, the faith to promote the equality of the skills and understanding of music with other subjects of study, the personality to cultivate a sense of wonder unimpaired by familiarity, and the confidence to develop an openness and responsiveness to the growing awareness of others.

A formidable list indeed, and one that matches in every way the demands of all other aspects of the music profession. Working in music education is not a soft option, nor is it a responsibility that should be taken lightly, for personal example is one of the most powerful forces in the learning process.

Routes into a career in music education will vary according to aspirations and experience, but for all teaching some form of professional training is advisable, and for full-time posts in schools and colleges Qualified Teacher Status (QTS) is virtually essential. This can be achieved through successful completion of a first degree or diploma, followed by a postgraduate certificate in education (PGCE), or the two-year mature access BEd degree, which requires a minimum age of twenty-one, and successful completion of one year of higher education. Alternative routes include the four-year BEd or three-year BA(QTS), and the licensed teacher scheme, for which the minimum age for entry is twenty-six. All of these are funded and monitored by the Teacher Training Agency for Schools. Teaching in Scotland has its own special requirements.

While QTS is not always necessary for instrumental teaching in schools and colleges, some training or experience is really recommended. For posts in higher education, possession of a higher degree and a developing research profile are fundamental, and professional success as a performer or composer is normally expected by conservatoires.

As reputation and experience grow, it is possible to develop a career in related areas, such as adjudication or advisory services. Further specialist training is available for, for example, examining, inspecting, community music teaching, educational liaison, and for performers and composers working in educational projects. For those who are interested in the very important area of special needs or teaching music to those with disabilities, specialist training is essential.

Schools, further and higher education

The establishment of music within the National Curriculum in England and Wales for pupils in maintained schools between the ages of five and fourteen has ensured the need for skilled and versatile teachers. At primary level (key stages 1 and 2), specialist music posts are rare, although there is considerable scope for teaching music throughout the school while retaining a reduced responsibility for general class teaching. There is more scope in the private sector, although a typical preparatory or junior school music teacher may also have to provide instrumental as well as class lessons.

Specialist posts are more widespread within the secondary sector (Key Stage 3), and often involve teaching through Years ten and eleven (Key Stage 4) and beyond. In some further education institutions (a sector which now includes sixth form colleges), music may be restricted to Advanced Level only, but alternative courses, such as national diplomas in performing arts or music technology, are now being offered, and these require relevant teaching skills in order that students can understand the common factors for music across related arts subjects or science and technology.

In schools and colleges, corporate music making at all levels plays an important part in developing both musical and personal skills. Indeed, the musical life of many private and public schools is most strongly based on performing activities, fed by individual tuition. In some cases, these offer considerable scope for teachers with interests and abilities in liturgical music. There are also a small number of openings in the specialist music schools for teachers who are also distinguished and experienced performers.

Competition is intense for lectureships in universities and conservatoires, and a high degree of recognised specialisation, or the capacity and reputation to attract the most able students, are among the important criteria for consideration. Entry to the university sector can sometimes be made easier by gaining a research studentship with associated teaching duties.

Instrumental teaching

The provision of instrumental teaching in schools and colleges, and related orchestral, ensemble and choral music-making, continues to be the area of music education that is subject to the most rapid change. Local management of schools, the direct funding of colleges by the Further Education Funding Councils, the subsequent reduction in resources available to local authorities for central funding and the capping of their direct government grants, have usually resulted in reviews of instrumental music services. Very few of these are now funded directly by local authorities. A new pattern is emerging, in which tuition is paid for by parents or institutions, with or without local authority subsidy. In some areas, completely independent agencies are selling direct services, or schools and colleges are using private teachers.

These types of arrangements have, of course, been in operation in many private schools for a long time, and also in most universities and conservatoires, although, in the case of the latter, vacancies are normally filled by invitation.

These continuing changes have made a marked difference to employment prospects and security. In particular, there has been a reduction in the number of full-time permanent instrumental posts, and these have been replaced by short-term, part-time, temporary contracts, or contracts on a self-employed basis. The situation is therefore fluid and flexible, but recent surveys seem to indicate that, despite these changes, more children than ever are learning instruments and the commitment to area youth ensembles is at least as strong as ever. There is challenging and fulfilling work here, best suited to those who have particular skills in performing, coaching and directing, matched by a progressive approach to teaching. Nevertheless, earning a reasonable living from instrumental teaching alone may not be possible, and it is in this area particularly that versatility, resourcefulness and an entrepreneurial attitude are necessary.

Community, adult and short course teaching

These areas share some common ground in that they are normally outside the conventional school or college system. The impetus for the growth of community music has arisen primarily through a growing realisation of the power of music in improving society, and the wider value of the skills it provides. Many community music teachers 'arrive' through the community services, and they need exceptional ability and experience in promoting the widest range of music to the greatest variety of clients. Special training courses are now sponsored through the community music organisations, such as Community Music London and Community Music Wales, and these deal particularly with important aspects such as awareness of disability or racial background. Although community music teachers may be employed through such organisations, they may also find contract work through social services, regional arts boards, the health service, youth services and private charities or commercial enterprises funding local or national projects.

The main employers of teachers for adults and short courses are the local authorities, the adult or continuing education departments of universities and colleges, the Workers Educational Association, the University of the Third Age and, occasionally, the Technical and Enterprise Councils. Students are normally looking for either a recreational approach or for the chance to obtain better qualifications.

There are also a remarkably large number of residential courses in music, which now seem to provide opportunities for study and further study in almost every aspect of the subject. In most cases, however, the organisers are likely only to engage, on short-term or temporary contracts, musicians who have established a recognised reputation in their specialist fields.

Advisers, inspectors, examiners and adjudicators

These categories of work are connected not only because they share the common processes of evaluation and judgement, but also because entry to them is generally restricted to those who already have considerable experience and an established reputation.

The number of local authority music advisers has dwindled with the reduction of central service provision and, although many authorities retain such posts, responsibilities nearly always extend into other subject areas or aspects of education.

The inspectorate has also changed considerably since the 1992 Education Act. There is now only a handful of specialist HMIs in England and Wales, and their day-to-day function as inspectors has been taken over in schools by part-time inspectors working through agencies contracted by OFSTED (the Office for Standards in Education) in England and OHMCI (the Office of Her Majesty's Chief Inspector) in Wales; the HMI system has been retained in Scotland. Inspection or assessment in further and higher education has become the responsibility of the quality divisions of the respective funding councils. In all these areas there is considerable scope for work for experienced musicians in education who fulfil the rigorous requirements of the training courses provided.

Examiners may work for a number of bodies, including those which provide public examinations, such as the GCSE Examining Boards, the Business and Technology Education Council (BTEC), National Vocational Qualification (NVQ), or the Royal Society of Arts (RSA), or for the specialist organisations which provide graded music examinations – the Associated Board of the Royal Schools of Music (ABRSM), Trinity College of Music, the London College of Music, and the Guildhall School of Music and Drama. There are also opportunities for external examining or moderating in higher education. Most of this is essentially part-time and mainly irregular work, which requires much accumulated experience and acquired status, as well as additional training.

Adjudicating is on the fringe of music education, although it may take place in or for educational establishments. Festivals and local, national and international competitions provide a variety of opportunities for the experienced and generally well-known musician, whose judgements are sound, self-confidence unbounded, and who possesses good public speaking ability. Payment is normally by fee, which generally grows in proportion to the reputation and desirability of the adjudicator.

Performers and composers

The realisation of the value of enabling pupils and students to meet practising musicians has happily coincided with a growth of opportunity during the last five years. This has been particularly noticeable in the large-scale performing organisations in Britain, and now virtually every opera company and orchestra has an educational programme. This provides fascinating work for education liaison officers, who act as facilitators, setting up networks and identifying needs for both their employing organisation and for the education service. Entry to this exciting work normally follows from a background in education or performance, or both.

Education programmes also provide enormous scope for individual performers and members of ensembles to share their particular skills in a wide range of styles, including jazz, commercial music and through music technology.

The demands of the National Curriculum in composing have also provided a useful opportunity for composers to work with children, and this is an area which teachers particularly seem to value.

Resources

The legal requirement to provide music education in schools has resulted in a wider range of learning materials becoming available to support the curriculum. These can take many forms and offer openings for writers, composers, arrangers and computer programmers, as well as for creators and designers of radio, television and video facilities. Successful direct experience, of both the learning process and the chosen media, are essential to ensure relevance and quality of the product, as well as to attract demand.

In conclusion

There are many and varied openings in music education and a wide range of opportunities for employment. Working in education has the advantage of being compatible with other types of musical activity. Generally, the financial rewards are modest, but for those who have the right qualities for success, there is real fulfilment in being part of a constantly developing mission to pass on the skills, understanding, knowledge of music – and, above all, enthusiasm for it.

THE INDEPENDENT TEACHER

TANYA POLUNIN

Tanya Polunin's Pianoforte School was concerned for many years with the training of concert artists and teachers. Students of the School, from all over the world, have won scholarships to study in the former USSR, Poland, Hungary and Czechoslovakia and have been finalists in many national and international competitions. Tanya Polunin was Warden of the Private Teachers' Section of the Incorporated Society of Musicians and was a founder member of International Piano Teachers' Consultants (IPTEC). She has been on the jury of BBC TV's Young Musician of the Year, and adjudicates frequently at leading music festivals. An Associated Board examiner for many years in the United Kingdom and the Far East, she is now retired and coaches artists for recitals and holds refresher courses and consultations for teachers.

So you have decided to teach independently, either a few hours a week, or full time; what does it take? Ask yourself the following questions and, if the answer is even a qualified 'yes' to most of them, you are in business.

1 Do you have faith in yourself as a person, as a musician and as a teacher?
2 Do you have talent, expertise and some experience?
3 Can you communicate easily; are you articulate?
4 Have you business acuity and organisation, or the ability to acquire them?
5 Do you love people, especially children?
6 Are you enthusiastic about music itself, and about musical skills and knowledge?
7 Are you keen to enthuse others and to pass on your joy and experience in music?
8 Have you had a thorough basic training and are you well qualified?

If you *are* in business, get going without hestitation. Much of what follows may seem complex, but it is possible to make a sound and gradual beginning with only the most basic equipment – a studio, an instrument, a telephone and a business-like approach. It is necessary to charge realistic fees (see below), and to be informed and well organised in your approach. It makes no difference whether you intend to teach for 5 or 50 hours per week.

Acquiring pupils

The best method is by personal recommendation – hard at first, but it is self-generating in time. Advertising in local papers and the musical and educational press needs to be continuous to be effective, but so can be a simple but nicely displayed card: 'Piano Tuition by Qualified Pianist'. Name, qualifications, address, telephone. One new pupil from this will pay for many insertions. Leave your professional card or printed notice in libraries, music shops and music clubs, in social clubs, schools and colleges. Contact leisure and educational associations for retired people (many of whom also have grandchildren!), adult education centres, University of the Third Age and such like. Playing for festivals and dancing classes as accompanist, giving recitals at local institutions, teaching part-time in a local school or college, will all help to get you known and talked about. Occasionally it is possible to buy a teaching practice from a retiring teacher, but this often means buying the house as well as the goodwill.

A practice takes time to build up, but eventually you will reach the envious stage of being able to audition and choose your new pupils, and gently to shed those who have not the talent or industry to benefit from your specialist work.

Adult beginners

Adult beginners, or 'begin-againers', often have to trudge round from teacher to teacher until they find one who will accept them; they are brave people, pitting themselves to learn what children learn with comparative ease.

The advantages of adult beginners are that they possess
  (a) a love of music which has driven them to seek lessons,
  (b) a long-term view of their aims, and the patience to work and progress gradually,
  (c) greater musical experience to draw on,
  (d) the ability to be more outspoken about their playing, and
  (e) expertise and superiority in their own fields, giving them self-confidence and belief in themselves.

Their disadvantages are stiff muscles and inflexible joints, laborious learning of skills a child can acquire, poor co-ordination, visible and intractable nerves, and the expectation that, because they are adult, they should progress very quickly. Sometimes slow progress causes much frustration, however, their love of music is so great that they persevere, and are tremendously worth while to teach; you will learn so much from them.

Adults are often ambitious in the music they wish to study, and may have to accept a modest standard of playing at first. They frequently wish to take examinations but I would never enter an adult for an examination under about grade 5 standard. Remember that they can be among your best ambassadors.

Your brochure or prospectus

To give accurate factual information about yourself and the services you offer, it is necessary to have a brochure or prospectus. This should be well laid out using only the most expensive paper and printing you can afford. It is desirable to look successful from the start, however diffident you may feel. Quite a basic lay-out can be used, which hardly varies, even when the prospectus becomes glossy later.

The simplest form is a sheet of A4 card or good quality paper folded in half; this gives four pages. On page one, the name of your school or studio, your logo if you wish, your name and qualifications, address and telephone number. Page two contains your musical curriculum vitae, excerpts from press notices of your work and from letters of recommendation, and brief details of pupils' successes. Do not be modest; be factual, but write in glowing terms – if you do not blow your own trumpet, no-one else will. Page three: clear descriptions of the courses available and the subjects of lessons and classes. Mention special tuition for children and adult beginners. Page four can contain a brief resumé of business terms. The fees list should be a separate insert of a different colour (which changes when new fees come into effect) stating current charges (on an hourly basis and pro rata) for consultation lessons, courses of lessons and classes. On the back of the fees list, give your business terms in full.

Setting up the practice

The most ambitious plan is a separate studio block or wing comprising a large studio, one or more smaller studios, a waiting room or area, toilet and kitchen facilities and an office. However, if you are using your own house, you can have a more modest arrangement, although a studio, a waiting area, an office and facilities are essential. The studio should be seen to be a *music* studio, not a hastily or temporarily converted family room where you have to turn out the family and the cat and deprive them of TV – but a studio used only for your work, and fitted up and sound-proofed as such. The decor should be light, airy and positive with close carpeting and pleasing curtains and pictures, generally music-orientated. The best piano you can afford should be well lit, free from dust inside and out, with clean ivories. You will also need an adjustable piano stool, a footstool for tiny pupils and a strong, efficient, adjustable music stand. Amenities should include shelves for your library, tapes and CDs, recording equipment, a music centre and an office with a desk, filing cabinet, telephone/fax and typewriter or word processor (learn to type!). Also have a telephone extension (with a very soft bell) within arm's reach when you are teaching.

These first essentials can be expanded gradually to include the use of several studios, or a house for your School of Music. More and better instruments (two grand pianos in your main studio are impressive and practical) and good pianos in your other studios. A waiting room or hall, warm and comfortable, with music books and a table where waiting pupils can do last-minute theory or homework, and can meet and talk. A library of books and music, and a lending library for sight reading. Recording equipment, records and tapes; business stationery, filing cabinets – and a part-time secretary.

Noise nuisance

Music entails the production of sounds which may annoy neighbours, and it is important to do all you can to minimise this. In a semi-detached house, choose a room on the other side from your neighbours which has no party wall. Sound-proofing may mean only keeping windows and doors shut during practice and teaching times. Secondary glazing can be effective where there is a gap of at least four inches between inside and outside windows. Absorbent acoustic panels can be used on walls and ceiling. Small rubber pads, up to one inch thick, underneath piano casters, close carpeting, thick curtains, all can help to insulate the sound. Prove to your neighbours that you have done a great deal, and spent money too, considering their comfort: state the times you teach each day and promise that there will be no music making before 8 am or after 10 pm and none on Sundays. Do not set up a practice next door to a bed-ridden granny.

It is wise to scan the local bye-laws on noise nuisance, as they can vary from council to council. Consider also the Town and Country Planning Act which designates areas which may not be used for business, and by-laws affecting the 'change of use' of a house. A mean neighbour can report you to the council as 'running a music school' and the council is bound to investigate. It could even prevent you from continuing your business.

Business matters

For clear understanding of the terms and conditions under which you accept pupils, it is wise to have printed agreement forms which are signed both by the pupil and/or parents and yourself; this means two copies which are exchanged after signature. Make sure these terms are understood by the pupil or parents, and invite questions before signing.

It is important to cover the following points:
(a) The pupil wishes to study and the teacher agrees to teach.
(b) The number of lessons in a course (usually ten) and the length of lessons.
(c) Teaching terms according to the school calendar, with holiday breaks and public holidays.
(d) Payment of fees in advance, at or before the first lesson of a course.
(e) Notice for the cessation of lessons: notice of at least one full course to take affect at the end of that course.
(f) Missed lessons, which will be charged for unless a month's notice is given. Lessons missed by the teacher are carried forward; the pupil does not lose them.
(g) Examinations, competitions, and public performance: the teacher will not enter a pupil without the pupil's or parent's consent; the pupil will not enter an examination or competition or perform in public without the teacher's consent.
(h) Increase of fees: the teacher reserves the right to increase fees from time to time, (to reflect increasing costs of overheads and inflation

and the teacher's added experience). Due notice will be given,
at least one course of lessons ahead.

How much to charge

You are not a benevolent institution – you are earning your living by your profession, and your fees need to reflect a realistic return on your investment, your talent and experience, and your devotion to your work. It is essential to charge realistic fees which bear comparison to what your colleagues earn per annum at universities and schools.

When deciding what fees to charge, consider the following:

(a) The value of your talent, years of study and training, your musical and teaching experince.

(b) The fact that you will not be earning during holiday periods.
Thirty to forty weeks' work has to show a profit on 52 weeks' living. Since you are self-employed there is no holiday pay, no sick leave, no unemployment benefit, and you must pay your own national insurance, self-employed pension and personal and studio insurances.

(c) Find out what is charged by experienced, qualified teachers in your district (the others do not count). Consider how many of them earn their full living from teaching, and *charge more*. Alright, *be* the most expensive teacher in the district. *You* know you are worth it.
You might even become fashionable!

(d) Start high; you can always lower fees, but it is much harder to raise them (except *as* a direct result of inflation, and that is *not* progress). Start high, but remember that 'high' is relative. What do dentists, lawyers, medical consultants and solicitors charge? Like you, all have had long, arduous, expensive training. How much do you pay the plumber or electrician?

(e) People plead poverty, even when they have two cars in the family, a second home or two holidays abroad a year, and colour television. *People will pay for what they really want and people value most what costs them most.*

(f) Experience is invaluable, is worth paying for, and should be reflected in your fees. Most recommended fees are for young, beginner teachers with little or no experience.

Once you have decided on your fees, make sure you have an effective billing system and keep clear accounts. You will be respected for your strict code of business practice.

If you have an agreed code of business conduct you can then, *as a concession only,* be a little flexible if *you* feel the pupil's situation demands it. There should be no concessions regarding fees, except insofar as you, the teacher, wish to help a talented and really needy pupil by giving a bursary. Remember that it is *your* livelihood, and you can only be as generous as you can afford to be. Bill pupils in full each time, and then deduct a proportion of the bursary. It is desirable that this should be a confidential arrangement, unless bursaries are awarded by open competition.

Accounts should be sent out to arrive at least two weeks prior to the end of a course of lessons. Bill forms should also carry a resumé of the business terms relating to payment and notice.

Do not accept payment per lesson (except for single consultation lessons charged at a higher fee). Do not give lessons without prior payment, or you lay yourself open to abuse and find yourself giving presents to unscrupulous people.

Finances

Consider your finances in two stages. First, those concerning your school activities: your income from teaching, and the cost of the day-to-day running of the studio and practice. Remember all expenditure, including rent or mortgage repayments, heat and light, and domestic help relating to the parts of the house used for your business. Don't forget the upkeep of your capital investment, the depreciation of assets, and insurance of the studio and effects.

Second, you will have to submit annual accounts to the tax-man. There are many allowable expenses for running the practice and it is wise to use an accountant from the beginning.

Consider your self-employed status and the resultant benefits and drawbacks. Consider national insurance payments and a self-employed pension. Consider insurance: house, fire and theft, and list separately instruments and valuable assets. Consider life and accident insurance, public liability, income protection; consider medical insurance which will enable you to *choose* to go into hospital in a holiday period and not lose too many fees in term time.

Running the practice

Get used to the idea, from the start, that much of your work will be at rather unsocial hours; from four to nine or ten in the evening when school children and working people are free, and on Saturdays. Many teachers take Sunday and part of Monday off, starting teaching at 4 pm. A few adults can come during the day, and some people have half-days free.

When planning your timetable, consider the age and school commitments of child pupils, the distance they travel and their homework (Fridays are therefore popular for lessons); also the early dark during winter.

Make a timetable that is reasonable for *you*, and does not impose the strain of over-long hours, otherwise your last pupils of the day will not get a fair deal – you will have little brain or patience left.

Length of lessons can vary according to pupils' ages and standards – 30 minutes for age 5 to 9, 45 minutes for 10 to 13, and one hour from 14 years onwards. Also consider the standard of work: to try to give a broad musical and instrumental education in 60 minutes a week at grade 8 standard is not realistic. Teachers may, and do, try to get by on less, but instruction can hardly be detailed and thorough, and we owe our pupils this. At this stage, two separate, one-hour sessions a week might suffice to cover everything.

Keep broadly to school and college terms, but there is no reason why you should not teach most pupils for up to 40 weeks a year, and this may be wise if you have a family to bring up. It is possible to have four ten-week courses of lessons a year running continuously across pre-arranged holiday breaks of, say, two weeks each at Easter and Christmas, five weeks in summer, and three separate weeks when schools have their mid-term breaks.

New pupils can begin lessons at the beginning of any ten-week course of lessons. Some teachers prefer to adhere to school terms, but they still have to live for 52 weeks – and take a holiday.

Courses and classes

The aim is a course of musical instruction and education, in the broadest sense, together with specialist instrumental instruction. 'I only teach piano – you must go to Mrs Bloggs for aural training, sight reading, theory, history, general musicianship and so on.' This is not good practice, dividing the indivisible. It took me years as a child before I realised that my classical pieces were full of cadences, or that the hymns I played at school prayers were traditional harmony... You need to be a jack-of-all-trades, though specialising in your main subject. If you feel you cannot teach the so-called 'fringe subjects', jolly well learn how to, at least up to a moderate standard; obviously you need educating. Only at an advanced level should you need help from specialist colleagues.

How are you going to fit it all in? The answer is with Saturday classes for much of the instruction. Groups of three to ten pupils of related standard can learn very fast, from you and from each other, and much fun can be had in the process: to the subsidiary theory, keyboard harmony, extemporisation, score reading, written harmony, part writing, chorale singing and aural work contained in the general musicianship classes I also add teachers' classes, technique jamborees, scale and study competitions, performance prizes (with outside adjudicators) at students' recitals, and progress prizes.

The courses of study need individual planning for each pupil, to suit their ability and needs and individual rate of progress.

Lesson content

Each lesson requires planning on a simple basis, with a clear idea (in your pupil's mind, too) of what you hope to achieve each term and in the long run. Each instrumental lesson can be divided into –
  (a) *Aural skills* A few minutes as the pupil comes in the door!
  (b) *Sight reading*
  (c) *Technical skills* Scales and arpeggios, exercises and studies
  (d) *Interpretation skills* How to study; study of works; performance; memory
and, for beginners:
  (a) *Aural skills*
  (b) *Reading skills, notation and timing* later combined into sight reading
  (c) *Exercises, scales, arpeggios, short studies*
  (d) *Pieces*

(e) *Playing old pieces from memory*

If any important part of the lesson is omitted for lack of time, arrange with the pupil to *start* the next lesson with it. Punctuality is vital both for you and the pupil. Start on time and finish on time. Just 'finishing the movement' steals time from the next pupil, or runs the whole day late.

Classes should have the same organised basis, and the same main principles apply.

Performance

Encourage the corporate life of the school by getting groups of pupils to play to each other frequently, starting in groups of three or four to avoid shyness, and later developing this into a gentle criticism class where they can help each other with suggestions and get used to playing to an audience. Informal in-house competitions can foster keenness, as can recitals, with parents and friends present and, finally, the more formidable end-of-term concert, all of which is a direct preparation for the important aspect of playing, freely and easily, for other people's pleasure. Have tea and cakes and a social gathering after the more informal events and get to know something of the family backgrounds of your pupils; parents can meet and can discuss their children – and you!

You will also gain a valuable insight into how your pupils react under performance conditions and a chance to see how well your lessons in platform deportment have stuck.

Parents

Parents are ambitious for their children; it is difficult for them to think objectively, and emotional ties confuse matters. Take the parents into partnership with the pupils and yourself. Discuss aims, progress, practice, the importance of examinations and competitions and all matters relevant to the progress and enjoyment of their particular child. Do not pronounce on prospective progress until you know something of the talent and application of the child; do not patronise parents, rather, share with them. Communication is vital here, and your attitude is always attentive and concerned. Occasionally, parents are not very interested in the child's music and, if so, the pupil needs extra support and encouragement from you. Arrange a time each evening when parents can telephone you – not during lessons...

In your business dealings with parents, keep strictly to the business code; do not be persuaded or cajoled into lowering fees or accepting late or part payment. We can all plead poverty.

Examinations, competitions, public performance: as mentioned above, there will be a clause in your business terms and agreement about these.

Regular grade examinations are a way of life for some teachers and pupils. Sadly, progress is linked to, or judged by, success in examinations, or pot-hunting in competitions. But you know better, and value them for the incentive to work and progress that they generate. Taken in passing, in the pupil's stride, they can be valuable and tangible assets, and the resulting certificate a source of pride.

A diet of examination music only is to be deplored, nor is it necessary. Keep it all in perspective, bearing in mind those examinations which may be qualifying grades for GCSE, A level or college entrance. If a child wants to enter competitions, the competitive spirit is to be realistically encouraged but certificate collecting is to be deplored and has nothing to do with music. Parents often suggest that their child *should* compete or take an examination. Discuss future plans so that all realise you are being constructive and not negative, but do not be bullied against your judgement. Some young people thrive on examinations and competitions. However, others of different temperament should rarely, if ever, do them, and should not be allowed to think themselves second class. They need to be allowed to go at their own pace.

You, the teacher, should have the final say; good results will reflect on the pupil (rightly); bad results reflect on you, the teacher (wrongly).

Qualifications and the music profession

Ambitious pupils who do well in final grade examinations often like to consider taking a diploma, or even entering the profession. Advise them to consider these facts:

Grade 8 is still an amateur examination, where the examiner will do his best to give good marks. Diplomas are *not* grade 9 or 10; they are totally different and are several years' study in advance of grade 8, and are the first professional examination. You have to *prove* to a panel of examiners that you are good enough. A diploma syllabus is also far more advanced and far-reaching in its demands and the standard of performance far, far higher. A brilliant grade 8 has little bearing on professional musician material, unless you are 12 or 13 years old – or less!

If a diploma is really desirable and, in your realistic view, attainable, then the pupil who has largely grown up within your comprehensive courses can be well prepared by focusing the various aspects of study towards the requirements of the syllabus. It may be advisable to ask for additional help from specialist colleagues if, say, your knowledge of history of music is not sufficiently far-reaching. Also, a mature musical approach is needed and your brilliant young pupil may take time to grow into this.

GCSE and A-level music can be valuable, but it is essential to co-operate with the pupil's school head of music and to agree how to divide the tuition. Extra time for lessons with you is essential to cover your part of the syllabus and to provide practical training as well, in the time the pupil has remaining after other school work. How many hours a week does the school give to maths A level, for instance? Music will take just as many.

Your answer to 'shall I take up music as a profession?' is generally 'to be realistic, I would not advise it'. It is not a soft, easy option: it is an overcrowded profession and very tough. There is room at the very top, but not for many as soloists. Is your pupil top-class material? It is misleading to foster hopes which may lead to struggle and frustration. So many talents are required of a professional beyond just outstanding musical and instrumental ability – above all, the determination not only to survive but also to make an individual niche for himself, and the ability to learn how to market his talents.

College entrance and diplomas are only the first hurdle. Immense musical ability with a well-founded and developed technique are required, together with resilience, a great dedication to work, and really robust health.

Professional associations

It is wise to belong to at least two national professional associations, one representing musicians as a whole, and one covering your special interests as an instrumentalist and teacher. Both these can give you invaluable advice and support in all aspects of your work, and even legal assistance. It is also helpful to join local music associations, clubs and festivals; these will help you to get better known and to meet colleagues.

I would particularly suggest the Incorporated Society of Musicians, the European String Teachers Association (ESTA) and, for consultation, the International Piano Teachers' Consultants (IPTEC).

As you build up your teaching practice, gradually work yourself into a consistent organised system which suits *you*. If your basic methods are clear, sound and strict, you can afford to be a little flexible. Try to create a corporate image of your school so that pupils identify with it with pride, and younger pupils have a clear idea of how they can progress in their music.

Here, then, is a brief outline of how to set up and run an independent teaching practice. You will have many ideas to try out and incorporate; here, to start with, is a basic method of approach that has worked for me and for my past students for over 30 years. I, for one, have found it to be the most satisfying and fulfilling work in the world.

WORKING IN THE COMMUNITY

PETER RENSHAW

Peter Renshaw is Head of the Department of Performance and Communication Skills at the Guildhall School of Music and Drama. Formerly Principal of the Yehudi Menuhin School and Gresham Professor of Music, he has lectured widely in Great Britain and overseas on music training and the professional development of musicians. He is a member of the Arts Council of England's Education and Training Committee, and is currently an adviser to the London Philharmonic, Royal Philharmonic Orchestra, Royal Opera House, City of London Sinfonia and the Firebird Trust. As a consultant, he has worked with the Ontario Arts Council, the Association of Canadian Orchestras, Banff Centre for the Arts, Youth Music Australia, the University of Sydney and numerous arts organisations in Scandinavia.

Responding to Change

The music world offers a diversity of opportunity and challenge to those musicians who are open-minded, adaptable and responsive to change. No longer can individual performers, composers, conductors, teachers, therapists and administrators hide behind a narrow musical and cultural conditioning if they want music to be a vibrant, dynamic force in society. Change is now the norm. Fundamentally new questions are being asked, traditional assumptions are being challenged, new skills are being developed, and newly defined goals are being pursued. Such a significant shift in attitude and perspective is essential if music is to become more accessible and serve a much wider community.

This revolution in philosophy and action is challenging the modern musician to become a flexible, creative resource, capable of responding to changing cultural, educational, community and performance needs. An instrumentalist or a singer can no longer just rely on traditional technical and interpretative skills to play in an orchestra or sing in an opera chorus, supplemented perhaps by individual teaching. Most major orchestras, opera companies and performance groups have developed educational and community policies which demand an additional range of social, leadership, communication, performance, creative and workshop skills. This is obliging the musician to become much more broadly based, both in terms of attitude and skill.

For musicians at the start of their career, or for those considering a change of direction, the prospect is exciting, but can also be daunting. The main point of this chapter is to identify some of the avenues which can be explored by those musicians wishing to work in the community. The examples are not exhaustive, but are intended to illustrate the range of options available.

Orchestras

Although rooted in a strong cultural tradition, many orchestras have begun to confront the challenge of their survival by adopting a more visionary leadership which views the orchestra as a group of musicians aiming to serve the widest possible community. Over the last decade, this thrust into the wider public view has been gathering momentum, often supported by sponsorship with an interest in urban and rural regeneration. This initiative has been encouraged by the Arts Council, Regional Arts Boards, Local Authorities and the Association of British Orchestras, with the result that many orchestras have evolved enterprising education and community policies responsive to local needs.

This community brief has generated an enthusiastic commitment from many players participating in these schemes and it has also demonstrated the need for orchestras to pay serious attention to the personal and artistic development of their musicians. Engaging in different kinds of performance practice has widened the opportunity for players to become more responsible for their musical actions. They have been encouraged to make artistic, social and educational decisions of their own, rather than just be an efficient cog in a high-precision machine, energised by a charismatic conductor.

Enlightened managements now recognise that serving the community and serving the players go hand in hand. In fact, each musician needs to be confronted by an internal creative challenge as a necessary precondition for working in the community. Responding to this growing emphasis on the rediscovery of the orchestral player as an individual, several orchestras have initiated ambitious training schemes which place their players at the centre of a rigorous research and development programme. Other orchestras are pursuing a range of activities in different community venues. In most cases, players are expected to work alongside composers or animateurs, and to lead workshops for children or for other groups. Invariably these activities culminate in shared performances, involving professional musicians and all participants collaborating in the project. Such partnerships help to establish a strong community of interest from which everyone can benefit.

Opera companies

Like the orchestras, most opera companies have an education department responsible for generating different creative projects, which are designed to make opera in all its forms widely accessible. Such projects vary considerably, but they range from devising large-scale community operas to creating music-theatre pieces or running a series of practical workshops. Singers, instrumentalists, composers, theatre directors, designers, writers, actors and choreographers come together as working partners with schools and community groups, often producing highly innovative and adventurous pieces of music-theatre.

Slowly, attempts are being made to integrate educational work with the artistic policies of the companies, with the implication that their singers and players ideally ought to have the necessary creative and communication skills to lead workshops in the community. Technical and interpretative skills alone are totally inadequate for this growing area of professional work.

Performance groups

Over the last decade, considerable initiative and imagination have been shown by an increasing number of smaller groups whose work embraces different forms of performance, accompanied by a wide variety of community activity. In some cases, their work has been supported by the Arts Council's Contemporary Music Network (CMN), which is an innovative touring scheme bringing the highest quality new music from around the world to the British public. CMN also has an educational function designed to increase access to new music through composing and performing workshops in schools, colleges and community venues.

In recent years, some music groups have displayed a growing interest in cross-arts activities which can also generate extensive community collaboration. Work with the visual arts often originates from the more visionary education departments in art galleries or arts centres. There is increasing opportunity for musicians to work alongside artists from other disciplines, but such projects demand the creation of a shared artistic vocabulary and a clarity of intention if they are to be successful both artistically and in a community context.

Similar collaborations have been taking place between Western and non-Western musicians, with the aim of exploring the possible connections between the music of classical Asia or of Africa and the Caribbean with that of the contemporary West. Such collaborative projects also present opportunities for creating new audiences and establishing strong links with different kinds of community groups. This places the principles of access to the arts, equal opportunity and cultural diversity high on any arts agenda.

People with special needs

Many organisations are now trying to establish greater access to the arts for people with learning difficulties or physical disabilities, along with people who are elderly, socially disadvantaged or in long-term care. This opens up enormous opportunities for musicians to give performances and lead workshops in special schools, day centres, residential homes, hospices, psychiatric hospitals and prisons. Many orchestras, opera companies and performance groups offer programmes in these areas, whilst additional work can be found through contacting such organisations as Shape, Artlink, Artshare, National Music and Disability Information Service, British Society for Music Therapy, Firebird Trust, Live Music Now!, Council for Music in Hospitals, Hospice Arts and Community Music Ltd.

Networking

For freelance artists or composers wishing to diversify and work in educational and community settings, it is essential to be fully conversant with the network of organisations which act either in an advisory capacity or have access to funding which enables them to initiate projects. The power base of each individual artist is very largely dependent on the strength and potential of that person's network.

Any network is likely to have a national, regional and local profile, and it could include the following kind of examples:

(i) *at national level* Arts Council, Department for Education, National Foundation of Arts Education, National Community Music Association, Arts Education for a Multicultural Society, Sonic Arts Network, Performing Right Society, Electro-Acoustic Music Association, Jazz Services Ltd, South Bank Centre;

(ii) *at regional/local level* Regional Arts Boards, local education authorities, adult education, youth centres, local authority arts and entertainment departments, community arts centres, theatres, concert halls, local agencies, Eastern Orchestral Board.

Training musicians for work in the community

It cannot be stated too strongly that this diversity of opportunity confronts all training establishments with a major challenge which demands a fundamental shift of attitude and perspective. At present, with one or two notable exceptions, very few colleges offer substantial training modules as preparation for work in the community. Those institutions which have taken this area of development seriously include University of London Goldsmiths' College, the new universities at East Anglia, Leicester, Newcastle, Liverpool, Middlesex and Kingston, Salford College of Technology, Colchester Institute of Higher Education, Leeds College of Music and Community Music Ltd.

Although the conservatoires constitute the main training ground for musicians entering the profession, at the time of writing only the Guildhall School's Department of Performance and Communication Skills (PCS) has developed a comprehensive range of courses for all its undergraduate students, together with a full-time, one-year postgraduate course (The Guildhall Ensemble) and several pioneering retraining programmes for professional orchestral musicians.

Such a training programme is one response to change. It is based on the premise that musicians now have to be open and adaptable to different musical and social contexts. Therefore, workshops in performance and communication skills, theatre, voice and body work, T'ai-chi, improvisation and composition, and new music technology need to be supported by a vigorous educational and community development programme designed to break down social, musical and artistic barriers. This should equip a musician to face most future contingencies.

THE CHURCH MUSICIAN

PAUL HALE

Paul Hale is Rector Chori (Director of Music) at Southwell Cathedral in Nottinghamshire, where he runs a vigorous musical establishment with a choir school and daily sung services. Previously, he has been Assistant Organist at Rochester Cathedral, Assistant Director of Music at Tonbridge School, and Organ Scholar at New College, Oxford. He has a passionate and life-long interest in church music and the organ, is well known as an organ consultant, directs the Nottingham Bach Society, and edits Organists' Review.

There are various options open to church musicians. Among the many paths to musical and spiritual fulfilment, there are none, it has to be said, to great wealth. If your motivation in choosing a career is to aim for an accountant's salary, then re-train to be an accountant – thousands have. The Church has never paid well, cannot now pay a truly professional rate to any organist or singer, and never will be able to reward its musicians as highly as it or they might desire. Having said that, a more realistic attitude to salaries and conditions now prevails in many quarters, of which more below.

You will only succeed in church music if you are utterly dedicated to it. This does not mean being narrow-minded so much as single-minded in your determination to arrive at the church or cathedral post you may always have coveted. That musical goal needs also to be allied to a religious conviction of some sort; a grasp of both the spiritual worth of the daily offering of musical praise to God – even if the congregation numbers only half a dozen – is central to the task, as is an intelligent and enquiring grasp of the liturgy and of the appropriateness of everything sung. Although men clearly dominate cathedral organ lofts, there is no clear reason why this should be so, and all Deans and Chapters would fall over backwards to show themselves to be 'equal opportunities employers'.

There are clearly two main avenues for a professional church musician the cathedrals and the parish churches. Most full-time career possibilities are within the Church of England, but there are some non-conformist and Synagogue positions (and thus, holders) of distinction, most of which are in London. The Roman Catholic church, in several of its cathedrals and oratories in this country, preserves and develops its liturgical music at the highest levels, including the maintainance of choir schools.

Let us examine first the cathedrals, and then the parish churches, in detail.

Cathedrals

There are approximately 47 Anglican and Roman Catholic cathedrals in Great Britain in which the organist's position is full-time or nearly full-time; these include some Oxbridge college chapels and the Chapel of St George, Windsor Castle. There are about 21 cathedral or cathedral-type posts (including the Chapel Royal) which are part-time, ranging from very part-time to well over half-time. There are basically two types of cathedral – those with choir-schools, which run daily sung services (typically seven to nine a week), and those relying on local children and having no choir school, usually employing a part-time organist and singing perhaps only four or five services a week. Most so-called 'parish church' cathedrals fall into the latter category. The majority of 'full-time' organists augment their salaries by teaching (privately, or in a school or college), examining, in giving recitals, running a choral society, broadcasting and so on, but there is a very real time limit on how much of this can be done. No-one should embark on a cathedral career expecting to be away every other week for a few days, unless they are organist at a 'part-time' cathedral, in which case it might work very well.

Salaries for full-time posts (as at 1995) range from £11,000 to £17,500, with a few 'top jobs' paying up to £25,000. In other words, only by being organist of one of the two or three most significant cathedral or collegiate establishments would one earn as much as an experienced director of music in a decent independent school. In addition to the salary, most employers provide a free house, and salaries have generally been increased to cover Council Tax. The Inland Revenue is generally willing to accept this arrangement as necessary for the proper performance of one's duties, and does not, therefore, charge income tax on the value of this particular perk. Fees are paid for extra and special services, and there is, increasingly, a pension scheme, or the willingness to contribute to a private pension plan.

Conditions of employment vary enormously, and are established in the contract which most organists have (and which all should insist upon having). Most contracts are without term, but fixed-term contracts are becoming more common. How this will work in practice has yet to be established. For a full-time cathedral organist, there will be typically six weeks' real holiday a year, often plus some at half-terms. Retirement is usually at 65.

The essentials of the job include the following:

The recruiting of boys (or girls) for the choir, and men to be lay clerks, a task which takes up an increasingly significant part of one's time, as there are now very few choral establishments towards which potential choristers or men flock. In recent years, the Choir Schools' Association has striven hard, with some success, to raise our public profile, and thus endeavour to reverse the decline in applications. Choristers are usually chosen at a voice trial, where the organist may be helped by his assistant and by school staff and clergy. Lay clerks are chosen at interview, and are appointed by the Dean or Provost.

Training and administering the choir, which involves a combination of musicianship, of voice-training ability, of personal leadership, and of organisational skills. No-one has a perfect balance; most organists incline to a particular strength in one area or another.

Playing the organ. I put this third because, for many organists, it is their assistants who do most of the playing. Whether or not this is a good thing is debatable, but most choir-trainers wish to conduct and mould a performance of something they have rehearsed with the choir, so it is understandable. Perhaps the organist and his assistant should reverse roles for one day or more a week. In most cathedrals there is at least one service a week at which only one organist is present, and the music is sub-conducted from within the choir. Arranging for tuning and maintenance of the organ is another responsible task; a working knowledge of the action and problems of one's own organ is essential for a happy and fruitful relationship with the tuner!

Choosing the music. It seems incredible to us that, within living memory, this vital task in many cathedrals was undertaken by the Precentor (the canon responsible for the music and liturgy). These days, the organist will usually submit his choice and may sometimes be questioned by the Precentor about a seemingly liturgically inappropriate item. The cost of buying music and library equipment is generally covered by an agreed budget.

Administration, which may take many hours. It is important to be efficient and to create an organised public image. There is often secretarial help available. There will usually be weekly staff meetings which the organist is expected to attend. These are vital for general lines of communication with clergy and lay administrators; it is remarkable how, even in an essentially collegiate establishment, a week can pass without a word being spoken between colleagues.

Work in the diocese. This must be accepted as an essential part of the cathedral organist's role, encouraging choirs and helping organists. Many cathedral organists are also diocesan organ advisers.

In part-time cathedral positions, most of the above applies, scaled down to different levels.

Assistant organists in cathedrals are often under-appreciated! They are never paid a truly full-time salary (typically between £5,000 and £10,000, with one or two higher exceptions), and thus tend to spend much time teaching. Many cathedrals (certainly most choir-school establishments) provide a house (some a housing allowance) and, in the majority of cases, the post is linked to a job in the choir school – which may involve teaching subjects other than music, together with sports and boarding duties. Probably all assistants have the chance to work with the choir; some several times a week, and some only occasionally. An assistant will often do most of the playing, and will thus need to be a truly liturgical organist. A player who is fundamentally a recitalist might not enjoy cathedral work nor particularly excel at it, for most of the playing is accompanying. A real feel for accompaniment and for the glories of the psalms is absolutely vital. After a few years as Number 2, many assistants naturally succeed in becoming Number 1, but be warned, promotion very rarely occurs within a cathedral.

'How do I become a cathedral organist or assistant organist?' is a question which is often asked. The necessary qualities are clear enough and may be discerned from the foregoing. Paper qualifications are, annoyingly, vital if you are to help yourself on to a short-list. A good degree will convince a Dean and Chapter that you have an intellectual grasp of things other than church music or playing the organ. Posts are usually advertised in the *Church Times*. A well-prepared, well-presented CV is essential, and you will usually need three referees – musical, clerical and personal. You should be a Christian; clerical employers are also concerned about your spiritual health! At the interview, be prepared to play the organ – typically a piece of Bach, another work, some transposition, some improvisation, and possibly the stylish playing of a hymn or psalm. You will probably have to rehearse the choir, or at least the choristers. This is obviously an unnatural occasion, as you will be nervous, but make the best of it; make sensible musical points, work them hard but politely and positively, be charming but not facetious, and don't criticise the way they sing already! These factors apply equally well to interviews for organist or assistant organist.

It has to be said that few become cathedral organists without having been an assistant first, however gifted they are. Be prepared to tread this path. Patience is a virtue, as is also the ability to learn from one's superior's strengths and weaknesses – the buck will stop with you all too soon.

Parish churches

Parish church posts fall into several categories. It could be said that there are enough categories to suit just about every standard of organist, but many organists are unable to move to find just the right church for them. There remain two parish churches with choir schools; another maintains daily services without a school. These are in the 'cathedrals' category, and many of the above comments apply.

Most towns and cities boast a parish church which runs a vigorous musical tradition. There are then thousands of churches with choirs of varying size and quality, and a huge number of small country churches with no choir. None of these churches supports a full-time organist, though a few pay as well as a modest cathedral post, and some may supply a house (occasionally in lieu of salary). Suggested rates of salary and fees are published by the Incorporated Society of Musicians, and draft contracts are provided by the ISM, the Royal School of Church Music and the Royal College of Organists, who can also help in other ways.

Many such posts can be truly rewarding, and can be held in conjunction with full-time teaching or performing work. An absolute requirement is the ability to strike a good working relationship with the parish priest. The patience to see the other point of view, to compromise from time to time, not to appear remote and detached from the congregation – all these are vital assets at a time when the role of the parish musician is increasingly under question. The humility to ask experienced and successful church musicians for advice should be developed, especially at a time when the recruiting and training of boys' choirs is rapidly diminishing. Observe someone who does it well – attend courses run by the RSCM, or ask a choir trainer you admire for some advice and a chat. Remember that a successful choir has a life outside the choir stalls too – trips, sport, tours, holidays, treats. You have to be able to offer as tempting a package as all the other activities now available to children. It is quite a daunting task, especially if you are also required to work with, and arrange music for, an instrumental group leading worship songs.

A word to singers

Singers will find a fully-professional existence as a lay clerk possible only in two or three London cathedrals. In cathedrals in which the choir sings every day, a lay clerk will currently earn between £2,000 and £4,500, and may be offered a house (either rent-free or at a reasonable charge). Thus he would need an almost full-time job to provide a living wage. The hours and locality of this job would need to be such that he could reach the cathedral in time for evensong during the week. Singing professionally outside the cathedral to any great extent would inevitably mean away engagements; these are only possible regularly if a well-established deputy system exists and the organist displays a rare degree of good will. Only in London does such a system really prevail. Thus, a singer would need to have a job near the cathedral (teaching and office work are common), and several larger cathedrals employ lay clerks in the office, in the shop, in the education centre, and so on. Sick-leave is generally paid, but a pension scheme is rarely offered. Holidays will tend to coincide with school holidays, but expect to remain singing up to Christmas and Easter, and be prepared for shortened half-terms. Most lay clerks have a contract of employment with no fixed term, but a retiring age of 60 or 65.

Required skills sought by most organists would centre on the ability to sight-read really fluently, on accuracy of pitch, and on a quality of voice which blends well and yet is characterful enough for solos ('verses'). A big operatic voice with a pronounced vibrato is not generally acceptable. Many cathedrals have only six men on the foundation, so a singer has to hold his part alone on his side. A sociable disposition is often looked for, as the lay clerk who 'rocks the boat' is a cathedral organist's dread, as is the man who, after a few months, always discovers that 'the grass is greener' somewhere else, and constantly talks of moving on. An element of stability is a key ingredient in building and developing a choir's style.

To conclude, it must be accepted that cathedral work at any level is something of a vocation. If an organist responds to that vocation and achieves the sort of post which he desires, he will find the work – though laden with problems, and with limited financial reward – immensely satisfying in ways not to be found anywhere else in the musical profession, nor, indeed, in the rest of the world.

The Incorporated Association of Organists

President: Dr Peter Hurford OBE

The IAO exists to bring together and encourage all who love the pipe organ and its music, players and listeners alike. It fulfills this role both in the UK and abroad through over 90 affiliated organists' associations and a personal membership section: new members are always welcome.

The IAO publishes *Organists' Review* quarterly, a quality journal containing articles, letters, reviews, photographs and news of forthcoming events. The IAO's major annual event is its Organ Congress, held in a different city each year to experience the finest instruments – a five-day festival of concerts, recitals, master classes and lectures. In 1996 it will be in London in late July and in 1997, it will be in Haarlem, Holland. All are welcome, whether they wish to improve their playing or simply enjoy the events. The IAO also promotes the London Organ Day in April or May each year and supports a wide range of other educational events throughout the UK.

To find out more about the IAO and its activities or to make contact with your local organists' association, please phone or write to **Richard Popple, Secretary, IAO, 11 Stonehill Drive, Bromyard, Herefordshire HR7 4XB. Tel: 01885 483155.**

THE RECORDING INDUSTRY

JOHN BOYDEN

John Boyden has worked in the business of classical music for 38 years and has produced some 1,500 commercially-issued records. Apart from continuing to produce recordings, he is also Chairman of three companies – Finesplice Limited, a high-tech company specialising in classical music digital editing and CD mastering, Manygate Management Limited, which represents artists and mounts concerts and tours, and Boyden Communications Limited, which is engaged in record production. John Boyden is also Artistic Director of the New Queen's Hall Orchestra, which he re-formed in 1992.

The great thing about the classical record business is the almost infinite number of opportunities existing within it for the well-motivated and imaginative person. Almost anything is possible when an individual, prepared to analyse his or her particular attributes, drives towards a chosen goal with single-minded zeal.

The performance of classical music, as with all human activities, is largely governed by fashion. Outsiders often mistakenly assume that such music, the stuff of genius and consisting of masterpieces, is unchanging and unchangeable, and that Beethoven's solitary violin concerto, for instance, floats unaltered in a universe of its own, grown dusty with age and familiarity. This is not so. Beethoven's masterpiece will appear to be as different as the number of its performers, let alone when exposed, as now, to the latest ideas in so-called authentic performance.

Such an understanding opens the door to anybody willing to back his own judgement. Once the individual sets his mind on entering the world of recorded classical music, he is as free to rearrange the furniture of the great composers as any other tenant. This is an important insight. With a single leap, the mind is freed from the intimidation of what has gone before, or from what is currently determined to be the right way, the proper way to reach fulfilment.

I say all this with a small degree of authority because I have always made it a conscious policy to be true to my own ideas, no matter how painful the temporary cost. Consequently, when asked to offer advice to someone contemplating entering our world, I find that I know next to nothing about the formal and more structured routes into the classical record industry.

Perhaps I should outline my own experience, not in order to score points, nor to solicit any emotional reaction, but merely to illustrate how I have survived in a changing industry for more than thirty years, and both enjoyed and fulfilled myself at the same time.

I spent the first ten years of my working life in a shop, during which time I made some recordings which I tried to place with anyone interested. However, and it is a mighty big however, it is necessary to appreciate that, at that time, the entire business lay under the control of Decca and EMI. Effectively, other than these two giants, there was no other significant player in the UK classical music industry. The public and the trade were deeply suspicious of any new companies, and opportunities for individual efforts were virtually non-existent.

Some patchy success came my way, but my first really important chance arrived when I made a recording of a couple of Beethoven violin sonatas which was sold, in 1967, to Music for Pleasure. On the strength of those performances, Klemperer appointed the young violinist to be leader of the New Philharmonia, and the consequent publicity was so attractive to Music for Pleasure that they offered me a job.

Once inside MFP, I beavered away to form a classical label. I achieved this in 1970 with the formation of Classics For Pleasure, the success of which was based on a major sponsorship deal which I was fortunate to have concluded with the LPO and Imperial Tobacco. This sponsorship meant that I had the budget to make 18 orchestral recordings over the next three years, and it gave me complete freedom. This brings me to another important element in business life: independence is everything. Without it one is always at the mercy of committees; and most of us know what committees are good for – designing camels. Of course, your disposition may fit you for a life sitting on committees, in which case stop reading now.

At that time and, indeed, throughout the 1970s and early 1980s, the major international companies were perceived, by the general public, to have a monopoly of the finest artists, to make the best recordings, and to project an image of vastly superior quality over their lesser competitors. This was largely due to the difficulties and expenses in producing old-fashioned black discs. Compact disc has changed all that. Today, anyone can produce a thousand CDs and store them for a smaller relative investment than ever before.

The technical side of classical recording has also changed. The highest attainable quality is now available from any number of independent engineers. In fact, many recordings produced by the major companies have been engineered for them by independent engineers. This means that, following the removal of any sense of technically superior manufacture which the majors enjoyed in the days of black disc (there being no difference in quality between one CD and another), a whole range of specialist labels, often far more enterprising than the larger companies in their choice of repertoire and artists, has arisen to the great advantage of the music-loving public and many newly-discovered artists. Such a situation has led the larger companies to adapt to market conditions instead of, as formerly, leading them.

As a consequence, anyone with determination, together with a knowledge of serious music, should be able to find his or her way into one or other of the many interesting aspects of the recording world now on offer.

Not every music student is going to earn his living as a performer; the music colleges process far too many students for that. However, instead of falling back on teaching as an alternative, why not consider joining the record business, a business in which you can help create employment for the ones lucky enough to make it? What could be better than to assist really talented people, from all over the world, who regard London as the centre of recorded music?

The major record companies, now all foreign owned except for EMI, require experts to devise artistic policy and to identify key areas of product development. Some people have been known to sneer at the 'commercial' aspects of the classical record business. Such people are misguided. The simple truth is that record companies have led most, if not all, of the innovations in public taste since the war. The initiatives which led to Vivaldi's *Four Seasons* becoming the enormous box office success of present times came from Decca's pioneering efforts during the very early fifties, and the general trends towards authenticity, whether in mediaeval music, the baroque or classical, have all stemmed from record companies.

Once record companies had come to accept that the new music being written was no longer commercially viable (at some time following Britten's War Requiem 30 years ago), they were forced to find alternatives to standard war-horses, such as Brahms and Tchaikovsky. This has been achieved firstly by exploiting the music of the Baroque, followed by that of the Renaissance and earlier and, most recently, by demonstrating the virtues of the authentic performance of early nineteenth-century orchestral repertoire.

During the twenties, thirties and forties, record companies recorded tremendous amounts of contemporary music, often forming close relationships with particular composers, such as Elgar and HMV, or Britten and Decca. The fact that they do not do so today is more a reflection of the realities of the marketplace than of the 'commercialism' of the record companies. So, given the public's apparent lack of enthusiasm for 'tower-block' music, record companies have been forced to discover other aspects of music more likely to strike a sympathetic chord among their consumers.

It would be unrealistic to suggest that such insights originated in the minds of ignorant savages devoid of knowledge and discrimination. The truth is far simpler. Record companies have been forced, by the need to sell records, to come up with angles and concepts which exploit existing needs. This is known as marketing. It is a commercial requirement which is ignored at the peril of any trading enterprise.

This means that record companies need people with ideas, knowledge and commercial insight with which to further their development over the next ten years or so. They also require people whose musical judgement, coloured with commonsense, can form a decent opinion of the musical qualities of a performer.

So how do you get started? I suggest that you work in a classical record shop during your holidays. Such an experience will bring you face to face with the only really important person – the customer. You will learn what sells and why. You may be in for a shock at the gullibility of the consumer and the true extent of his knowledge. But such a dose of reality will prove to be worth a great deal to you. You may even come up with an original idea, or perceive an opportunity that nobody else has identified.

Secondly, read all the record magazines. Read them from cover to cover, even the bits you dislike. Find out how recordings are made. Try to go on recording sessions and see whether you believe you are capable of guiding a group of individual artists through a performance while keeping within the commercial restraints of time. Good producers are rare. Listen to recordings in an analytical way. Try to understand which sort of recording you prefer – develop an attitude towards, and even rationalise an actual philosophy of, sound. Do not simply react to a recording, but make every effort to identify why you prefer one approach to another.

Perhaps, if you are of a technical inclination, you may wish to look at engineering. Courses exist at several universities and polytechnics – Surrey University, University of East Anglia, and so on – or you may wish to tag along, during your vacations, with an independent recording engineer as a barely-paid assistant. Experience is the most essential commodity. Without it you are an outsider, looking in.

You can always follow my example by setting up your own little recording operation. Mine consisted of a pair of microphones and a couple of Revox tape recorders. Today it is far easier: DAT machines produce excellent results, need virtually no maintenance, and weigh next to nothing. If you have the enthusiasm, you will find there is no shortage of schools whose choir needs recording, or a local organist who wants to sell his own cassettes at concerts. Remember, one thing leads to another. Once you start, everything else will follow. If you fail to start, you must expect nothing to happen – you will not be disappointed.

The point is to acquire experience. In the end, nobody cares whether you are qualified or not. The rules are the same as those which apply to a performing musician. All that matters is 'can you do it now? Today?'

If, on the other hand, you find the travelling, the terrible hours and the pressures of responsibility, too much to handle, why not go into the office of a record company and become a member of the headquarters team responsible for sleeve notes, translations, copyright and logistics? Advertising, packaging design and marketing are all areas requiring knowledge and imagination. There is hardly a classical record company which does not have at least one person on its staff sufficiently qualified to ensure that horrendous mistakes in textual information are avoided. The gaffes of the uninformed are legion. How often, for instance, do photographs of orchestras appear composed entirely of left-handed musicians?

Not many openings do occur, it is true. The intelligent thing is to be sure that, when you do apply for a position, you can demonstrate your enthusiasm and knowledge by the experience you have had. Over the years, I have had many people apply to me for a job, some of whom have not even bothered to remember the name of the company whose ranks they claim to be so keen on joining. Such applicants have received short shrift. Never forget that there are many more people, with stars in their eyes, trying to break into one of the most exciting careers in the world, than there are openings available. No classical record company needs you, not until you have proved your worth – then it may be a different story.

To sum up, recorded classical music is a business which has to be run on lines of complete commercial integrity, or it will fail to come to terms with the realities of the market-place. The market-place determines the success and failure of every business venture and, in a properly organised record company, many experts are needed who are able to make their own contributions to achieve artistic and financial success. Such a relationship is no strait-jacket but is, rather, a formula which allows the individual to promote his own ideas and to see his own life fulfilled far more promptly than in most of the other areas of musical life.

MUSIC THERAPY

HELEN TYLER

Helen Tyler is Chairman of the British Society for Music Therapy. She completed a BA in music at Reading University, followed by an MPhil on Mozart's chamber music. She also studied piano and violin. Subsequently, Helen Tyler trained as a music therapist on the Nordoff-Robbins training course, qualifying in 1989. She now works as a music therapist at the Nordoff-Robbins Music Therapy Centre, where she is Assistant Director.

> Music alone with sudden charms can bind
> The wand'ring sense, and calm the troubled mind.
> (Congreve)

The power of music to bring about change and healing has been known throughout history and literature. One of the earliest descriptions of music used in this way is in the Bible in the Book of Samuel: '... whenever the evil spirit was upon Saul, David took the lyre and played it; so Saul was refreshed and was well, and the evil spirit departed from him.' Centuries later, professional music therapists seek to use this same power to relieve pain and suffering, whether in a young autistic or disabled child, an adult with schizophrenia or depression, people with Alzheimer's disease, or someone with a terminal illness in the last stages of life. All these people, and many others, from babies to those in extreme old age, with physical, mental or emotional problems, can respond to music therapy. In the following pages, I hope to show how the combination of musical skill, a training in music therapy, and a desire to help people in need can lead to a satisfying and enriching career.

Why music?

In all societies and cultures, music is an integral part of public and private life, and is also the basis of ritual, whether spiritual or ceremonial. Music adds another dimension to occasions of national importance or personal significance, and supports or transcends the spoken word in worship, celebration and mourning. Few people would deny the important part music has played in their lives from infancy to old age, and that it is a powerful medium for communication. It is important, however, not to view music simply as a vehicle for the emotions, but also as a complex creation of the intellect.

Stravinsky wrote: 'I know that twelve notes in each octave and the varieties of rhythm offer me opportunities that all of human genius will never exhaust.' Here, Stravinsky acknowledges the potent force contained within pitch and rhythm, the basic ingredients of music, which, combined with the composer's ingenuity and inspiration, can create musical patterns and structures of infinite variety.

The music therapist has the opportunity to use not only the spiritual and emotional aspects of music, but also its inherent form, structure and logic, thus linking the artistic and the scientific, the intuitive and the intellectual. Powerful tools indeed!

The music therapist is working on the proven premise that within every human being there exists the capacity to respond to the elements of music, and that this innate responsiveness remains intact and accessible despite damage or trauma to other organs, even brain damage or coma.

In the womb, the foetus reacts to rhythm and pitch, and researchers have found that a new-born baby can already distinguish the tone of its mother's voice, as well as being calmed or aroused by different rhythmic sounds or movements. Psychologists have used the term 'baby song' to describe the earliest attempts of a baby to 'talk' to the mother. The two-way dialogue that ensues is the basis of language development, yet is closer to song than to speech. This links the world of organised sound, or music, to the basic need to communicate, even at the earliest pre-verbal level, and this knowledge is used and developed in music therapy.

What is therapy?

At this point, a question may be raised as to how music therapy differs from other forms of musical activity which have been found beneficial. The uplifting experience of singing in a choir, the satisfaction of performing with fellow musicians, the enjoyment of listening to music, live or recorded, or the inspiration given by a gifted teacher, are all therapeutic, since they promote feelings of well-being and enhance the quality of life. However, music therapy practised as a profession has certain features which separate it from more general musical experiences. Central to the therapy is the relationship which is built up between therapist and client or patient (either word is used, depending on the work-place). This relationship is based on mutual trust and acceptance, and takes place within a therapeutic setting. This means regularity and consistency of the time and place of sessions, confidentiality, and the pursuit of therapeutic goals.

In musical terms, the client/therapist relationship is developed through the use of musical improvisation. The free-flowing exchanges which can be facilitated through clinical improvisation allow the therapist to be the listener, the reflector, the enabler and the supporter of the client, with the flexibility to move to new musical areas as the therapy demands. Although pre-composed and recorded music can be used in therapy, clinical improvisation provides the shared language of the communication. Similarly, therapist and client may speak, either about the music or feelings evoked during the session, but the music will retain its position at the heart of the therapy.

Whether the therapy lasts for a few months or several years, the therapist will be working to enable inner change, growth, fulfilment of potential and improved quality of life.

For each client, the gains and experiences will be different. A withdrawn and remote autistic boy reaches out to play the piano with the music therapist, and so takes the first step out of his silent, isolated world. As the sessions progress week by week, shared pleasure in the musical experience leads into other forms of communication, eye contact, singing, and the beginnings of speech. A suicidal teenager expresses her rage and despair through chaotic outbursts of drumming, and is supported by the therapist with strongly dissonant music. As trust develops, the girl is able to allow other feelings to emerge, of fear and insecurity, and these, too, can be expressed in the music. A patient dying of AIDS uses his music therapy sessions to get in touch with the importance of music, both in his life and as his death approaches. At this point, words are no longer enough, and the music takes over.

In these examples, changes brought about in the music therapy sessions will be felt as benefits in the patient's everyday life and relationships.

Another aspect of therapy which sets it apart from other musical experiences is the necessity to accept and work with negative and resistant feelings, whether these are expressed musically or verbally. If a client appears to reject the therapy, this is not necessarily a sign that it should end, but could be an indication that an area of difficulty has been reached which needs further exploration. Analysis and evaluation of the sessions through studying video or audio recordings assist in this, and, as with psychotherapists, music therapists also go to fellow professionals for supervision and discussion of their cases.

Where and how does music therapy take place?

The diversity of places where music therapy can be found is a sign of the development of the profession over the last fifty years. Music therapists work in medical and psychiatric hospitals, in special schools, nurseries and mainstream schools, in prisons and in residential homes, including hospices and those for psycho-geriatric patients. They can also be found in clinics and units for drug users and young offenders, for people with cancer, HIV or AIDS, and for children or young people with anorexia or who have been abused.

The therapy is very often one-to-one, but with a young child, or with a profoundly disabled or violent client, two therapists may work together. Music therapy can also take place in groups, particularly in schools or hospitals.

The therapist will use his or her own instrument, be it piano, strings or wind, and there will be a range of percussion instruments for both the client and therapist to play, ranging from small, delicate bells or shakers to dramatic gongs, drums and cymbals. Tuned instruments, such as xylophone, marimba, melodica, lyre or guitar, are also used, as appropriate to the situation. The client, adult or child, does not have to be musical or musically skilful to benefit from music therapy, so it is important that the instruments can produce a range of satisfying and expressive musical sounds without creating a barrier or feelings of musical inadequacy.

Music therapy training

At the time of writing, there are five postgraduate training courses in the UK, with more in the planning stages. The entry requirements vary slightly for each course, as does the orientation and emphasis of the teaching and clinical work. Normally, music therapy students are only accepted if they have a musical training equivalent to a degree or diploma from a university or music college. A high standard of musical performance is also essential, and auditions for the training will include the playing of repertoire and improvisation, as well as an intensive interview. Because of the demanding nature of the work, candidates need to have personal insight, self-awareness, maturity of outlook and a compassionate personality. Successful completion of the training after one or two years leads either to a Diploma in Music Therapy or to a Master's Degree, depending on the length and intensity of the course. Following initial qualification, there is a period of mandatory work under supervision before being accepted for full membership of the professional association. All the courses give the students experience of working under supervision with adults and children with various special needs, disabilities and problems. Lectures give a background to the medical, psychological and psychiatric conditions of the clients they will meet, and to child development, mental and physical illness, and other related topics. Improvisational skills are taught on the courses, and the students have their own experience of music therapy, either individually or in a group. The curriculum of each course varies, and different degrees of emphasis are placed on particular aspects of therapy work. The training will also include voice and movement classes, and observation of experienced music therapists working with clients.

Entry to the music therapy profession is particularly encouraged from mature students, who have had some experience of life and are well-motivated to use their musical gifts in the service of others. For full details of the current training courses, write to the British Society for Music Therapy, whose address can be found in the *British Music Yearbook.*

As a career, music therapy has moved from being seen as a form of relaxation or a distraction from pain to being an accepted part of a treatment programme for patients. In hospital, a music therapist is part of the medical team, attending ward rounds, meeting with doctors and nurses, and co-operating with other professionals such as occupational therapists or physiotherapists.

Music therapists setting up in private practice receive referrals from many sources, including from GPs, who are becoming aware of the importance of treatment other than drugs for many ailments of emotional origin.

In all areas of work, the goals of the treatment will not be specifically musical, but aims such as developing confidence, concentration or self-expression undoubtedly stimulate the development of skills and the satisfaction of achievement through the music.

Music therapy is still a young profession, and there is a long way to go before it is available to all who need it. The Association of Professional Music Therapists (APMT) has campaigned successfully to establish fair pay and conditions for its members, to increase employment opportunities, and to achieve a status for music therapy alongside other professions. The British

Society for Music Therapy (BSMT) has worked for the last thirty years to spread information about music therapy through workshops, conferences and publications. Public awareness is increasing, and interest in training as a music therapist is growing all the time. As the end of the twentieth century approaches, research into methods and results of the treatment are seen as vital to the academic and medical standing of the profession, and more universities are showing interest in establishing music therapy research posts. This growing professionalism is both positive and necessary to ensure a healthy future, but does not invalidate that indefinable power of music which is an essential part of music therapy.

> Music has charms to sooth a savage breast,
> To soften rocks or bend a knotted oak.
> (Congreve)

THE MUSIC LIBRARIAN

HELEN FAULKNER

Helen Faulkner was Manager of the BBC Music Library between 1985 and 1994. Educated in Sussex and at University of London, Gold-smiths' College, she has a BMus and MMus in Musical Analysis. After taking a post-graduate diploma in librarianship she was, for some years, Music Librarian at Goldsmiths' and a lecturer in the music department there. As President of the Broadcasting and Orchestral Libraries Branch of the International Association of Music Libraries, she frequently speaks at national and international conferences and is a regular contributor to journals and other publications in the field.

There are many types of music library, and many routes to employment in music librarianship. Whilst the majority of professional music librarians enter as new graduates, it is perfectly possible to join the profession at a later stage, either following a course as a mature student, or after relevant work experience. In some types of music library, it is quite common to find staff who have previously worked or trained as performers or academics. In others, most of the staff will have arrived by a rather more direct route from school via further education. The two routes to 'qualified' status as a librarian are either a degree course in librarianship, which can sometimes be combined with another subject, or a degree course in any subject followed by a one-year postgraduate diploma in librarianship or information science.

In general, librarianship these days is almost entirely a graduate profession, except for posts at the lowest clerical level from which it is very difficult to progress without some kind of formal training. However, *music* librarianship is not entirely typical of the profession as a whole because of the range of libraries which cover the subject and the fact that many of them fall outside the more common areas of public or academic institutions.

The image of the librarian as a very quiet, conservative person is, these days, a myth. There is, however, one surviving vestige of the image which is real and important: anyone with a distaste for order and organisation would probably not be happy working in a library. Any substantial collection needs to be kept in such a way that its contents can be quickly and easily located.

Common to the staff of all types of music library is a fundamental interest in, and enthusiasm for, the 'materials' of music, whether performing material or sound recordings (or a combination of both), and a knowledge of the repertoire which is related to the needs of the users served by a specific collection. An understanding of the music publishing and recording industries can be very useful – indeed it is essential for some types of post – and you will obviously be at an advantage if you are yourself a regular user of a range of libraries. Good communication skills are very important because a librarian often has to deal directly with users and suppliers of material. You may also be working to tight deadlines, so it is important to be able to keep going under pressure.

Public libraries

Most local authorities have collections of music and sound recordings in what are commonly termed 'public libraries'. The scope of these collections varies considerably but some, particularly in the major cities, are extensive and serve a wide range of listeners and (largely amateur) performers. Many of these libraries or, in the case of county services, groups of libraries, have specialist music librarians whose job it is to select and maintain stock and promote it to potential users. The extent to which these librarians have contact with the public varies tremendously, and in many cases they will also have responsibility for other areas of the stock, such as drama or video collections, or for other library functions, such as cataloguing or circulation. At more senior levels in public libraries, staff tend to be much less subject-orientated and very much more managerially deployed over a range of functions. A decision has to be taken at some point about whether one wishes to stay with one's subject or become a more senior, but more general, librarian.

Most professional staff in local authority libraries have followed the conventional training path of a degree in librarianship from a university or polytechnic or a degree in another subject, followed by a postgraduate diploma in librarianship or information science. Many posts carry a requirement that the holder is 'chartered', that is that they are a member of the Library Association and have qualified to a level approved by the LA. Usually this is achieved by the route outlined above but, exceptionally, a charter can be awarded for extensive experience and evidence of achievement without a formal qualification.

Academic libraries

In order to support specialist courses in music, many colleges, polytechnics and universities have music collections. These tend to be aimed at the academically biased student rather than the performer, though where performance is an important part of the course the collection will reflect this. In some academic collections the music librarian will also be responsible for obtaining performing material for choirs and orchestras.

Subject specialist staff in academic libraries need to have a sound academic background themselves, at least to first-degree level, and specialist skills in the bibliography of music. They are likely to have to advise on, and locate, a lot of more obscure repertoire, and to provide material, and help to form research strategies, for students and staff up to doctoral level. They are also likely to be involved in teaching undergraduates how to use library facilities and reference materials.

Posts in this type of library are not numerous, and career progression will generally depend on a willingness to take on more managerial responsibility over a wider area, dropping the subject-based tasks.

Conservatoire libraries

The music colleges and conservatoires aim to produce performers and teachers of practical musical skills. The service provided by their libraries is, therefore, mainly the acquisition and supply of performing material, from solo and chamber works through to large-scale orchestral and choral works. Apart from supplying works from their own stock, these libraries deal extensively with other collections and particularly publishers' hire libraries. Additionally, many conservatoire libraries hold archival collections of national importance, often containing autograph manuscripts and materials associated with particular composers or performers, which will be of interest to scholars and researchers.

It is less usual for staff in these libraries to be formally qualified as librarians. In the main they will be trained musicians with wide repertoire knowledge, though some staff will be employed to perform the more technical library tasks such as cataloguing, for which some training is usual. Career progression in these libraries is limited by the size of the staffing establishment and a generally rather low level of staff turnover.

National libraries

These collections have two functions: they are archive repositories for material published in their countries, and they provide support for all other libraries by operating or co-ordinating inter-library loan schemes. These libraries may also mount exhibitions, both of items held in the collections, and also thematic exhibitions including items borrowed from other collections, so the staff develop a curatorial role.

The staff of the national libraries tend to have advanced academic qualifications and formal library training and, whilst there are some subject specialist posts at a high level, most promotion is into managerial areas.

Broadcasting libraries

The libraries which support the broadcasting of music supply both sound recordings (commercial recordings and material from sound archives) and performing material. Perhaps more than in any other kind of music library, staff of these libraries work under a great deal of pressure to meet deadlines, and this is particularly true in libraries of sound recordings. These libraries range from some of the biggest collections of music or records in the world to smaller regional collections with perhaps only one or two staff. They are essentially 'working collections' but function also as broadcasting archives. All areas of the musical repertoire are covered, so staff with many different areas of specialist expertise are employed. From time to time staff have to attend recording sessions, and music copyists are employed to make performing material for new works or other works for which no material exists.

There tends to be a balance between formally trained library staff and people with a performing or more practical background. In the larger libraries there are opportunities for internal promotion, and many staff progress to other areas of broadcasting.

Orchestral and opera libraries

Most of the major orchestras and opera companies employ librarians to provide material for performance. Some have extensive collections, whilst others have smaller collections but will obtain works as required from other sources. These librarians need a combination of good practical skills from the viewpoint of the performer, and also a good knowledge of the repertoire with which they are dealing. Good copying skills are often required and a willingness to work unsociable hours.

As a rule, staff working in these libraries will not be formally trained librarians but will often have been trained as performers. Career progression is usually into orchestral management, though orchestral librarians tend to be amongst the longest serving music librarians, so vacancies are rare.

Publishers' hire libraries

A significantly large proportion of the orchestral, choral and operatic repertoire is only available as hired material from music publishers. All the major music publishers (many of whom act as agents for other, usually foreign, publishers) employ staff to run the music hire operations which generate an important part of their income. The staff in these libraries need, in addition to a knowledge of the particular publisher's catalogues, an ability to handle the complex agreements on hire tariffs which cover hire both to professional and amateur bodies. The ability to interpret copyright law, both domestic and international, is particularly important, as is the ability to prioritise sometimes heavy workloads.

Music Information Centres

These are collections which promote the music, mainly contemporary, of a particular country. The staff of these centres also organise concerts and other events to publicise the works of the composer that they represent. These libraries are usually staffed by only two or three people whose main attributes must be extensive repertoire knowledge, experience of the contemporary music scene, and a desire to promote new music.

There are many other types of library, school libraries for instance, which do not have specialist music librarians. If you are committed to a career in librarianship, it is important to consider the possibility of moving outside music. Certainly your career possibilities will be greatly increased if you allow yourself a wider range of options, and a formal training in librarianship will give you a bigger pool of jobs from which to choose.

The Library Association is the main professional body for librarians in the UK, and can provide more information and up-to-date details of courses in librarianship. Help and advice is also available from the International Association of Music Libraries, Archives and Documentation Centres (IAML), which holds annual conferences and other study days specifically aimed at music specialists.

THE MUSICIAN IN THE SERVICES

LIEUTENANT COLONEL C J ROSS

Lt Col Ross joined the Band of the Black Watch in 1958. Following a course of study at Kneller Hall as a student bandmaster, he was appointed Bandmaster of The King's Own Border Regiment in 1973, subsequently serving as Director of Music, Royal Electrical and Mechanical Engineers and Director of Music, Welsh Guards Band. He was appointed Principal Director of Music (Army) in 1994.

In recent years, all three of the Armed Forces have suffered cutbacks which have reduced the number of bands quite drastically. You would therefore be forgiven for thinking that they are no longer recruiting musicians. Fortunately, you couldn't be more wrong.

The Armed Forces run one of the largest single musical organisations in the world, with over forty bands employing more than 1,500 musicians. The skill, musicality, and versatility expected of their musicians is probably equalled only by London session players. Military music offers young musicians an unrivalled breadth of playing experience. The three services teach and play all instruments of the symphonic wind band, as well as strings and harp. They teach harmony, orchestration, conducting, orchestral management, and repertoire. They play all kinds of music, including jazz, swing, middle-of-the-road, pop, light, baroque, mainstream, symphonic and operatic. To say that military musicians are versatile is an understatement.

Consider the option

If you have the dedication, ambition and drive to take up the challenge of a career as a musician, you probably already have many of the qualities required of a musician in the Services.

Military musicians share the same dedication to excellence as do professional civilian musicians. However, that's where the comparison ends. As a musician in the Services, you will not experience any difficulty funding your musical education – it's paid for! Even better, you are paid to undertake it! What's more, you will be taught by some of the country's leading instrumental and academic professors.Once you have qualified with one of the three services, you will immediately have the opportunity to play professionally – and not just in a marching band.

In the services, you will have the whole world of music open to you. There will be plenty of encouragement to advance your skills, your salary and your status in both your professional musical and military careers.

From battlefield to Brahms

Before the invention of the telephone and radio communication, drum, bugle and trumpet were needed for the very serious purpose of sending messages (perhaps in code incomprehensible to the enemy) to distances beyond the range of the human voice, so as to be able to co-ordinate the actions of large numbers of men on the battlefield. Men could be told what to do by a pattern of drum beats or a bugle call.

Today, although musicians in the Armed Forces are no longer required to act as battlefield communicators in the way their forebears were, their role has expanded and grown in importance. Musicians are the public face of the three Services – not only in this country, but all around the world.

Pageant and spectacle are an important part of what makes military music exciting to watch and inspiring to listen to. Few can fail to be moved by the great occasions: the Royal Tournament at Earls Court, for example, or the celebrations to commemorate the anniversary of the end of the Second World War. But, for musicians in the Forces, these occasions are not the whole story.

A Wap Babba Loo Bop, A Wap Bam Boo

Little Richard's phrase is not one which you would normally associate with military music! However, military musicians are every bit as capable of playing the gamut of rock, pop or jazz as adeptly as they are the classical repertoire.

Military musicians could find themselves playing as part of a marching band for an important ceremonial occasion, providing dance music for any one of a number of social engagements, backing music for a visiting entertainer, or playing in an indoor or outdoor concert.

Whether performing as part of a symphony orchestra or jazz combo, military musicians play to the highest standards.

Working life

As a military musician, your working day is filled with what you do best – music. That means a programme of daily rehearsal, practice and performance. Naturally, as a musician your working hours are governed by the type of engagement your band is undertaking, so at times you could be working evenings and weekends. However, time off in lieu is given where possible.

Engagements can range from performing at a civic dinner to an overseas tour. Wherever you go in the world, you'll have plenty of opportunities to experience the local atmosphere of the countries you visit – and in the best of company.

All musicians are encouraged to take part in private engagements for which they are paid accordingly – over and above their normal Forces salary.

Military discipline

Despite what you may have heard, you will not find yourself being shouted at all day long – we'd all soon get very bored with that! For the most part, military discipline is about personal discipline – in other words, common sense. You will be expected to conduct yourself accordingly.

Pay and conditions

Rates of pay in the Services are comparable with orchestras, and are reviewed annually. Military musicians are supplied with accommodation at a fraction of the cost of civilian housing.

Signing on

Essentially, the Armed Forces are young people's organisations with a flexible career structure. Musicians join on an open engagement for twenty-two years, but, just like any other job, you can give notice to leave. One year's notice is required after serving for a minimum of two years; the minimum engagement is thus three years. One year may seem a long while, but this is the time it takes to find and train a replacement and, just as importantly, to train you for an alternative career.

There are also opportunities to withdraw from service within your first few months.

Bursary scheme

Currently, all military musicians are trained in music at one of the three Military Schools of Music after entry into the Armed Forces. As a result of a recent review of music training in the Services, it has been decided to carry out a trial, over a period of three years (1995-1998) to have military musicians taught through the national further and higher education systems.

The scheme commenced in September 1995, and bursaries offered are as follows:

(a) A three-year bursary for a course leading to a recognised degree in music.

(b) A two-year bursary for a course leading to a National Certificate qualification.

(c) A one- or two-year bursary for students already at college, to the completion of their courses.

The bursaries, worth £1,500 annually, will be paid in termly instalments of £500. Additionally, by using HE and FE validated courses, HEFC and FEFC money will cover tuition fees. However, candidates should confirm the availability of the additional funding with their colleges.

It is the responsibility of the bursary candidates to obtain a place on a suitable music course, and evidence of a provisional place must be produced before a candidate may attend an audition.

After completing their studies, a minimum return of service will normally be required before a candidate will be free to leave military service without having a liability for repayment of some of the costs of the bursary. A candidate may leave during the first three or six months of service (depending on age at entry), but must repay that proportion of the bursary costs which have not been amortised by service in the Armed Forces.

For consideration for a bursary, candidates must have a place, or the offer of a provisional place, on a suitable college course. They must undergo a musical assessment, prior to attending a full audition at one of the three Military Schools of Music. Additionally, as with other Service recruits, they will have to reach a certain standard in the recruiting test, and will undergo a selection interview. Candidates will be medically examined, and must be security cleared before attending an audition.

Bursary candidates who are already at, or due to attend, college may apply directly to one of the Military Schools of Music, and will be musically assessed before undergoing processing in the Careers Offices.

Further details and an application form can be obtained by writing to the Army Careers Adviser Bands, RMSM, Kneller Hall, Twickenham, Middlesex TW2 7DU (telephone 0181-898 5533 extn 8638).

Training for life

As a military musician, you will, of course, have to perform normal military (soldiering) duties. You will not be asked to lead an assault on an enemy position in the same way that an infantryman would! However, you would be trained to carry out vital roles in the event of a national emergency or war. Army and Royal Marine musicians are trained to be medical orderlies, whilst the Royal Air Force musicians carry out security duties.

To prepare for life in the Services, all military musicians undergo a period of basic training. The skills learnt during basic training will stand anyone in good stead for the rest of their life, even long after their military career is over.

During basic training, men and women study map-reading, weapon training, the discipline of the parade ground, and care of uniform and equipment. During this time, the level of fitness is gradually raised (this does worry some people, but it is nothing that any reasonably fit young person can't handle).

Training the professional musician

Each of the three Services has its own School of Music. The length of time spent undergoing musical training varies between one term and two years, depending on which Service the musician joins. Tuition at these Schools of Music is delivered by some of the country's leading instrumental and academic professors. Indeed, many of the professors are the same people who play in the great London symphony orchestras and teach in the leading music colleges. This is important, not only for the reputation of military music, but also because it ensures strong contemporary links with the world of civilian professional music.

As a military musician, you can be sure that your training will be comparable to any leading college of music in the world.

Shape your own career

Once musical training is completed, you would be posted to a band of your choice (subject to instrumental vacancies). At the band, you will receive on-the-job training and experience under the Director of Music and the Bandmaster/Training Officer. This is where your career really takes off. You will have the opportunity to enjoy all the many facets of Service life; the travel, the sport, the comradeship, the experience of playing and contributing as a band-member, and, of course, opportunities for promotion.

Although the three Services have slightly different rank structures, with all of them you must attain various qualifications within your trade to progress higher. Several higher training courses are held at the Military Schools of Music. The shorter (four to six week) promotion courses include subjects such as musical leadership and band management, conducting and orchestration.

Musicians who are recommended by their Directors of Music have the chance to audition for a Bandmasters Course. These vary in content and length. The Army trains its Bandmasters for three years, covering composition, orchestration, transcription, interpretation of a score, rehearsal and conducting techniques. Within the course, potential Bandmasters are given the chance to learn, largely by doing, the human and administrative skills needed to manage a symphonic wind band. Success in the Army Bandmasters course leads to the award of a BA degree from Kingston University.

Women in bands

The Armed Forces are equal opportunity employers in all senses. Women are a primary and important source for recruiting woodwind and string players. Currently, females are employed in all three Services in mixed bands. It is hoped that there will eventually be no single-sexed bands, although this will take some time to achieve. The career opportunities open to women are no different from those of their male counterparts.

Entry requirements

The three Services are looking for young people who are enthusiastic for music, and who have a real desire to make a musical contribution. A good musician without qualifications is more use than a poor musician with a lot of qualifications. It is thus possible to qualify by audition alone. In common with other trades in the Services, it is potential that is the key quality.

To enter the Armed Forces at any trade, you need to pass a medical examination and some other entrance tests. An audition could take place either before or after these tests. The length of audition varies between the three Services, averaging two to three days. Auditionees will usually sit written theoretical and aural tests, as well as being interviewed by a Director of Music. The practical element varies between Services, but would generally include performance of two contrasting pieces on both primary and secondary instruments, sight-reading and scales. Precise details of the audition process is given well in advance. During your stay, you would also be given a chance to 'Look at Life as a Military Musician'. As well as seeing (and often participating in) what daily life consists of as a military musician, you have the opportunity of meeting musicians currently under training in an informal situation out of working hours. This is your chance to ask anything you like about the job, with no feeling of being pressurised.

Furthermore, you won't hear the famous phrase 'Don't call us' – you are told the result of the audition there and then, with no eternal waiting for a letter that might never arrive.

What to do next

Contact your nearest Forces Recruiting Officer or Schools Liaison Officer. Alternatively, write directly to one (or all) of the following addresses:

Army Careers Adviser (Bands)
The Royal Military School of Music
Kneller Hall
Twickenham
Middlesex TW2 7DU
(Telephone: 0181-898 5533)

Principal Director of Music
Royal Air Force School of Music
RAF Uxbridge Uxbridge
Middlesex UB10 0RZ
(Telephone: 01895 37144)

Principal Director of Music
Royal Marines School of Music
HMS Nelson
Queen Street
Portsmouth
PO1 3HH
(Telephone: 01705 722351)

SECTION 2

BUILDING A CAREER

THE ART OF AUDITIONING

A Handbook for Singers,
Accompanists and Coaches.

By Anthony Legge

£10.95 + £2.00 p+p in the UK

Order by post - simply send your cheque
(made payable to Rhinegold Publishing Ltd) to:
Book Sales Dept, Rhinegold Publishing Ltd,
241 Shaftesbury Avenue, London WC2H 8EH.

CREDIT CARD HOLDERS MAY TELEPHONE
0171-333 1721 DURING OFFICE HOURS

THE ART OF AUDITIONING

ANTHONY LEGGE

Anthony Legge is a highly-regarded international coach and accompanist. He has wide experience in the operatic field, both in the United Kingdom and abroad, working regularly with the principal British opera companies, Australian Opera, and with many European companies. He recently prepared Wagner's Der Ring des Nibelungen *for performance at Bayreuth under Daniel Barenboim. He is now Head of Music at English National Opera, and is the author of* The Art of Auditioning, *published by Rhinegold.*

Whatever the art of auditioning may be, I can only provide guidelines to help you find your own method for dealing with this difficult part of your career. Unfortunately, it is highly unlikely that you can avoid facing up to the problem of auditioning. If an organisation is not aware of your talents, the only way for them to find out about you is by audition. It would be much easier if they could hear you in performance, but this is not always possible, so we are left with a less than ideal system. Even for established artists, auditions may occasionally rear their ugly heads when it is necessary to hear the artist in a certain acoustic in order to discover how their sound carries – as, for example, when an opera singer needs to be heard in the special environment of Bayreuth. Auditions are often arranged or rescheduled at short notice dependent on the availability of the audition panel or the venue, so it is advisable to have your 'warhorse' audition pieces ready and up to scratch at all times: you never know when you may hear on the grapevine of a chance to audition, and this may well lead to an opportunity that will further your career.

It is important that the audition repertoire that you have chosen is completely within your grasp. An experienced panel will always be able to judge whether you could be stretched further, or if you can cope with more complicated music. What they find difficult to do is to reverse the process and to imagine that you can play or sing simpler or more lyrical music only from hearing a virtuoso or an overdramatic piece. An ideal piece is one that contains contrasting sections demonstrating your different abilities. Of course, for many instrumental auditions, there is a set piece followed by sight-reading. If this proves to be the case, bring as much of your personality to your playing as possible. The panel may only wish to hear one section, so do not be put off by this.

Sight-reading also forms an important part of many auditions, especially those for instrumentalists. The most important element in sight-reading is to keep the pulse going and, at the same time, to stay calm. When preparing yourself for sight-reading, try to find an efficient way to scan the music as a whole, so that you can anticipate the difficult passages. For singers, the parameters are somewhat different. For a start, you are usually allowed to begin with a piece of your own choice, but the panel will then expect to be able to choose from a selection of your repertoire, so make sure that you bring pieces covering a range of styles. Do not be disconcerted if the panel does not hear you sing to the end of the music – it may be that they have heard sufficient to make an informed judgement, or else they could be pressed for time. Be honest with yourself and decide where your true talents lie and present them clearly to the panel. You can never guess what the audition panel is really searching for, so there is a lot of luck involved.

If you need to prepare a curriculum vitae, try to keep it concise, ideally on one side of an A4 page. The panel does not have much time to read it – and, anyway, you do not want them to be engrossed in it while you are performing brilliantly! For singers, a photograph is not always necessary, but you might care to place a passport-size picture on the top left-hand corner of the c.v. Make sure there are no misprints or exaggerated facts to distract the panel. You may find the following a useful guide:

CURRICULUM VITAE

Name: Use your professional name if it differs from your own.

Instrument or Voice Type:

Date of Birth: State this rather than your age – otherwise you will have to update your c.v. more frequently.

Address: Make sure this is an address at which you can be contacted, not the one from which you are just moving.

Telephone: The same applies.

Agent: Only include this heading if you have one.

Qualifications: Use abbreviated form – 9 GCSEs; 3 A-levels; ARCM – don't spell them all out, subject by subject.

Teachers: List your current teacher first and how long you have studied with him or her, then any previous teachers with dates studied.

Repertoire: (for singers only) Make this succinct: Title (Venue/Company, Date).

Concerts and Recitals: State venues/societies and dates.

Masterclasses & Competitions: Show classes under name of tutor, with dates, and list competitions, prizes won and dates.

Future Engagements: Only include this heading if you have any!

Other Performing Experience: List any other experience, for example, film, television, and anything else which may be relevant.

Referees: These are not always needed. If they are, and usually two are expected, ensure that they are agreeable to act as referees, and that they are available for comment when contacted.

On the day of the audition, plan your schedule. Aim to timetable the day so that you are never rushed, but sufficiently occupied so that your nerves do not take control. Practise slowly and use any relaxation techniques that you know. Choose something to wear which is simple, comfortable and not distracting. Avoid loose hair: the panel will want to see you clearly!

The most difficult aspect of auditioning is learning to cope with nerves – auditions are very unnatural and there are many things that can put you off your stride. After gaining from the security of a calm timetable, arrive at the audition venue in good time in order to acclimatise yourself to the atmosphere – this allows the nerves to calm down. It is possible that the auditions will be running early, and you may have to perform before your allotted time: look on this as a bonus, and not as something to throw you – it will all be over so much the sooner! If, on the other hand, there are delays, be patient and immerse yourself in your music in order to keep the adrenalin flowing. You are there to present yourself in the best possible light – either the panel likes you, or it is looking for something else. Remember that the auditions secretary is in communication with the panel and, from the moment of your arrival until your departure, your manner will be noticed.

Many auditions will be organised with an official accompanist, so make sure your music is well marked up with cuts, cadenzas, places where you take time, and any other signposts which will help the pianist to play as well as possible for you. The state of your music copy is vital – it is worth five minutes to bind it well or stick it into a scrapbook. A folder where music can be slipped inside transparent pages is not such a good idea since light is often reflected off the pages, making them hard to read. If you are able to rehearse with the accompanist, be very clear about what you need, and allow him or her time to get to know you. This time is of great benefit to your performance – do not waste it by using it as a warm-up session. Only choose to bring your own accompanist if you feel this will be a marked improvement on the official one, or if you are performing very unusual or difficult repertoire. There is a danger that the panel could become more interested in your pianist than in you!

As you walk in, make the panel feel at ease – surprisingly, they can be nervous of your attitude. Remember that they are hoping to find someone good – it would solve all their problems. Give yourself time to adjust to the acoustics by selecting a solid opening piece, if you have a choice, which will allow you to be at ease and help you to find your sound. The panel ought to allow a bit of grace at the beginning for you to settle in – after all, whoever performs in a hall with no rehearsal and with half-a-dozen people sitting somewhere at the back? If they ask you a question, project your voice well without shouting, in order to demonstrate your self-control and confidence – if you are a singer, this will also show that you are able to project dialogue.

The purpose of an audition is to hear what you can offer now. Let the panel decide what you may be capable of in the future. An audition is not the place to overstretch your ability. You need to look and sound confident, capable and able to cope under pressure. Whatever the outcome, endeavour to give a performance. Even if the panel do not choose you this time, your approach to the audition will be remembered and may be of benefit to you in the future. I wish you good luck.

COMPETITIONS

GRAEME KAY

Graeme Kay is editor of Opera Now *magazine, and a former editor of* Classical Music *and* Arts Management Weekly *magazines. Before becoming a journalist, he spent eight years as an arts manager working for Scottish Opera, the Manchester International Festival, London Contemporary Dance Theatre and Southern Arts Association. He has organised two national music competitions; he has served as an adjudicator for the final of the BBC Young Musician of the Year, and since 1991 has been a member of the panel for the Australian Musical Foundation awards.*

Quarter of a million dollars for a competition you didn't even know you'd been entered for? Sounds like a Cinderella story, but that is exactly what happened to the British pianist David Owen Norris.

In March 1991, it was announced that Norris had won the Kalamazoo, Michigan-based David S Gilmore competition, which was conducted in secret. Nominations were solicited privately by the organisers, some 700 hours of tapes were listened to, and a team of assessors toured the world in secret, attending concerts given by the short-listed candidates. The rationale for this unusual procedure was to reward real, enduring talents without the intense pressure generated by the 'often gruelling experience of head-to-head, stand-and-deliver piano competition'.

While many music competitions are conducted 'blind'(i.e. the candidates are screened from the judges' view), the Gilmore award stood out because it tackled head on the criticism that competitions are a pressurised, sudden-death experience which distorts musicianship and has all the subtlety of a crowd-pleasing gladiatorial contest. But even as David Owen Norris (a deserving winner if ever there was one) collected his cheque, recorded the sixty unanticipated engagements in his Filofax, and put to immediate use the publicity and 'career-related expenses' which came with the prize, it could be argued that the disadvantage of this selection technique is that its impact depends on the status of the competition, and what the organisers say about the winner.

By contrast, what makes it worth while entering high-profile competitions, such as the Leeds, the Tchaikovsky, the Carl Flesch, the Cardiff Singer of the World, or the Van Cliburn, is that the finals bring together artists, judges, and an audience which will comprise a large number of opinion-formers and talent-spotters in the profession, such as journalists, agents, promoters, and TV, radio and record producers. All are gathered under one roof in a shared experience, and all in their own individual ways can have a major effect on a developing career.

The debate about the morality of competitions will continue to rage. To question whether the Gilmour method is more or less valid than the Leeds system is surely the same thing as asking whether classification by continuous assessment is better than by formal examination. There is room for both. Individuals are not born with equal gifts and aptitudes; uncontrollable economic and environmental factors – and sheer luck – play a part in shaping our destinies. A competitive atmosphere stimulates people to rigorous self-assessment and self-improvement.

If you are ideologically opposed to competitions, then it is unlikely that you will flourish by exposing yourself to them. For better or worse, the pragmatic view must be that competitions are sewn into the fabric of the music business. Not all of them are worth while; it is up to you and your teachers to weigh up the pros and cons by carefully assessing a number of factors: *What do I have to do, and be prepared to sacrifice, in order to enter this competition?* You have to assume that you may be required to attend throughout the competition, and you must be prepared to take out the appropriate block of time from your schedule. You may be asked to supply a demonstration-quality recording for the competition. Can you organise that, and pay for it? Look carefully at the financial arrangements. Is your travel and accommodation paid? (This is important if the competition is being held in Kalamazoo, Michigan.) If the competition involves travelling away from home, what are the practising arrangements? If you are an instrumental soloist or singer, what is the provision for accompanists? Do you have to accept the accompanist provided, or can you bring your own? Who pays? (This is a good point at which to make the observation that, if no official accompanist is provided by the competition, you do need to equip yourself with a first-rate accompanist; this is especially the case if you are going to play duo works.) *What do I stand to gain from this competition (a) just by participating, or (b) if I eventually win?* While some competitions still resemble a cattle-market, others nowadays are keen to stress that participating will, in itself, be a worth-while experience: three such competitions which spring to mind are the BBC Young Musician of the Year, the Sainsbury's Choir of the Year, and the London International String Quartet Competition. You have to look carefully at the prize on offer to make sure that it is actually what you want. Prizes come in the form of cash, engagements, scholarships for further study, agency representation, publicity and promotion, broadcasts and recordings; a pianist might win a Steinway grand, which is the sort of thing you have to think about if you live in a cramped, fourth-floor flat in Stoke Newington. If you win a competition in a foreign country, and the prize involves a series of engagements in that country, what are the financial and subsistence arrangements?

Some of the questions will not be answered in advance of your entry. However, these matters have to be addressed at some point, and it's as well to be aware of what might crop up.

Given the ubiquity of competitions these days, you can be sure that your colleagues in the music business will not be short of opinions about the relative merits and demerits of various events. The press can be helpful, too: *Classical Music* magazine, which addresses itself primarily to people working in the music profession, regularly previews competitions and talks to the organisers about the governing philosophy. You will be relieved to know that, when a new competition is announced, journalists always ask why another one is actually necessary.

Let us now assume that, taking everything into account, you have decided to enter a competition. It is worth making a few general observations about mental preparation and attitude. Be sure that you are confident about entering this kind of arena. Every time you appear on a public stage, you are, in a sense, auditioning. While music colleges get you used to performing in front of a knowledgeable and hyper-critical audience, the college atmosphere is womb-like: performing in competitions is exposure in the cold, harsh light of the outside world – it is rather like doing job interviews the whole time. You are confident enough to have applied for the job, you want to give of your best, to look your best, and to give the best possible account of yourself. Never mind the judging panel, you are testing yourself; you have got to have your own standards, and be able to measure yourself by them, knowing when you're doing something well, and when things are going wrong. This helps to get things in context for the occasions when judges deliver themselves of potentially devastating written or oral assessments.

You may remember that the Polish competitor Piotr Anderzewski disqualified himself during the 1990 Leeds International Piano Competition because he was deeply disappointed with his own performance. This was clearly a sincere gesture and is not recommended as an attention-seeking ploy – the subsequent interest in the man-who-walked-off would not have been sustained if people were not already convinced (as many were) that this was a formidable talent. It is quite another matter if a judge stomps off in disgust, of course, as Marta Argerich once did in support of Ivo Pogorelich ...

Bear in mind that, even if you are not successful in competitions, the preparation involved will prove invaluable in whatever corner of the music world you end up. While a competition panel will inevitably be looking at you in a very critical way, everyone wants you to do well. It is rarely pointed out that audiences hate to be embarrassed and disappointed even more than performers do. An audience is generally willing you to succeed – that's what they've paid for, after all. Nevertheless, you have to be emotionally tough – you have to want to do it more than anything else in the world.

Choice of repertoire is bound up with mental attitude. While competitions often specify repertoire (this should influence your decision on which to enter), there will be many opportunities for you to select your own. Getting the choice right is the most important factor in entering 'free' competitions. You must read the repertoire rules and rubric very carefully, choosing works to reflect the things which you do well, both from a technical and interpretative point of view. Make the competition guidelines work for you.

It is often worth including unusual or rarely-heard works of quality (thus, your performance will not be compared with every great musician since the dawn of the recording era). Do not choose repertoire which is outside your emotional or intellectual range (e.g. a 22-year-old singing Schubert's *Winterreise*).

Now for the thorny topic of presentation. You have to treat each stage of a competition as a real concert performance in matters of stage deportment and dress. Always choose clothes which are smart and tidy, and un-distracting, and in which you feel comfortable, both from a practical playing or singing point of view and as regards style. Try to evolve a personal style of dress and stage manner which complements your musical personality. Being outrageous will only work if you are a genuinely outrageous personality.

For women: it will be immediately obvious if you are a tomboy – used to loose tops and leggings – who has been poured into a Laura Ashley floral print number specially for the competition judges. And singers, please note that strings of pearls are now a cliché!

For men: Nigel Kennedy's infamous 'hopcat' fiddler persona was grafted on to a career that was already fairly secure. When Nige was of competition age, he looked like an angelic choirboy. Ivo Pogorelich, on the other hand, had a tempestuous style more or less within conventional bounds, and which matched his personality. Assuming that you'll be having to cope with a suit at some point, one tip which comes from a seasoned auditioner is that suits should be buttoned when standing; pianists, of course, usually undo jackets when they sit down.

It is time to make some observations from the judges' point of view. The first point is never to underestimate the panel. Panels are usually selected to represent a cross-section of musical experience and view-points. Panellists may be practising musicians familiar with your instrument, or they may not. They may include journalists, critics, agents and administrators. They live in the real world and are human beings who know what you are going through.

Technical proficiency will be taken for granted, but it will not be raised to the status of a sacred cow. Panels are not composed of people like the curmudgeonly Sixtus Beckmesser in Wagner's *Die Meistersinger von Nürnberg* – gleefully chalking up faults by drawing five-barred gates on their note-pads. Although a somewhat stern adjudicator I know once commented, 'Ah, we specialise in wrong notes, do we?', playing wrong notes will emphatically not disqualify a competitor.

At a national singing competition I administered, the panel was confronted with a young singer who really was suffering from an appalling cold. She won, and is now a household name – Marie McLaughlin. The judges, as always, were looking for that elusive quality which separates the sheep from the goats – musicianship. It is musicianship which – as one judge-watcher told me – makes panellists stop fidgeting, put down their pencils, and really listen. Being able to recognise musicianship, and – most difficult in a competition – to evaluate and quantify it, comes only from experience and a certain musical maturity. That is why the judges have been selected, after all, and in part explains why panels occasionally make selections which appear to a general audience to be eccentric. 'Audience prizes' are a useful safety valve, and always say something about performers' success in communicating directly with an audience. It is especially gratifying when the audience's selection coincides with the judges' first choice.

Sometimes first prizes are not awarded. If it happens to you, it's nothing to get hung up about. Unless the general standard really is lower than expected, it is equally possible that a high standard has been achieved overall which would require the first prize winner to be of such stratospheric achievement that it might put past and future winners in the shade. This is exactly what happened in a competition for which I was responsible, and which was conducted by 'blind' audition at every stage; the only person who was deeply upset by the decision not to award first prize was the sponsor. Coming second in these circumstances does not blight a career.

Much has been written about the effect of the 'competition performance' (crudely, an attempt to dazzle the judges into thinking that, on the strength of a well-rehearsed party piece, a competitor is perhaps more gifted than a painstaking process of continuous assessment might reveal). Judges are wise to this, of course, and you should bear in mind that people who do well over the course of a competition are not necessarily the ones who do best in the first round.

Consistency is the virtue most likely to be rewarded in the long run. The pianist Peter Donohoe is a case in point. He made an ambitious bid in the Leeds competition a few years back, and many were surprised that a musician with such an obviously formidable technique did badly in the final. However, he went on to score a spectacular triumph in the Moscow Tchaikovsky competition, and that proved to be the foundation of his future success. Now, with a secure career and many recordings to his credit, Donohoe is still better at some types of repertoire than others; nothing he does is less than excellent, but such variety is a fact of musical life.

Another hard fact of musical life is that (except for singers who mature later), if you haven't made it to whatever your goal is by the age of 25, you are probably going to have to settle for less. But if competitions have put you on the up escalator, you will need an increasing amount of support and advice from people who can help foster your talent: an agent, a publicist who will help with print, photography and press coverage. Competition success is a leg-up, rather than an end in itself; God, as ever, helps those who help themselves, and it is up to you to maximise your success. There are a lot of competition winners out there – don't forget those who've gone before and those who will come after.

But above all, don't take competitions too seriously. Any arts manager can tell of talents which have been spotted at every stage of competitions, and have been flashed around the music profession's informal Internet. Word of mouth is a far more potent barometer for a career than 'mere' competition success.

The author gratefully acknowledges the assistance of Roderick Lakin, Director of Music at the Royal Over-Seas League, in the preparation of this chapter.

120

ORCHESTRAL FREELANCING – MAKING THE CONTACTS

TREVOR FORD

The telephone rang again. I picked up the receiver and gave my number. 'Hello,' said a rather cross-sounding young female voice, 'I wrote to you two months ago about work – I'm a violinist.' I asked if I'd replied. 'Yes,' she said, sounding surprised that I wasn't sure, 'and you said you would put my name on your list.' This sounded ominous. 'And I'm telephoning', she continued, 'to see what's happening. It's been weeks now and I haven't heard from you!' I explained, as I had done so many times before, that things were quiet and that I couldn't guarantee work to everyone who contacted me. There was a pause. And then: 'How many violinists are there on your books?' I thought for a moment and guessed at 500. Another pause, a disappointed 'Oh ... ', a click and she was gone.

This true story illustrates the wrong way to follow up a letter and I could easily fill many pages simply quoting from correspondence and conversations which have been disastrous in the extreme. So, how should you go about making yourself known to those of us who are responsible for booking orchestral personnel? First, please remember that we fixers, like you, are human. Most of us have been, or are still, orchestral players, and many of us have written exactly the same type of letter which you are now trying to compose. In general, we understand your problems, and are just waiting to be convinced that you are the perfect musician that we have always been looking for.

Identifying the target

There really is very little point in making up a giant mailing list by adding together the orchestras and fixers sections in the *British Music Yearbook* and sending everyone the same letter at the same moment. An hour or two of intelligent research can save you a small fortune in postage, and can also make the whole operation a little more worth while. On many occasions I have received five copies of the same letter, four of which have been forwarded to me from the offices of the orchestras who employ me. First, therefore, knock out the duplicates; if Wilf McThackhacker fixes for half-a-dozen orchestras, you will achieve little by writing to him at six different addresses. And if he is called Wilf (or John or Peter or Ann), please don't start with 'Dear Sir or Madam', as do about a quarter of the letters I receive. It doesn't get you off to a good start.

Then, establish what sort of organisation you are contacting. Orchestras are, on the whole, contract or freelance, and I would be inclined to treat the four London symphony orchestras as being contract orchestras for the purposes of this chapter. Additionally, many fixers only contract for commercial organisations, such as film and TV companies: unless you are already well established or can secure a personal introduction, you will be wasting your time by writing to them. The contract orchestras will usually have some sort of system for dealing with applications to get on the extras list. Often, a copy of your letter will be passed to the section principal and he or she will decide whether you should be called for audition. And, since they audition, they are worth writing to, even if your professional experience is very limited.

Things are quite different with the freelance orchestras. Usually, the fixer is far too busy to spend time reading your letter over and over again looking for the good points, and will have to rely on your ability to show that you are already a trustworthy and reliable professional. The chances are that there will be no auditions and, therefore, there is an element of risk for the orchestra if you are booked. If you have no professional orchestral experience at all and had a mediocre career as a student, why bother writing at all at this stage? You would probably be better off waiting a few months until you have played in a few concerts and actually have something worth writing about. If you really are an absolute beginner, speak to professionals you already know, either as teachers or as friends, and try to get them to recommend you. Alternatively, see if you can play to some established freelance principal players with the same objective.

What to say

The golden rule is: *be brief.* The fat letter bursting from its envelope at the breakfast table rarely reveals a list of international solo engagements but more often details of ten GCSE passes (with grades) and a directory of all the pieces played by the writer since she was 12 years old. Handwritten. On lined paper...

Your job, as I said earlier, is to convince me that you are just the player I am looking for. Your primary school, Sunday school, secondary school, GCSEs, weight-training classes and ability to crochet an electric blanket are of no interest. Equally useless is a list of conductors you have played under (anyone can pay to go on a music course, and my youth orchestra was once conducted by Sir Adrian Boult), a list of orchestral repertoire (are you implying that you can only play these pieces, or that we should plan our programmes around you?) and (ladies) a very sexy photograph (although, speaking personally, I don't really object to these). And don't say you are a regular extra with an orchestra which booked you once and didn't call again: we often find out.

What we do want to know is:

1 What you play – guess how often you forget to tell us!
2 Where and with whom you studied.
3 Awards and prizes at college and since you left.
4 Concerto appearances, recitals and responsible positions while a student or after (e.g. principal second violin).
5 Professional orchestral experience. Deputising with the Sprongthorpe

Symphony Orchestra is *not* professional experience. Neither is getting together with a couple of dozen unemployed ex-students.

Generally, if you weren't paid for it, don't mention it.

6 Where you can be contacted easily. Easily doesn't include a deaf grandmother who can't write, or a permanently engaged telephone at a student hostel.

If you are living with your parents, warn them that you may be telephoned at odd hours. I was once abused by a parent for attempting to telephone his daughter at 10 p.m. He put the phone down on me and I didn't bother to try again.

The letter

Having decided what you want to say, you now have to write a letter. On the face of it, this seems easy. In theory, I would agree. Experience has shown that many of you don't know where to start.

First, decide if you are going to enclose a curriculum vitae or if you are going to incorporate everything into the letter. Then establish to whom you are writing, and make sure you can spell his or her name. Establishing gender is also a good idea. Don't use (a) ruled paper, (b) file paper, (c) torn paper, (d) paper with flowers or pictures of cats on it, (e) toilet paper (the off-white highly absorbent stuff from Woolworths). Then simply say what has to be said as quickly and as neatly as possible. I will give some actual examples of bad wording later. Don't address fixers by their first names unless you really know them well. Don't say that you are an undiscovered genius or you will remain one. Don't say how brilliant you are – you might be lying.

If you have references, by all means enclose copies. Please make sure they are in English and are legible. If you are listing referees, it helps if you spell their names correctly – you will, of course, have asked their permission first. Enclose a stamped, addressed envelope; it doesn't guarantee a reply but it can help. However, an envelope four inches by three inches isn't much use. Or why not be really nice and say that you don't need a reply? If someone who works regularly for the orchestra to which you are writing (and who, preferably, plays the same instrument) has told you to write in, mention his name, but only if he is really prepared to recommend you.

Finally, 'yours sincerely' is acceptable; very few other things are. And, please, sign or write your name legibly at the end of the letter. Then check it carefully, put it in an envelope, address it correctly, put a stamp on it and post it. This all sounds terribly obvious, but at least two of these last points are often neglected.

The CV

Personally, I rather like a well-produced, typed or printed CV. It can be the most efficient way of conveying what you have to say and the reader can easily find the information he wants. However, the majority of CVs are far too long and contain quantities of irrelevant information. Go back to the list of things to say

and, if you are tempted to include something which does not come under one of the six headings, think again and (usually) leave it out.

Set out your single page of A4 with your name, address, telephone number and instrument at the top. Please don't write it like a programme biography ('she then spent an enjoyable three years in historic Vienna studying with ... ') but keep to the facts. If you photocopy 500 and then move, change your name or decide that you have missed something out, start again: crossings out, comments in boxes with long curly arrows spidering their way across the page, and stapled-on scraps of paper are not a good idea.

Last of all, if you know you can't spell, get someone to check it for you. If you can't type, don't try – ask (or even pay) somebody who can do it properly.

The telephone call

Some people insist on telephoning, usually during lunch, mainly when I am not in the office and, inevitably, when I don't want to be disturbed. The conversation usually starts with 'You don't know me, but ...' or with a long silence. Someone once said 'a number of people have told me to phone' and, when I asked who, couldn't think of anyone.

Unless you really have a wonderful way on the telephone, it is usually better to write; the recipient of your letter can read it at a time which is convenient to himself, but he can't choose when you are going to telephone. If you do decide to telephone, think of what you are going to say first – long silences are embarrassing for everyone. Make sure you know who to ask for, preferably by name, and then establish if you are calling at a convenient time before beginning your soliloquy. Don't stay on the phone too long. Ask if you should follow up the call with a letter.

Keeping in touch

First, don't be too disappointed if you don't receive a reply to your letter. An orchestra can easily receive 500 letters in a year from aspiring musicians, and the cost of answering these in both time and money is considerable. From a small organisation, at best a duplicated reply may be expected; many just don't (or can't afford to) answer as a matter of course. This doesn't mean that your letter hasn't made an impression.

Letters are usually filed away by instrument and referred to when necessary. This may be months, or even years, after your original communication, and all your work will have been wasted if you have moved house without telling anyone. The fact that you have not had any response from an orchestra does not mean you never will, and you should retain your original mailing list and update it regularly. Then, if your address or telephone number changes, you can easily notify everyone who might be interested.

A change of address can also be a good opportunity for updating your CV. If you are now working regularly for the LSO and have recently recorded a concerto with the Berlin Phil, say so (as briefly as possible), but don't send any information which was in your original letter. However, if you really have nothing new to say, don't try to make something up, but just send a postcard, either handwritten, printed or incorporating a stick-on address label.

Following up your original letter with a telephone call achieves very little. For one thing, you are implying that your letter was incomplete. If you are expecting to be told what sort of impression you created, then forget it – we are all far too polite to tell you what we really thought. Don't call to complain if you aren't offered any work – there may not be any.

Diary services

Just a brief word about these. The original diary services were for session players but, in recent years, the idea has spread to the freelance orchestral fraternity. A diary service exists to take messages for you. It does not (and should not) promise – or even try – to get you work. You should only consider joining a diary service when you have enough established freelance contacts to justify the expense.

A number of rather misguided younger players seem to think that the appearance of their name on a service's clients' list gives them some sort of professional status. This is far from true and, in fact, the opposite can be the case. Writing to your fixer and letting him know that you are now a proud client of Julian Bakersmith's diary service can simply imply that you are getting no work and are becoming desperate.

If you do decide to join a service, first ask around to find the one best suited to your needs. Speak to the proprietors and see what they can offer you. Don't be talked into joining a service by offers of a sudden rush of concerts – it won't happen. If you are planning to go to a newly-established organisation, make sure that their telephone is manned at all times – I once called a service and was greeted by an answering machine.

Once signed up as a client, make sure you can be traced at any time – don't disappear for a week without leaving a contact telephone number, and make sure that the service passes on to you immediately any messages received from fixers. Keep your diary up to date by phoning in any work which comes direct to you, and also take out holidays, personal engagements and your great-aunt's funeral, otherwise you may find yourself double booked.

Getting asked back

The longed-for telephone call has come, and you have a date in your diary. How do you make sure that you get asked back? This, of course, depends to a large degree on the impression you create at that first rehearsal. Naturally, your technique and musical ability have a lot to do with it, but you are probably no better than a dozen others. Here, then, are my ten commandments:

1 Be on time. If you are late, the chances are you will never be asked back.
2 Make sure you can sight-read well. Rehearsal time is very limited and if the orchestra has to wait while you try to practise a difficult bit in

your bars' rest, they will become a little disillusioned with you. Remember that the BBC often starts rehearsing at 10 o'clock and recording by ten past – and you won't have seen the music before.

3 Don't practise concertos in the bandroom or sit in the orchestra with a book of impossible-looking fingering exercises on your stand.

4 Don't complain about being bored during the rehearsal; everyone else has learned to put up with it and so must you.

5 Don't practise someone else's part where he can hear you – even if you think you *can* play it better.

6 Don't tell the person sitting next to you that he is out of tune.

7 Unless you have been booked as a principal player, don't ask the conductor questions. Refer them via your principal.

8 Don't deliberately play at a different pitch, in a different style or at a different speed to the players around you, even if you are sure that they are all wrong. They have probably been in the profession for years and may, by now, know what they are doing.

9 Be friendly, but not patronising. Offering to get the teas in the break is probably the best thing that you can do!

10 Don't tell everyone how short of work you are. They may all be in the same position.

I hope you don't mind me writing to you like this

When the first edition of this book appeared, I quoted from some letters I had received, partly for amusement but more as a warning. Since then, the number of really funny letters has dropped considerably, which is, I suppose, a pity – or maybe this *Handbook* is doing its job.

If you missed the previous editions of the *Handbook*, do try to find one: most music college libraries will have a copy or two on the shelves, and those original, well-matured quotes are definitely worth reading. This morning, however, as if in answer to a prayer, I received what is probably the most awful letter ever sent to a fixer. I hope the writer will forgive me for reproducing it, together with some of the accompanying CV (which doesn't mention an instrument, by the way). See how many disasters you can spot (and the wonderful spelling mistake *is* authentic). The author's name and personal details have, of course, been omitted for security reasons ...

Dear Sir/Madam

I am a talented and versatile violinist who has just finished a Performing Arts degree. The music business now needs my playing and my personality. Any work you have would be wasted on others. I enclose my C.V. and look forward to hearing from you.

Yours faithfully

XX

CIRRICULUM VITAE

Name:

Address:

Nationality:

Date of Birth:

Education:

Qualifications: GCSE 1988

Subject	Grade	Subject	Grade
English Language	C	Music	B
Oral Communication	1	Psychology	C
English Literature	C	Religious Studies	E
French	D	Science	D
Home Economics	C	Double Subject	D

ADVANCED LEVEL 1990

English Literature	D
Music	D

Pianoforte Associated Board	Grade 5	1991
Music Aural Associated Board	Grade 5	1987
Violin Associated Board	Grade 8	1987

Award of merit life saving certificate
Pad1 international open water divers certificate
Advanced resuscitation certificate

Work Experience:

1994	Bloggs & Co High Road Newark Notts	General packing and computer
1989/90	Cat & Fiddle Public House Smith Street Newark Notts	Bar Person
1987	Crest Hotel Lansdown Road Bournemouth	Breakfast waitress and chambermaid

Resume: The activity that dominates my life is music ... I started in school where I was the leader of the orchestra for many years and played for the annual pantomime.

Recently I have organised a string quartet with three other players ... This has been rewarding both musically and financially.

During school I became very involved with Sprongthorpe Life Saving and Swimming Club and achieved several awards from there. Teaching children requires patience and tact but teaching adults at the same time needs a great deal of sensitivity of which I didn't realize I possessed until then. I left to travel Australia, but it is something I miss very much and would like to get involved with again once my life is settled.

I worked around Australia for seven months and learned a lot about the country and myself. ... When I returned, I took a one year course in music at Sprongthorpe College where I started learning the piano. Whilst there, I performed in a variety of ways on the violin.

I have gained considerably from working with and watching different teams of people including the 'Tomorrows World' team from the BBC. I feel confident when I need to put across a point of view or calm a potentially 'explosive' situation. I would be an asset to any group be it new or established.

MARKETING YOURSELF

KEITH DIGGLE

Keith Diggle is the Marketing Director of Rhinegold Publishing Limited and author of the book Arts Marketing *(published in 1994). He was a promoter of music and the performing arts when director of Mersey-side Arts Association and was co-founder of the English Sinfonia.*

The product and the market

If there is one essential, never-to-be-forgotten rule in the marketing of individuals or groups of individuals, it is 'always put yourself in the shoes of your customers'. Just as writers have to learn to be readers if they are to assess their work effectively, so the performer must develop the objectivity that will enable him to see himself, his professional colleagues, his programmes and performances, even his style of dress and speech, clearly and unemotionally. Most important of all, the performer must assess where he stands in his profession, how he is rated as a performer (by those who can influence his career) and how well-known he is (by those whose interest he seeks to arouse). Only when we can 'see ourselves as others see us' can we begin to apply the concepts of marketing to a career.

We must take this even further and imagine what it is like to be a person who, for pleasure or professional reasons (I grant that the two are not mutually exclusive) employs, engages, or in any other way makes use of the services of, musicians. What is he like? How much does he know about music? About your kind of music? About you? Under what pressures does he labour? Is he motivated towards achieving success? What does 'success' mean to him – is it a full house, irrespective of the artist engaged or the music played, or can 'success' mean something else? At the heart of who he is and what he does, what does he really want?

I have started by touching on the first and most important considerations in marketing: the *product* (that's *you*) and the *market* (that's *them*). I have made the point that your assessment of both must be ruthlessly honest; you must see things as they are and not as you would like them to be. Note that I have not defined the market as being those blessed people with good ears and good sense that make up your audiences. They would be your market if you were yourself promoting music (either your own or someone else's). For the moment, let us assume that the promotion of your performance is being handled by someone else, so your task is to sell yourself to those people, the promoters, whose responsibility it will be, later on, to market you to the public.

What does your market know of you?

Consider what passes through the mind of a promoter as he opens an envelope

and takes out a brochure. Secretaries of music clubs, local government officers in departments of arts and recreation, university music societies, all tell us how many of these brochures they receive every week. Some say they just throw them in the bin without a second thought (sometimes unopened) and others say they give them a second thought and *then* throw them away. How many are opened, read carefully, acknowledged by post, filed away for future reference, we shall never know. Yet, artists *are* engaged and concert seasons *are* booked. How?

The temptation to refer to the parable of the sower is very strong at this stage. The sower accepted the random nature of what he was doing. However, when we consider the concepts of marketing, we are trying to keep the element of chance to a minimum: we have to seek out the fertile soil and set about creating more, not being able to afford to waste the seeds that are our advertisements on the rocky ground.

When the promoter opens an envelope and takes out a brochure, or opens a magazine and sees an advertisement, he relates what he sees to what he already knows. His state of *awareness* in relation to you and/or what you have to offer is crucial to what he does next. If nothing strikes a chord with him, nothing is what he does in response (apart from reach for the waste-paper bin). If the promoter has already heard of you, or if what you are offering is something which is of *interest* (preferably both) your brochure or advertisement will be given the benefit of closer examination and may result in action – or a decision to take action at a later date (so you go in the filing tray rather than the bin).

The part played by the brochure

Does the brochure itself not play a part in this? Surely, a well-designed, well-written, attractive piece of print will stand a better chance of making an impact than one that is plain, lacklustre and boring? Indeed it does, but it will go no further than attracting attention (that is, it will attract for no more than a fraction of a second) unless it is attracting attention to something that the reader knows something about, is interested in and, preferably, has need of. Are *you,* the reader, not constantly receiving through the post wonderfully well-designed, expensively-printed sales brochures for things in which you have no interest and for which you have no need? And what do you do with them?

Am I saying that, if one is a complete beginner whom no-one knows, a brochure posted to a promoter has no chance at all of obtaining an engagement? Not quite, but I *am* saying that there is only a very small chance. The promoter's awareness of you is non-existent and his need for you is probably non-existent as well – unless he is looking out for beginners.

So, goodbye to brochures? No, not at all. But, if you are a beginner, goodbye, perhaps, to investing all your hopes and a fair amount of your savings in a mailing to every known promoter in the land in the belief that engagements will immediately follow. You will still need a brochure because, as you create awareness of yourself and as you learn more of what individual promoters are doing, you will require a piece of paper that tells people who you are, what you do, how well you do it, and how they may make contact with you. You will need to revise that piece of paper regularly as you add to it news of your developing career and remove from it that which is out of date and, one hopes, now unworthy of you. And, as we shall see, these pieces of paper will play a part in creating fertile soil for your subsequent advertising.

Publicity – how to become famous

These considerations are all concerned with your *publicity,* a word which is often very misunderstood. Publicity comprises two closely-related activities: *public relations* (not a very helpful term unless you remember that your public in this instance is made up of those who may engage you – a better expression might be *market relations* or *promoter relations*), and *advertising.* Advertising (sending out brochures, for instance) only works if the ground has been prepared, if the people to whom you are aiming it know something of you, and if there is a good chance that they will believe what you are asking them to read. More than that, what they know about you already must be essentially favourable.

Most artists only ever concentrate upon their advertising. Once a career has matured, this may well be enough but, at the start, PR is crucially important: you are attempting to build a favourable awareness of yourself in the minds of those who can give you work. The various opportunities that exist for young artists to display their talents, the competitions, awards and 'platforms', do not necessarily create work instantly, but they make the artists better known: they create 'fame'.

It is worth dwelling briefly on this word 'fame', which literally means 'to be spoken of'. Fame is not a matter of being either famous or not-famous; it usually builds slowly with each exposure in the media gradually being added to by each successive appearance, until eventually an artist becomes someone who is known by many more people than he knows himself. Of course, there are the exceptions: those wonderful occasions when someone wins a major international competition and becomes a star overnight with every promoter in every civilised country clamouring to offer engagements. Mainly, however, it happens over a period of time. As one famous actor commented, 'It took me at least ten years to become a star overnight!'.

Promoters need audiences, and that is why fame is important to them and why it is important to you. You need the promoter to know of you and you also need the promoter to believe that you are known to enough people to make an audience.

Building one's fame is a matter of making the most of every opportunity. If, by hook or by crook, you have obtained an engagement (whether paid or not doesn't matter) you should spend as much time exploiting this as you do rehearsing for the performance. Your first interest will be with music critics in the hope that they will say good things about you and your performance, but the chances are that they will all be far too busy to come to hear you. As a general rule, music critics only show interest if they have already heard something good about you on the grapevine (you have to face the problem of awareness with these folk just as you do with the promoters). Start with the people you have met in the business, preferably people who engage musicians and people whose opinion counts with them (don't forget your own friends in the music world). Call them, get them to come along, make sure someone meets and greets them and gives them an interval drink. Afterwards, write to them and ask them what they thought of it all. If they say anything complimentary, see if you can quote them in your letters and brochure.

Weeks before the event, start thinking if there is anything about you and what you do that might interest the newspapers and radio. If you were born in Bristol, write and tell the Bristol papers and local radio what you are doing – even if your performance is going to take place in Southend. Are you planning to play anything written by a person with local connections? What about the Bristol music clubs? Why not invite them to attend? Why not hire a coach and suggest that they come along to support you? Then telephone the local radio stations (at both Southend and Bristol) to tell them that your supporters' club is about to descend on Southend. Make sure that you have some photographs taken of the occasion, not just of you performing but of you with the music club members *(laughing)*, you with the local government entertainments manager who booked you (still laughing), you with a group of local children who are studying music (still laughing) – and then have enough prints made to send to the local papers (in Bristol and Southend) and to magazines such as the 'county glossies', those monthlies that are devoted to local activities. A brief reference to you in a local publication, with a picture, will not make you a star but it will give you something to copy and send on to other promoters. *And* it will add to their perception of you, making you more than just a name at the bottom of a letter.

Obviously, I do not mean that you should slavishly follow this example. I give it as a simple illustration of how you can be creative using a straightforward engagement that would otherwise be over when the last note had been played. Read the national newspapers and you will see how bright ideas are constantly being used to put artists into the public eye.

Degrading and time-consuming?

To the serious musician this will all feel rather degrading and, in a sense, it is: you are a musician because you want to be a musician and not a buffoon desperately seeking attention. But such is the nature of the world in which we live that the majority of people, even very talented people, have to develop a knack for attracting attention. It is desperately unfair, but it also helps to be physically attractive: when you are wholly unknown, the people whose attention you are seeking need something to latch on to. You must help them do this by paying attention to how you look. Make the most of yourself! Most people's first sight of you will be in a photograph (this tells us something about the importance of your professional photograph). Only later, when you become better known, will it be your talent that comes to mind first rather than your appearance.

Marketing yourself will also strike you as being very time consuming. It is.

Perhaps one of the only advantages of being a beginner is that you will tend to have time on your hands (when you are not practising, naturally) and the task should not be overwhelming. Later, it would be wise to consider paying someone to do this work for you. A PR specialist can say things about you that you would never dare say yourself and he will also know far more people to say them to than you do. A good agent (see the chapter entitled **Finding an Agent**), should you be successful in persuading one to take you on, will carry out many of the PR functions for you because, at this later stage, telling people about you and selling you to them is pretty much the same thing. But, if you are failing to make your career live up to your talent, consider taking on a PR specialist who knows the music world.

Advertising – using your fame to obtain engagements

Try to think of advertising not as something separate from PR, but as an activity to be practised together with PR. It is an inseparable companion to the process of making people aware of you. The brochure you send out may not find you an engagement immediately but, if it is well conceived and executed, it is playing its part in helping your market know you are there. As you develop your own fame, so your advertising will become more effective. What advertising methods are open to you?

The multi-purpose brochure is clearly an essential. It can be used to introduce you to a large number of people who, up until that time, have never heard of you. As I have said, it will not yield much in the way of engagements initially but it builds awareness. It can be used to leave a permanent reminder of you with people that you have met – people who have attended one of your performances, for example. If the telephone is used as a means of seeking engagements, a brochure can be used to accompany the letter which follows up the conversation. As your fame grows, it becomes more and more an instrument that will sell you.

How, then, does one set about creating a good brochure? Keep at the forefront of your mind the thought that the brochure has to carry three basic pieces of information: it must convey a clear and attractive impression of who you are and what you do, it must carry information that gives you credibility (so that people will believe that you are good at what you do), and it must provide the interested person with a means of making contact with you.

People who work in advertising tend to apply the mnenonic AIDA when planning advertisements and sales literature. *A* stands for *Awareness* – the instant that the piece of paper is seen it must make people aware of it; it must be eye-catching. *I* stands for *Interest* – once you have caught the reader's eye you must then hold his interest. *D* stands for *Desire* – then the reader must begin to want what is advertised. *A* stands for *Action* – the reader must then be encouraged to do something, preferably pick up the telephone to see when you are free. Good copywriting and design contribute enormously to all four parts of the process.

Copywriting and design

The best thing to do at this stage is to disregard every other artist's brochure you have ever seen and try to think of original ways of describing yourself that will excite the reader. Most people start with their name. But why? Unless their readers already have some awareness of them, why should a name excite them? They also slap a photograph immediately under their name. Wonderful! Now we know what this unknown person looks like. Where's the waste-paper bin?

You are a double-bass player, your name is Eric Smith and your appearance, although neat and tidy, is not striking. (If double-bass players of unstriking appearance, called Eric Smith, read this, their time will not be wasted.) The envelope is opened and what do we read? All by itself, on the first part of the paper that we see: LOW NOTES ON A HIGH LEVEL – that is all. The letters are printed in an unusual typeface in bright orange on a buff coloured background (or buff on a bright orange background, or in any other striking combination of colours that are compatible with legibility). What does it mean? It means we are made *aware* and, because the statement does not tell us enough, we are *interested*. We need to know more so we turn the page. And what do we see? A sketch of a small person, holding a double-bass, apparently playing it on the top of a New York skyscraper. There are more words alongside the sketch: A DANGEROUSLY ENTERTAINING EVENING IN THE COMPANY OF ERIC SMITH AND HIS AMAZING TALKING, DANCING DOUBLE-BASS. Beneath these words there are more words, written smaller (now your attention is held, the words do not have to shout at you):

'Dragonetti would have loved every minute of it'
The Manchester Gazette.

'He held his capacity audience enraptured – and the double-bass was good as well'
Peterborough Post.

'Thank you Eric Smith, you brought life to this tired old town'
Councillor John Jones, Chairman of the Entertainments Committee, Borough of Oldville.

The brochure goes on to tell you what Eric Smith does for his money. Having caught you, it does not waste any more of your time; it tells you that Eric Smith does a light-hearted lecture recital on the history of the double-bass, illustrating it with a wide variety of music, old and new, and any amount of amusing anecdotes. It tells how long the entertainment lasts and what sort of facilities are needed (for example, if an accompanist is used, a piano might prove useful). It mentions some of the more interesting places visited in recent times. It also adds credibility by quoting at greater length some of the laudatory comments that have been made by promoters, musicians and music critics. Because Eric Smith is not very prepossessing – no photographer has ever taken a halfway decent picture of him – no picture appears in the brochure apart from one or two more sketches.

The interested promoter will now need to be told how much Mr Smith charges for his services and how to contact him. It is hard to say when a fee should be stated in print and when it should be left to emerge in a subsequent discussion. As a general rule, only the very famous need to be coy about how much they charge (either because they are embarrassed about how large the fee is, or because they do not wish to pre-empt a discussion that could result in it being even bigger). It helps a promoter to know where you stand on the matter of fees (and expenses), so say what you want.

Whether or not you should invite a response directly back to you very much depends on your personality. Eric Smith, as you can tell, is quite happy to deal with enquiries himself – indeed, he rather enjoys it. If you are a quieter sort of soul then you might, in the absence of an agent, obtain the assistance of husband, wife, father, mother or friend who lives in the same house. I know one musician, a guitarist, who performed under a stage name and acted as his own agent under his real name. He kept the bluff going for years.

But what about the *design* of the brochure? First do the real spadework: decide who you are, what you do, and how you want people to perceive you. Reject all the conventional approaches and invent something for *you* which is true, original and most likely to attract. The brochure has to convey as persuasive a picture of you as possible and that means that it must immediately make you stand out from the crowd.

Consider giving a title to your performance. Or devise your programmes on a thematic basis and give them titles. If you are part of an ensemble, choose a good, original title for the group, a title that will stay in people's minds. See how memorable are titles like The King's Singers, The Scholars, The Fairer Sax, Trio Zingara and Fortune's Fire.

Once you have decided how you want to present yourself and, by implication, the style of your presentation, the matter of design becomes relatively simple. It is a mistake to present yourself unprepared to a designer in the expectation that a personality will be created for you – you must do this work yourself. Then it is simply a matter of producing an original piece of paper so designed that it will immediately create *awareness*, arouse *interest* and so on. Look out for different ways of folding the paper to tempt the reader into the brochure; decide which words will shout and which words will speak quietly and in more detail. The best brief that you can give a designer is the *copy* – the actual words you want to use. From your words, the designer can create design using the tools of typography, illustration and colour. And if you cannot afford a designer? Do it yourself – it is not impossible.

Design leads to printing and this is expensive for most people. It is a necessary expense, however, and provided you have done the preparatory work before you approach a designer, and given that the designer knows that you want to keep printing costs to a minimum, it should give value for money.

Advertisements

Advertisements in magazines such as *Classical Music, The Singer, Classical Piano* and *Early Music Today,* and in the *British Music Yearbook,* should be approached in exactly the same way as the brochure. If you just stick down your name and standard photograph, do not expect huge results. The only difference between brochure and advertisement is that the advertisement is almost always in black and white, is flat (that is, no folds), is always in the company of other advertisements and is printed and distributed by someone else for you.

Using the telephone

An advertisement or a brochure cannot do any more than project its message. It cannot respond, answer questions or steer the reader into a more productive frame of mind. If the advertisement or brochure tempts the promoter into calling you, or the person you have deputed to act as your intermediary, then there is the opportunity to turn the interest into a commitment of one sort or another. The commitment may be an agreement to engage you on a certain date for a certain fee; that is the ultimate as far as you are concerned. A commitment to attend one of your performances, to meet you afterwards for a drink and a chat, is the next best thing. The aim must be to obtain one sort of commitment or another from the caller. If this cannot be done then and there, note the telephone number and name of the caller and arrange to call back – and call back within a few days with a better reason why they should engage you or come to see you.

Should one ever take the initiative and call promoters before they think of calling you? Again, it depends on your personality or that of the person acting for you. If you can do it well, you will ultimately find it very rewarding: even if you do not get engagements at first, you will learn about the promoters, how they work, how they make their decisions. Be systematic. List your targets, names and telephone numbers (Rhinegold's *British Music Yearbook* is an excellent source) and make out a file card for each. As you telephone, check that you have the correct person, address and telephone number, and make notes on each call. Find out and note the best time of day to call. Summarise your reception and record what action you agreed would be taken: 'send brochure with covering letter inviting her to attend next performance in nearby town', 'call back in September' and so on. As you progress, you create a file of contacts so that, as time goes by, you can telephone people easily, in a relaxed manner. Do not telephone anyone unless you have something specific to tell them and have a specific commitment in mind for them.

Development

As I have said before, the whole process takes time. Your work in generating an awareness of yourself through PR activities, your self-advertising, your engagements, all contribute to the growth of your career. With determination and a level of common sense the talented musician can carve out a career. Many before you have been successful; good luck with it!

BRITISH
AND INTERNATIONAL
MUSIC
YEARBOOK

For those who choose it, perform it, make it, manage it, market it, tour it, supply it, fund it and house it.

THE DIRECTORY OF THE CLASSICAL MUSIC INDUSTRY

Published each November
£19.95

ADDITIONAL POSTAGE AND PACKING CHARGES
£4.00 to UK addresses,
£7.50 surface mail worldwide,
£7.50 Airmail in Europe,
£16.00 Outside Europe.

Send your cheque, made payable to Rhinegold Publishing Ltd to:
Book Sales Dept, Rhinegold Publishing Ltd, FREEPOST, London WC2H 8BR

CREDIT CARD ORDERS TEL:0171 333 1721 FAX:0171 333 1769

FINDING AN AGENT

JOHN BICKLEY

John Bickley developed an early interest in music as a chorister at Westminster Abbey, and, after Cambridge, founded Magenta Music International, of which he is now Managing Director. His involvement in the legal, marketing and financial aspects of the music business led to an MBA. He is Chairman of the International Artist Managers' Association, and has too little time to indulge in his marathon running and skiing interests.

'How do I find an agent?' and 'What should I expect from an agent?' are two questions asked by almost every artist setting out on a career as a solo performer. Are these the right questions, though? Does the artist mean 'agent', or rather 'artist manager'? And what about the manager's expectations of the artist?

If I were asked to explain the difference between the terms 'agent' and 'artist manager', my answer would be that the expression 'agent' is perhaps now rather old fashioned, implying someone with a long list of artists who are simply slotted into jobs which happen to come the agent's way. Artist managers have wider horizons and, usually, shorter lists of artists. They have a pro-active, more involved, and longer-term attitude to their artists' work, and usually have a global perspective. What could better signal this difference than the fact that the British Association of Concert Agents has recently changed its name to the International Artist Managers' Association?

Before discussing this further, we need to be aware of what the marketplace is like in which the artist manager – and thus the artist – is working. It has changed markedly recently, and continues to change – not, of course, at the same speed and in the same way in every country, but changing nevertheless. An understanding of the marketplace is crucial to knowing the kind of artist manager you need. Not only is it fragmenting, but also expanding and contracting at the same time, depending on where you look. Live performance remains the backbone of any career, but consider the potential employers, even in this area: orchestras, opera companies, venues, festivals, choral societies, music societies. And then there are the record companies, radio and TV organisations (public and independent), production companies, and a myriad other potential employers. All these are replicated in all the countries where Western classical music has a market – thousands of potential employers and thousands of contacts.

It is these contacts that a young artist expects of an artist manager; and, whilst no manager can know everyone, the best have the widest connections or, at the very least, a policy of continually widening them, through travel and other company development policies.

OK, so the market is huge and complex, but, you ask, how do I decide whom to approach to guide me through it, and how do I make that approach? If there were a simple answer to this, I would give it, but there isn't: every artist manager has his or her own way of selecting and building an artist list, and few additions are made through unsolicited approaches. My own company receives many letters each week, supplemented by biographies, repertoire lists, sheets of reviews, brochures, photographs, tapes and videos. These packages reflect a wide range of presentational skills, from the over-sophisticated to the downright tatty. Far too many tapes are poorly recorded or documented. Very occasionally, an imaginatively prepared demo-tape will make it on to our office stereo system, but this is rare. A few might get listened to in the car *en route* to collect the children or to the supermarket. It is depressing but true, I fear, that the effort put in by the artist gets such scant attention. This is partly to do with strike rate: because it is almost unheard of to take on an artist on the strength of such a promotional package, the mounting pile of tapes, photos and biographies next to the in-tray gathers dust.

So how to have any chance of getting attention, let alone an audition (and how many artist managers have formal auditions these days?) or an appointment? Like any selling or marketing activity, the first approach has to be very well researched. Don't approach a singers' agency if you are a violinist: blindingly obvious, perhaps, but a policy more honoured in the breach. Do find out the name of the person you are hoping to impress: mass-produced 'Dear Sir/Madam' letters get the shortest shrift. Do follow up with a telephone call, but don't get irritated if it takes a few attempts to reach the person you want. The majority of the good artist managements are overstretched and under-staffed for the amount they are trying to achieve, the economics of the business being what they are. IAMA publishes a useful directory which indicates each member's fields of activity and, from the lists of artists, you can work out who might be the most appropriate.

There are short cuts to this process, and do exploit them if you can. Personal recommendations, either by other artists already represented by the management or by very well established artists who might also be teachers and who are prepared to help, might speed things up. But, quite frankly, the best way to get noticed is to get performing. Management staffs spend a lot of time going to concerts and other performances, as do recording company staffs, promoters and anyone else who is interested not just in seeking new talent but also in keeping abreast of the scene. And all these people talk to each other all of the time. So it doesn't matter how lowly the circumstances, take any performing opportunity, for, cumulatively, if you have got something to offer, you will get noticed.

Let's assume you have been noticed by a manager you think might be right for you at the beginning of your career; what can you expect? Whatever the arrangement with the manager, do not expect to be able to sit back and wait for work to come in. It is definitely a collaborative process, and this is something you should discuss in depth at the start of the relationship. It is more than likely that you will be asked to sign a contract giving the artist management company exclusivity. Exclusivity means what it says and, under most circumstances, is the only way for a relationship with a general manager to work. At first, it might seem that you are simply handing over your own contacts, but there will not be many contacts which an artist has which the manager does not also have, and if the management company is to get to immediate grips with developing the career, this early period needs to be highly collaborative.

You should take independent legal advice before rushing into an agreement, of course, and most managements would suggest this to you. All contracts are negotiable, so feel free to discuss the detail. It should cover levels of commission for various kinds of work, the responsibilities of the general manager *vis à vis* local managers in particular territories, and any costs which the manager will recharge for publicity material and other direct expenses. Commission rates vary, but certainly in the UK are in the 15-20% band. An artist with a long-term contract could expect to pay a lower rate. Rates in the USA can be 25%+, and, when local managers are involved, even when commission is split, the total payable is likely to be higher than the general manager's usual rate.

It takes time to develop a career and, although some general managers have strong connections with particular agencies in other countries, the usual practice is to bring local managers on stream gradually, not least because, if the general manager is worth his salt, he is going to be selling directly until your career is more established. The relationship between a general manager and a local manager often seems a little mysterious, so, again, discuss whatever is proposed. A general manager will only suggest using local managers where they believe you will be better served, but, as explained in the previous paragraph, there are usually cost implications to be taken into account.

You should discuss together what your objectives are for a year or two ahead, but be a little sceptical about grand talk of career strategies: so much depends on chance, or a series of moves, most of which cannot be foreseen too far down the line. The amount of individual attention you can expect is highly variable, and obviously relates to the management's staffing levels and the size of their list of artists. Keep abreast with what is happening in terms of marketing your career, but be realistic: however hard-working the management, they can never do half the things they would like to do, for the reasons already discussed. Managers nowadays are expected to be experts in everything – many artists cannot afford top legal or taxation advice, for example – and the more you ask them to do outside of finding you engagements and servicing those engagements, the less time will be available for the career development activities.

The artists who make the most consistent progress early on are those who develop ideas of their own, who are prepared to explore every opportunity, and who make a steady stream of suggestions. It is particularly important, for example, to participate enthusiastically in non-performing opportunities such as educational events. And, if you have a quiet patch in the diary, make the most of it to study new repertoire, think about future projects or other self-development, perhaps languages. You are also your own best sales-person when you are working: be punctual, well prepared and friendly with the promoter, and ask your manager to get feedback on these aspects afterwards.

Once you have a manager, you will still need to invest in an array of promotional material, particularly first-class colour and black-and-white photos, and promotional DATs and cassettes. Not every photo can be unconventional, but do try to be imaginative. It is rare that a single photo can distil your own 'self-image' and be, in the management's view, a perfect promotional tool: there are technical considerations to take into account, such as ease of reproduction. But most people can recognise a photo which grabs them, so spend time (and extra money, if necessary) getting this right. You can certainly expect your artist management to have strong views on this subject, and some experienced, objective advice can be useful.

Invest in the basic technological aids which are becoming standard: fax, computer with a modem, and a mobile phone. Keep your manager aware of where you can be contacted: being able to respond to short-notice enquiries early in a career can lead to significant breaks.

These, then, are some of the practicalities. But what is almost more essential is an understanding of the psychological relationship. Selling or marketing products must be so much easier than trying to promote artists: they don't have minds of their own and don't answer back! But the challenge and excitement of working with people is what most artist managers find stimulating, despite the stress caused by constant changes of mind, by the need for confidence building, and the enduring capability of artists always to believe that their peers are doing better than they are. Artist managers and artists often do become friends, but sometimes a more reserved approach works better.

An artist also needs to find a way – and few find this easy – to accept criticism when it is due, and to realise that, almost without exception, taking a long-term view leads to greater fulfilment and success. In my experience, artists often try to overreach themselves, leaving the manager with the task of having to persuade them to pace themselves – although the general perception would tend to suggest that the reverse is true. Artists who change managements every couple of years, who find it difficult to develop a continuing relationship with any of them, and who become aggressive at every set-back, are unlikely to do themselves any good. Obviously, people do change managers, as relationships do not always work out, but, if this happens to you, do try to handle the situation in an open and positive way. The previous manager might have put a great deal of effort into developing your career, and may very much regret losing you when the rewards are beginning to be reaped. Sometimes, if things are not working out, it will be the management itself which will make the decisive move. Your contract will, if properly drawn up, detail the procedure for such a change-over, but it is concomitant on both parties to act sensitively.

Such an overview as this can only give the most general guidance, but, if I had to summarise the whole process of working with an artistic management, it would be not to expect the earth, to be realistic, and to remember that your career depends on joint effort.

145

CONCERT MANAGEMENT AND PROMOTION

JEFFREY LONG

A former theatre stage manager, Jeffrey Long's experience in concert management, touring, promotion and public relations was gained with the London Sinfonietta, Universal Edition and the London Symphony Orchestra among others. He now runs a graphic design company catering for music and general clients.

Before you begin to consider promoting a concert, you need to be very clear why you are doing it. Music is unique in the interpretive arts in that you can do it without an audience. But the minute you ask people to pay to hear you play live, you had better realise that you have just joined the entertainment industry. If your primary objective is something other than presenting an entertaining experience to people you have never met, please think again. Motives such as wanting critical notices, the chance to run through works in public before supposedly importantly performances, or simply fulfilling an exhibitionist need, just will not do. So be honest with yourself!

Promoting your own concert is an expensive business. It consumes far more time than you imagine and is virtually always a loss-making activity. Before you begin, be sure that you can afford to lose everything you spend, unless you have a guarantee against loss.

Booking a hall

With your projected programme in mind, you need to book a hall, considering its availability, cost, seating capacity, location, acoustic, interior suitability and its status in the public mind as a place of entertainment. These factors may affect what you can play. You may be asked to support your request with tangible evidence of financial or artistic credibility. There will probably be a non-returnable deposit.

How do you choose a hall? One of the best ways is to find an event similar to one you would like to promote and to attend it; this should give you a good idea of existing potential in a few seconds. Note if you were able to see and hear properly, if the players had any practical difficulties, if programme sales, box office, bar and ushering were efficient. Count the audience accurately; estimates may exaggerate the numbers. Disadvantages, such as uncomfortable seating or poor local infrastructure, may cost you attendance. Ask the hall for recent attendance figures.

Concept

With the hall in mind, you must now look at the whole concert concept, matching art against budget. Be realistic: you will get neither audience nor critics for a Reger programme on a Maundy Thursday evening at a church hall in Wolverhampton. You will get both if you discover Mozart's 42nd symphony and première it in the Royal Festival Hall on a November weekday. Your concert is in competition with other activities which might occupy people's leisure time. Ask yourself, would *you* make an effort to go? If you feel that nobody will come, however well you publicise it, you might as well have a rehearsal instead.

Having established a suitable programme, you need to check for clashes with similar concerts and the availability of artists.

Practical problems

You may have chosen a hall with what appears to be a suitable piano or organ, but you should check the tuning arrangements. A=440 is normal in Britain but, if you are managing a concert abroad, you will find that concert pitch is frequently higher. This can cause major problems if you are touring other keyboards or tuned percussion, and baroque music groups playing at lower pitches may find they must tour everything. Access should be measured: a doorway wide enough for a piano on its side may be too narrow for 32-inch pedal timpani. Major orchestral tours to purpose-built halls have had to be changed on the concert day through failure to ascertain the amount of stage space. Some halls have their own music stands, some don't.

Adequate heating is essential and very rare outside recognised halls, but lighting may be your worst problem. Concert lighting is quite different from that employed in the theatre – you need plain white light from overhead and plenty of it. If you tour a lot to strange venues, it may be worth investing in quartz halogen lamps on long stands. If you are putting on anything staged or semi-staged, you will need lit music stands, as well as properly designed spotlighting for the performers. Note how you want to organise the house lighting during the concert. Reduced house lighting helps audience concentration, but they may need to be able to read words in the programme.

In all cases, establish that the venue has an adequate power source from which cables may be run without causing a fire or a safety hazard. Do not forget that this applies to vibraphones, live electronics, amplifiers and any other electrical equipment.

Check to see if you need public liability insurance – you will require this if you are not covered automatically by the hall's insurers.

Budget

The budget for the concert should be written as a simple income and expenditure account. The income side will look a bit short: probably only projected gross ticket sales, subsidy and a deficit to make the thing balance. It is appropriate to keep separate accounts for activities associated with, but isolated from, the actual performance: programme sales, bar takings and so on.

The expenditure side can be a catalogue of woe but optimism will make it worse! Expenses should be considered under two headings – those which relate to ticket sales, including all advertising and marketing (indirect expenses) and those upon which the performance itself depends, including players' fees (direct expenses). Begin with the hall hire fee and the commission charged on ticket sales, with VAT on top. If your ensemble is VAT registered, you will be reclaiming some or all of the latter. All promotional expenditure is incurred for the purpose of selling tickets, as are the costs of box office staff, ticket printing and ushers. Divide your promotion budget into advertising and publicity. Advertising includes all media costs from design to space bookings, all printed material, including design, artwork, typesetting, layout, printing, delivery and distribution. Publicity embraces all public and media relations activities from press conferences and news releases right down to extra commission you might need to pay on complimentary tickets, or the car your conductor takes to a local radio interview.

Next come the players' fees. Conductors, soloists and chamber groups usually receive a flat fee, with or without expenses. Contracts are advisable. Orchestral fees begin with the leader, followed by sub-leader, section principals, principals, sub-principals and rank-and-file. Each receives a concert fee to include a three-hour rehearsal on the day. Extra rehearsals are charged at half the concert fee plus a small supplement if you are having a single rehearsal on a day other than the concert day. For professional players, you will need a schedule of rules from the Association of British Orchestras or the Musicians' Union, which establishes minima for different kinds of performance. Certain players, including cello, double bass, harp, timpani and percussion, also receive established rates of porterage to contribute towards their transport costs. Some players are registered for VAT, which they will charge you. All payments must be made within a month of the concert date, and remember that musicians, once engaged, will have to be paid, even if you cancel the concert or decide subsequently that their services are not required. There may be a need to make special payments for learning a new instrument or undertaking a particularly difficult part. Broadcasting fees will appear in both income and expenditure accounts.

Your fixer will normally charge you 10% of the players' remuneration, excluding broadcasting fees and certain expenses, for booking the personnel.

Players travelling further than fifteen miles from their centre of employment will be paid distance money, in addition to the costs incurred by moving the entire group to the venue. If return to base by rail, or by the transport you are providing, is not possible before 2 am, you need to budget for a hotel and a subsistence payment for each player. The ABO, MU or your fixer will provide full details. Your travel costs should be calculated on the basis of second class rail fares (or the appropriate mileage rate announced by the ABO or the MU), or scheduled economy flights if abroad. If you fly, you will need an additional seat for each cello, something to remember if you are bringing a piano trio into the UK, for example.

Instrument hire, transport and tuning is your next consideration. Percussion hire is a matter of negotiation: some players run their own hire businesses. Music hire or purchase, composer's commission fees and performing rights fees (frequently included in hall hire, but check) come next. You will also need music stands, chairs, stools, tables for percussion sticks or electronics, rostra, heat and light.

Librarians, stage staff, flowers and gratuities complete a long list. You should calculate your administration costs (time, office, schedule distribution, telephone, post, etc) realistically. They won't go away.

It is normal to add a contingency figure to the expenditure account: somewhere between 5% and 10% of the total so far.

It is better to budget for programme books separately, including the cost of notes, design, typesetting, layout, printing, finishing, delivery and programme sellers. This can be balanced by income from programme sales and advertising and, quite possibly, another little deficit.

Organisation

Once you have booked the hall, you are committed, so you had better make a plan of action. You will already know how many rehearsals you need so, if your ensemble is anything more than domestic, tell your fixer and book a rehearsal hall immediately. The concert hall itself is ideal and even busy venues are sometimes available. Otherwise, you will need somewhere with a reasonable acoustic and the same facilities as the concert venue.

You now write a provisional schedule, available to anyone who needs it (other than your competitors). The final version will include dates, times, venues with exact addresses and contact numbers, maps where necessary, recommended sources of sustenance, your address and contact numbers, fax, telex, programme, artists, orchestration, notification of broadcasts, rehearsal order, dress, travel and hotel arrangements and special instructions or reminders concerning visas, passports, instrument transport and so on. A word about dress: all professional musicians are equipped with dinner suits and short black dresses or tails and long black dresses. Choose anything else, and you will be subjected to a wide variation of tastes so that, to establish uniformity, you will need more money and time.

Promotion

Marketing strategy is discussed elsewhere in this book, and Keith Diggle's *Arts Marketing* is *de rigueur*. Appropriate ticket pricing is a crucial matter. If you need to print tickets, do not delay; your price structure is unlikely to be better tomorrow. Many recognised concert halls request a reduction policy for parties, youth or the disadvantaged. Remember that disabled people go to concerts too! If there is no seating plan, make one. You may need to offer bulk deals to your own contacts, club or orchestra members. There are several specialist firms producing numbered tickets quickly and cheaply. Consult the box office staff on the format – they may want a system with several stubs. Estimate the number of complimentary tickets you need, not forgetting your sponsors, board of management and critics, draw them and list them for reference. You must know where your chairman is sitting. Always keep two pairs of house seats for emergencies.

Once these matters are under way, you can turn your attention to the main business of filling the hall with people. Selling the arts is qualitatively different from selling soap. In the first place, there are no funds for individual market research. However, they are hardly necessary because much has been done for you. We know that audiences for classical music show remarkable consistency. They are mostly people who are, or will become, educated decision-makers. In terms of *sales,* classical music reaches less than 5% of the total population. It is unlikely in the extreme that you have the funds to make an impact outside the established target market, however much we all wish you could. And the more you spend beyond a certain figure, the more money you will lose. Such is the nature of deficit finance.

Second, the possibility of changing your product as a result of research is restricted. If a manufacturer finds that the customer will not buy his rough, purple soap, he goes back to the lab to make a smooth, white product. Your position is less flexible. And your product talks. I have never known it possible to advertise a conductor as 'new, improved, and with added rostrum style'. Promotion of classical music is product-oriented, so you had better live with it. That we would prefer not to, is obviated by the enormous range of diatonic music now being rediscovered. Can you image the rush if someone discovered a Mozart opera written between *Figaro* and *The Magic Flute?*

Your concert tickets have a shelf life. Consider this: as a supermarket manager, you are asked to sell some yogurt. You are told that it will be lychee flavour and nothing else, all to be sold in one store. Five hundred pots only are available. Few people have heard of lychees and even fewer are known to like it. It will be delivered on 23rd October. It has a sell-by date of 23rd November, but your customers can eat it only on the sell-by date. You might feel you had a problem. But when your group manager tells you that each pot costs £2.50 to produce and that you have only £100 to spend on promotion, you might feel in need of an idea or two.

Do not be disheartened. Several people have been actively seeking lychee-flavoured yogurt all their lives. All you have to do is find them.

Advertising is the obvious method, but by no means the only one. Nevertheless, it is a method over which you have some kind of control, so the secret is cost effectiveness. Your first priority is to decide what will attract the audience. The late Eric Bravington, a very successful managing director of the LPO, had a useful rule of thumb for programme planning. He said that to fill a hall, two out of the following three factors should be box office certainties: content, conductor, soloist. I recommend you to decide which are the most attractive parts of your offering and use them as the basis of the message. Then use that message consistently in all your promotion. Try to restrict the effect of artistic ego. I cannot count the number of ineffective leaflets I have seen featuring a large, bad, picture of a hopelessly unknown pianist, name writ large, and somewhere in 12pt light, the word *Beethoven.*

Space booking in newspapers is often done in association with the hall, resulting in savings from bulk buying. You should always take advantage of these schemes. You can also use an agent. Their experience, especially with wording, will more than pay for their fee. They will advise you on the merits of lineage, semi-display and display, as well as position and the correlation of readership and target market. With specialist music, entertainment or tourist magazines, it is probably simpler to deal direct, linking display advertisements with the graphic design of your leaflets. You should also place listings in area entertainments or concert guides.

Leaflets and posters can be the best way to spend your money, but only, and I stress only, if you pay as much attention to distribution as production. Print nothing you cannot distribute. Be warned that, like some press advertising, posters and their sites are often expensive for the effect you get. This is because your advertising is competing against multi-million pound campaigns, and reaching many who will never attend a concert. There are agencies available to place leaflets and posters where they will be seen, but I regard that as the beginning of a task which will consume large quantities of your time, imagination and dedication. Use your friends, clubs and business acquaintances. Copywriting, design and printing are specialist skills of sophistication. Mistakes are costly, so be prepared to accept advice and make changes. Calculate lead times carefully. Ideally, you need your printed material delivered about two months before the concert. My best advice is to use people experienced in music promotion: they know what you can afford and have seen most of the problems before. As with many other things, you can use your talents to break the rules successfully only when you know why they are there.

For small, one-off concerts, use of TV, radio and cinema advertising is prohibitively costly, but should be considered for series and festivals.

As the most useful adjunct to advertising, but by no means a replacement for it, is a dedicated media relations campaign. Sometimes you will hear the phrase 'free advertising' used to describe successful public relations activity. Nothing could be further from the truth. There are many pamphlets and books available for consultation, as well as skilled practitioners who will give value for money. Organising press conferences, writing news releases and distributing them, and placing stories, are once again highly specialised skills. It would be more than a hint to say that there are people who can do these jobs effectively for you.

Briefly, if you have to write your own news release, it should be set out with meticulous accuracy on your A4 letterhead, one-and-a-half- or double-spaced, with wide margins. One hundred words of crisp copy should begin by answering who, what, where, when, how and why, the last being a cue for you to write a story which demonstrates why your concert is so worthy of the attention of sub-editors, who pride themselves on their world-weariness! There should be a short, unambiguous heading, with a date and a contact name and number at the foot. If you have photographs or cassettes to offer, say so. The Arts Council publishes a reasonable press list, but PR practitioners should include more contacts. Enclose your leaflet. Send review tickets to arts editors or chief music critics with their copy of the release. In the case of new music, invite critics to the general rehearsal. Music critics are employed freelance by their newspapers. They seldom visit the newspaper office. Do not forget the free events listings.

The monthlies will have to be informed separately three months in advance, otherwise six weeks is about right. If you can find a second, different story as you go along, there is no harm in having another go. Follow-up with telephone calls, so that you can arrange interviews, photo-calls or lengthier articles. Above all remember that neither critics nor media owe you anything.

Programmes

You will need a programme book or leaflet, unless details are included on the promotional leaflet. If you are commissioning notes, you will need to know how long they can be. Writing good programme notes is difficult. In my opinion they are often unnecessarily analytical, sometimes over the heads of even the musicians. Take care not to alienate the audience before the concert begins. Make a dummy programme to calculate how much copy can occupy each page. List the credits you need. Make the biographies short, but more than a list of achievements. Include the selling price and the fire regulations. Use photographs which your designer advises you will make reproducible half-tones. When you send copy to the designer/printer, it must be accurate and legible; you cannot expect him to read your mind as well as your words, let alone have your musical knowledge. Computer discs can be a great help. Author's corrections will be charged to you. Keep an eye on the lead times: the printer owes you nothing. Tell the programme sellers the price of the programme so they can organise their floats.

Programme advertising needs a special sort of salesman – there are few good commercial reasons for taking space. Remember that big companies move much slower than the music business, and that you will pay for setting and layout if anyone does not send camera-ready artwork.

As the day approaches

During the run up to the concert, monitor ticket sales on a graph. They may be slow. Only experience will tell you if there is a problem, but there may be some action you can take if there is. One such is judicious gifts of free tickets, known as 'papering the house'. Of course, blanket papering can give the impression that your concert is not worth attending, but the right amount can create interest which may even stimulate a few sales. It is best to choose people who would not normally come to a concert, but who might have friends who would. Papering works only well ahead of time, and is itself time-consuming.

As the rehearsals approach, attend to the little details. Write desk numbers on the string parts and give them to the leader for bowing, or to individual players. If you are having flowers in the hall, check that your soloists do not suffer from hay fever.

Rehearsals

If you are responsible for setting up at the hall, you must make certain you are there early. An hour is not too long to give you time to check out everything you need. You will know if the heating and lighting are acceptable, but there's always a chance that something will have been switched off – boilers after 1st March, for example, irrespective of awful weather conditions. And check that noisy air-conditioning will not be turned on automatically as soon as the audience's temperature begins to rise. You may find that someone has removed the chairs or music stands you thought were there, or that an item of percussion has not been delivered.

Set the stage out according to a written plan – it should summarise the number of music stands, chairs, low and high stools. Don't forget that the conductor and some players may need something very substantial for contemporary scores. Cello players like to have their bottoms on something firm, and frequently prefer piano stools. Lute and guitar players usually need music stands lowered further than those in many halls will go. Bass and cello spikes wreck parquet flooring – the usual solution is a triangular piece of hardboard or plywood with a hole in one corner to fit round a chair leg. Has the piano survived its move into position, and did you put the brakes back on?

Now find the toilets and, if you need dressing rooms, check they are unlocked. Touring? Take toilet paper and soap, towels if possible. Check that the interval coffee will be available when you want it, and find the nearest working telephone (unless you have a mobile). You need coins, a phonecard or other tokens. Check that a latecomer can actually phone through to the rehearsal to let you know – the number is on the schedule. Check that instruments and other valuables are secure during the break or between rehearsal and concert. Find a place where the musicians can rest or warm up.

If there are pieces where the visual relationship between players is crucial, take some chalk or plastic gaffer tape of different colours. Mark out the stands or instruments on the floor during the rehearsal, when the players have decided on the format. Note the marks on the stage plan.

If you are the fixer as well, you will have a list of the players, the times they were called and their telephone numbers. If they all arrive on time and the rehearsal begins with no problems, find the location of the nearest photocopier, in case there are part problems. With new or difficult music, it is advisable to pack manuscript paper, plain paper and a stock of pens, Tipp-Ex, pencils, erasers, paper clips, sellotape, Pritt, masking tape, magic tape, scissors, knife. There are essential if you are doubling as librarian. Playing out of doors? Four clothes pegs with springs per music stand, and an umbrella to hand. If you are using electrical equipment, straight and cross-head electrical screwdrivers, a fit-all plug, an assortment of fuses and a pair of pliers would probably help you to kick-start a reluctant vibraphone, but don't tackle anything like that unless you are sure of your ground.

Think about how much of a nursemaid you need to be. A friend of mine left Heathrow on a fine warm February morning without a coat. He was flying to Helsinki. A car rug and big sweater should complement the jump leads in your boot.

During the rehearsal you need to be silent but available. Tell the leader or director where you will be. Give the director and stage staff reference copies of your stage plans. You also need to ensure that extraneous noise is kept to a minimum, and to keep a weather eye on unexpected guests. It does no harm to be suspicious in a friendly way – you can prevent theft and bootleg recordings. If things go wrong, try to remain unruffled.

Most problems have a quick solution and you are not flying an aeroplane. Ask yourself – if I were playing, what would be annoying me most at the moment? If you can think of something you can act on (and we all know those you can't!) you need to take care of it straight away. Your function is to create a safe space in which musical risks may be taken.

Be firm about breaks, because they are essential to everyone, even if they don't think so. You must have fifteen minutes in three hours. Make sure you know where your players have gone: there is nothing more embarrassing than a misunderstanding about letting the trumpets go just before the conductor decides to go over a piece again.

If you need to make announcements, make sure that they occur at a convenient time and that the director is aware of their imminence. Musicians who have absorbed the input of a rehearsal have their attention elsewhere, so keep what have to say short, simple and unambiguous. You will find that the acoustic of a good concert hall is cruel to the spoken word, so project your voice to the front of the mouth and speak slowly, without fading away at the ends of words or sentences. Good use can be made of the fact that people remember anything funny, especially if sex is involved!

Be clear about requests and suggestions made to you. Act stupid, rather than assume you have understood someone. You need certainty.

Rehearsals are useful for administrative procedures, such as paying out, presentations or photocalls. Plan in advance: nobody likes waiting around. Suppose you want photographs of the ensemble. A new set of considerations arise: lighting, reflections, use of flash, colour, access, dress, interruptions to valuable rehearsal time and camera noise, besides questions like – can you photograph the whole band when the trombones have already been sent home? Consultation is the key. Ask the photographer what is necessary. Check with the hall to see if you need a pass for him.

Are you undertaking any radio interviews at the rehearsal? If so, you will need a soundproof environment away from the music.

Bear in mind that everything takes longer than you think, and you cannot be in two places at once.

Accidents are rare, but if you know where the first aid kit is kept, you are forearmed. The biggest problem in the UK is sustenance, especially on Sundays in the provinces. A box of fruit and convenience food can take the edge off a cause for upset.

At the end of every rehearsal or concert you should check the whole area for items left behind. If you are acting as librarian, you need certainty in your relationship with players who keep their music. During the rehearsal, you should prepare for its end and deal with the problems to be encountered at the next one or at the concert. One will be curtain calls. Some musicians have a natural presence which makes their interaction with the audience an integral part of their performance. The rest need rehearsing. The players should be quite clear about the way they enter and leave the stage. Sloppiness here can wreck a concert.

At the general rehearsal, time the pieces as they are run through, and inform the stage and front-of-house staff so they know when to prepare for the interval or the end. Tell them if you are playing encores, and also the names of the publishers of the copyright works. Check that piano retuning will take place as arranged and that time is available for soloists to warm up in the hall before the house is let in.

If you are selling records in the foyer, you will need staff, stock, a float of change, safe storage, a display, and instructions or facilities for taking cheques and credit cards. Mention the opportunity in the programme, if possible.

The time has now arrived to ask yourself if you have that special feeling – the one where you feel you have done everything you could possibly have done.

The concert

Be at the concert hall an hour and a half in advance. Check that the programmes have been delivered to the hands of the sellers, draw the complimentary copies you need for your guests, soloists, orchestra and so on. Leave envelopes of complimentary tickets to be collected from the arranged place. Establish that the stage is set up correctly, clear of extraneous articles and with music in the correct order on stands. Find the person who will present flowers to the soloists to be certain of the arrangements. Make sure your players arrive, change and are aware of the time. In the theatre, it is normal to call the half (35 minutes), quarter (20 minutes), five (10 minutes) and beginners (5 minutes) before the show. You may not need this formality.

If you are paying out on the night, have the cheques prepared in advance; there will be no time at the concert. You may be arranging a party afterwards; now is the time to make sure that everything is in order.

Dealing with VIPs needs special consideration, depending on how 'I' they are. A further schedule may be necessary, and is indispensable for royalty. In any event, you should be available from the quarter to greet arrivals, hand them a programme, find them a drink or take them to their seats.

When you are satisfied that all is well, and not before, you can set the concert in motion.

By now, it should run pretty smoothly. But your work is not over. You must use the interval to set the stage and music for the second half, to check that there are no problems and to entertain your guests. At the end of the concert, see that the stage and backstage areas are properly cleared. Few musicians leave without their instruments, but a trail of wallets and clothes is not so uncommon. You may be needed to help some players with the get-out. You should have sufficient money to tip helpful stage staff. Thank the musicians and anyone else who needs acknowledgement. Make arrangements to collect spare programmes for future promotional use. Now go for a drink.

Follow-up

Next morning, buy all the papers and scan for reviews. Send copies to the relevant people. In the old days of primitive technology, concert reviews appeared on the following day. Not so today. You may have to wait – six days is the maximum in my experience! A press-cuttings agency will make sure you get them all, but you will have to wait a month.

Invoice the programme advertisers and bulk ticket purchasers. Pay the participants and invoiced services and prepare the accounts. Thrill to the reviews, groan over the deficit and take a holiday. You deserve it.

SPONSORSHIP – THE RIGHT APPROACH

TIM STOCKIL

Tim Stockil was educated at Oxford and trained as a director at the Bristol Old Vic Theatre School. In 1981, after a variety of jobs in the theatre, he joined Merseyside Young People's Theatre Company as administrator, where he became interested in, and successful at, raising sponsorship. He joined the Association for Business Sponsorship of the Arts in October 1984 as one of the Programme Directors of the Business Sponsorship Incentive Scheme. He became Director of Business in the Arts, ABSA's major initiative, in November 1988.

Sponsorship is the payment of monies by a business to an arts organisation for the purpose of promoting its business name, its products or its services. It is not charity, and neither is it public subsidy. Many statutory bodies – the Arts Councils, the Regional Arts Associations and Boards – have an obligation to fund the arts. Businesses do not. It follows that it is a great deal easier to get subsidy from a public funding body than it is to get sponsorship from a business.

A business will use sponsorship for increasing name-awareness, client, customer and VIP entertaining, reaching a specific target market, enhancing corporate image and community relations, improving relations with staff, and associating its name with quality. Increasingly, there may also be an element of philanthropy or corporate responsibility in a business's sponsorship policy. If you can't offer some or all of these, you probably shouldn't look for sponsorship. If you can, the following guidelines should be helpful.

Self-analysis

First, examine your own operation. How are you established? What do you do? Why do you do it? Why is it important? Are you successful at it? How do you wish to develop? The last two questions are particularly important – if you consistently play to 40% houses, you would do better to improve your marketing, partly because selling more seats is the easiest way for you to increase your earnings, and also because a business is unlikely to sponsor an organisation which is not successful in audience terms. Development is also crucial; business sponsorship should be a supplement to public subsidy, not a substitute for it, not least because available business funds depend on market conditions outside your control and may be withdrawn at any time. A search for sponsorship for the extras – those things you would really like to do but for which you have never had the money – may have more chance of success than for your core needs. This may seem like wishful thinking, but a successful sponsorship of a special project should provide benefits, financial and otherwise, for your core operations.

The deeper your self-analysis, the better armed you will be. Is your board of directors going to be useful? Perhaps you ought to consider establishing a sponsorship sub-committee made up of business men and women sympathetic to your aims, and prepared to work to raise sponsorship for you. Do you really know your audience? You should consider doing an audience survey. But take advice on how to formulate one – the Arts Council may advise on this.

Such self-analysis takes time – but sponsorship is a time-consuming business. Most businesses with sponsorship budgets commit themselves to their expenditure for one financial year in the middle of the previous year. For example, if you approach a business whose financial year runs to 31st December to sponsor your gala concert in December 1997, you should be talking to them at least by early summer 1996, eighteen months before.

You may publish a brochure about yourselves, covering your history, constitution, *modus operandi,* catchment areas and audiences, and past successes, and such brochures are very useful in making approaches to businesses who may never have heard of you. You might even attract sponsorship to pay for such a promotional brochure.

Packaging

If your self-analysis has led you to believe that you can, and should, search for sponsorship, the next step is to develop sponsorship packages. It is rare for a business to sponsor the whole of an arts organisation's operations as it is usually more effective in terms of name-awareness to associate a company's name with a specific project – a tour, a special series of concerts, or a gala, for example. Each of these is a potential package, and each offers something different; a tour may reach towns where a sponsor wishes to be seen, a series of concerts might get high media coverage, a gala might be a particularly good entertainment opportunity. Each may reach a different audience.

Every package should be written up separately – type neatly, give each paragraph a number and a heading, and do not ramble (two or at most three pages are ample). A proposal should cover:

(a) *What the project is*
(b) *Who you are*
(c) *What you do*
(d) *The dates of the project*
(e) *The places you will be performing*
(f) *The number and make-up of your likely audience*
(g) *The publicity* Be fairly specific: give an idea of print runs, size of posters, where they will be displayed, newspapers in which you will advertise, direct mail leaflets, etc. Remember, however, that you cannot guarantee editorial coverage.
(h) *The benefits to the sponsor* Be specific but flexible: will you incorporate the sponsor's name into the title of the project – 'The Fred Smith Orchestra/Jo Bloggs & Co Tour'? Are there opportunities for

entertaining? Will you offer the sponsor tickets at reduced prices? Will you have their logo displayed prominently on all publicity material? Will your sponsor have a free page in the programme?

(i) *The cost* (and don't forget the VAT) This should relate to the value of the promotional opportunity, and not to the actual cost to you. It is perfectly possible for a concert to cost you £2,000 but be worth £30,000 to a sponsor or vice versa. A range of costings can be sensible – obviously, if you and your sponsor want to have a bus-shelter poster campaign, for example, it will cost more.

The purpose of this brief proposal is not to give a comprehensive break-down of the whole project, but to get to meet your potential sponsor. The neater, the more succinct and the more professional it is, the more likely you are to achieve that aim, not least because some of the big sponsors get upwards of 300 proposals a week. Include some background material (this is where your brochure comes in) but not vast reams which may well be filed in the waste-paper basket.

A valuable addition to any sponsorship proposal is the Pairing Scheme (formerly the Business Sponsorship Incentive Scheme), which is administered by the Association for Business Sponsorship of the Arts (ABSA) on behalf of the Minister for the Arts. The Scheme is intended as an incentive to businesses either to sponsor the arts for the first time, or to increase their commitment to the arts. It offers both government endorsement and financial support. Pairing Scheme funds can match new business money – money that has never been allocated to the arts before – pound for pound for first-time sponsors, or one pound for every two or four pounds of new sponsorship from second-time or established sponsors, depending on circumstances. Full details of the Scheme are available from ABSA. The next stage is to determine which companies you will approach.

Research

You cannot research too much. Find out what a business has sponsored before and what its policy is now. It is pointless to send a proposal for sponsorship of a high-profile gala performance to a firm that only sponsors projects involving the arts and education: this is why you create separate packages. Is the business making a profit? Are they keen on corporate, as opposed to product, advertising? What is their target market? Where do they operate? Write and ask a business for its annual report – public companies should send you one on request. Read the financial papers and the PR and marketing magazines. Use some commonsense – a company that is the object of a takeover bid is unlikely to be increasing its sponsorship portfolio.

This process should determine which business to approach – try starting with a shortlist of six.

The approach

Once you have decided on your shortlist, ring up and ask who deals with sponsorship. If the switchboard doesn't know, ask for the PR department. Once you have the name (check the spelling) and the correct title, ring the person up and ask what the company's sponsorship policy is. Do not try to sell your proposal over the telephone. Be brief, and specific – 'Are you still interested in sponsorships in Leicester and Milton Keynes? You haven't sponsored any jazz for three years – is this a policy decision? Will you be celebrating your 150th anniversary in any special way?' If it is clear that you are not wasting your time and theirs, say 'Thank you very much, I'll be writing to you'.

The letter you send to accompany your proposal should start 'Further to our telephone conversation ...' which should mean that it gets read. The rest of the letter consists of a short paragraph saying who you are, another short paragraph saying what the proposal is and why it is particularly appropriate for them to sponsor, and a final paragraph saying that you would like to discuss your proposal further and to that end you will ring up in a few days' time to arrange a mutually convenient date to meet. If you get an immediate reply saying no, you will at least waste no more time and money. If you hear nothing, you have a tacit agreement to meet, so ring up again and arrange a meeting.

Your shortlist may have to grow significantly before you can get someone to agree to meet you. Do not despair – polite persistence is the key to successful sponsorship raising.

Negotiation

Once you have an agreement to meet, go prepared. Dress smartly and arm yourself with back-up material. Be flexible. Begin by asking questions – it will allow you to see if you need to change your tack at all. You should have the authority to make immediate decisions as to whether your organisation can or cannot do something they suggest.

Make sure that, at the end of the meeting, you know what the next step is. Do they want further information? Do they want to come and hear your work? Will your proposal be put to the committee? Write and confirm what you understand to be the outcome of the meeting, and thank them for their time.

Management

Your proposal has been approved. Write a thank-you letter and specify exactly what the benefits will be, which of you is responsible for what, when you expect payment, and so on. Alternatively, they may send you a contract or a letter of agreement. One of these is essential – a 'reasonable number' of free seats may be ten to you but forty to them. Do they want to see proofs of artwork? Who is going to send out invitations to a press launch? You will need further meetings – you must keep in touch. If one of your venues burns down, tell them. If the opportunity arises for TV coverage of a concert, tell them. This is common courtesy, but it is also essential if you are to retain your sponsor. If you have kept in touch, if everything has gone smoothly, if you have both got out of the deal what you wanted and expected, if you have developed a relationship of mutual trust and understanding, your chances of retaining the sponsor for next time are good. Work at it – you never know what a goldmine you might have unearthed. And it is far easier to keep a sponsor than to find a new one.

Some last points

Individuals Sponsors very rarely support individuals. If you are a soloist looking for your big break in a London concert hall, a sponsor is much more likely to sponsor the venue than you.

Joint sponsorships There may be conflicts of interest here – make sure it is absolutely necessary.

Touring abroad It can be more difficult to raise sponsorship for touring abroad though there have been significant strides in this area over the last few years. CEREC, the European Committee for Business, Arts and Culture, based at 60 Rue de la Concorde, 1050 Brussels, may be able to advise.

Sponsorship consultants If you are looking for a great deal of money, it may be worth a consultant's while to take you on. Equally, sponsors may wish to employ a consultant. Increasingly, you may find yourself dealing with a firm's consultant rather than an in-house sponsorship department. Try to establish a relationship with your sponsor as well as the consultant – its good for all concerned.

ABSA Development Forum ABSA has set up the ADF, a forum for over 600 arts managers for whom sponsorship and development work are key parts of their jobs. The ADF provides ideal opportunities for networking, learning from your peers, and training.

Business in the Arts, ABSA's major initiative, brings business skills rather than money, to the arts. If you find, for example, that you need to know more about your audience if you are to be successful in raising sponsorship, Business in the Arts can probably help by matching you with a market research specialist from business – free of charge. There are twelve Business in the Arts offices covering nearly the whole of the UK – ring the head office for further information.

Bibliography

For general research, read *Campaign, Marketing, Marketing Week, PR Week, Sponsorship News, The Times 1000, Who's Who, Who Owns Whom,* the *Stock Exchange Yearbook* and *Key British Enterprises,* most of which should be available at a public library; so should the *Directory of Grant Making Trusts,* which is useful if you are looking for charitable donations, rather than sponsorship, as is *A Guide to Company Giving,* published by the Directory of Social Change, 24 Stephenson Way, London NW1 2DP. ABSA produces a number of publications of particular use to sponsorship seekers, including the 'ABSA/W H Smith

Sponsorship Manual' and 'Principles for Good Practice in Arts Sponsorship'. ABSA also runs regular introduction-to-sponsorship workshops all around the country.

Final note

Please, as your experience in raising sponsorship grows, share it with other arts organisations – you won't lose a sponsor as a result, and the concept and practice of sponsorship will be more widely understood to the benefit of all.

APPROACHING A RECORD COMPANY

ANNE RUSHTON

Anne Rushton gained a BMus from Cardiff University before working in the orchestra manager's office at the Royal Opera House, Covent Garden. She joined the staff of Collins Classics six years ago, and has been Managing Director since 1993.

As technology continues to secure a greater importance in our lives, and as, so we are told, concert audiences dwindle, musicians see it as increasingly important to pursue a career on tape as well as in the concert hall. Recordings are undoubtedly important, but the young artist must not lose sight of the fact that a recording career should complement a career on the platform and not be seen as an end in itself. Many people in the record industry feel that too many records are made, and an artist should therefore have a very clear impression of how recording balances the other elements in his or her career in order to have the best chance of success.

In most cases, the initial contact between a record company and an artist is through an agent. The services and styles of management are as varied as agents are numerous, and any artist seeking an agent should carefully consider what is most suitable. A good agent is an invaluable asset in building a career, and this obviously includes development of a recording profile.

The charitable organisation Young Concert Artists Trust (YCAT) offers services of general management to young artists who are embarking on a career, and they have had notable successes with musicians who have risen to great prominence. Artists are selected through annual auditions, and usually spend about three years with YCAT, during which time their careers are nurtured until the artist can secure the services of a commercial agent.

A good agent may, however, be hard to find, and the budding recording artist may thus find himself in the position of wishing to make a direct approach to a record company. This method is, without doubt, a tougher nut to crack, as companies will plan many years ahead with their established recording agenda – although working practices of record companies vary depending on the size and nature of the company. The following section relates primarily to the independent classical labels, but much will also apply to larger, multi-national organisations.

The company

Before you even think of putting pen to paper, research in detail the profiles of the various companies in which you are interested. Perhaps more so than ever before, labels are favouring specialisation in certain fields, and you can save yourself, and the prospective A & R (that's 'Artists and Repertoire') department, much time by not trying to fit a musical square peg into a round hole. Alternatively, it is highly unlikely that a label which already boasts long-term relationships with other artists specialising in your field will wish to forge a relationship with another performer dealing in similar repertoire.

Catalogues are readily available, either from record shops or direct from the record companies, and these should be consulted in depth to secure a knowledge of the companies' main areas of interest. A regular reading of the music press will bring you up to date with the various labels' most recent activity through news items, reviews and the advertisements which the companies place. These advertisements will often reflect the projects closest to a company's heart (and, hopefully, sales figures). Many record companies feature both full-price and mid/budget-price labels, and it may be that there is more opportunity for the younger artist on the lower-price label of the company.

The repertoire

More and more often, companies are looking to expand the recorded repertoire and, again, there may be areas of particular interest to certain companies which the artist should consider before making an approach. Having said this, bear in mind that the unheard of genius from medieval Bolivia whom you may wish to champion on record may not be so familiar to the A & R department, and any approach, therefore, will have to be supported with information.

What to send

You have to supply the company with enough material to outline your interests, but without inundating them with so much paper that you single-handedly threaten the existence of a rain-forest or two. You will, undoubtedly, be writing to someone who has great demands on their time, and they will certainly be put off if they have to wade through enormous amounts of written information. Therefore, *concise* supporting material will help in explaining the magic of your newly-discovered Bolivian madrigalist, but *do* keep it concise. Your initial approach should be with a view to getting a company sufficiently interested in your project so that you might have the opportunity to meet and expand on your ideas.

Demo tapes are very much the domain of the pop world but, if you do wish to submit a recording, bear the following tips in mind:

(a) Clearly mark the tape with your name and address to avoid the disappointment of its being separated from your letter, and with details of the programme.

(b) Indicate whether or not Dolby noise-reduction has been used, in order to avoid the tape's being distorted through being played in the wrong mode.

166

(c) Organise your recording with strong material at the start, and without spoken introductions or interludes explaining what you are going to play next.

(d) Only send a tape if it is of professional standard. This applies both to the technical standard of recording and also to the standard of performance.Only use an accompanist who can accompany you well, and not someone whom you happened upon at the local piano showrooms.

(e) Address your letter in full to the relevant person at the company. Letters beginning 'Dear Sir/Madam' are lazy, and those addressed to a first name only are presumptuous, unless you know the addressee personally.

Tapes should be accompanied with some biographical information and reviews. Personally, I prefer whole reviews rather than extracted quotes, which can so easily be transformed with a creative use of '...' – but do keep it to a minimum. You should also include details of forthcoming concert activity, both at home and, notably, abroad, with a schedule showing dates as far into the future as possible. This will be important, as it gives an indication of the level and breadth of your concert profile, and might help in enticing a company to release a disc in support of planned tours and their associated marketing opportunities.

Of course, the most effective way of displaying your talents is in concert, when the A & R manager can hear and see an artist for himself. If you can, time your written approaches so that they can include an invitation to a performance, and remember to give a fair amount of advance warning so that the manager has a chance of being free.

This country boasts a number of pioneering organisations which can extend opportunities for young artists to appear on the concert platform. Bodies such as the Park Lane Group and the National Federation of Music Societies can provide valuable advice and opportunities for artists seeking public performances. Some artists choose to promote their own concerts by hiring a venue, but this should be considered with care, as the risks at the box office can be great.

The finances

Money is a harsh reality of the recording industry (it is a business, after all), and the firm promise of funding may be a great asset in your approach to a company. In addition to artistic costs, which will obviously vary enormously depending on the size of the project, money will be required for venue, instrument and music hire, producer, engineer, editing and packaging. Mechanical royalties are payable on recordings of music which is in copyright, and this royalty is charged at the rate of 8.5% of UK dealer price.

The most expensive single item will be orchestral fees, if these are applicable. Based on 1995 Musicians' Union rates, the average cost of a full symphony orchestra for a three-hour recording session is something in the region of £6,000, during which a maximum of twenty minutes' music can be recorded, although in practice fifteen minutes is more likely to be achieved. With period-instrument orchestras, the musicians' costs are usually higher, and the amount of music which may be recorded in a session is more in the region of ten to twelve minutes. If, for an orchestral disc, you could offer sponsorship to cover the orchestral fees, the record company might be prepared to meet the production and packaging costs itself.

For chamber or solo recital discs, an alternative approach is to offer the company the opportunity of licensing a finished master tape produced by the artist. Here, the artist need only raise finance to cover the production costs and perhaps minimal artistic costs/expenses, and there is the potential of earnings from record sales through royalties. The negative elements to this approach are that the company will want to see that the recording is made to their usual professional technical standards, and that repertoire choices will obviously have been finalised before the company becomes involved. Either of these points may dissuade a company but, certainly for smaller labels, this is an easier way for them to produce a disc to feed their hungry release schedule.

If you are considering licensing a tape to a record company, you should review the company's strengths in distribution – particularly overseas, where most records are sold – and in marketing. In most cases, the company should offer a small advance against which future royalty earnings will be recouped, and, as you have made the initial investment in the recording, you will want to see what sales potential exists. Levels of advances and royalties vary enormously, and the rate of royalty on offer may be affected if the company has to pay mechanical royalties on copyright material. Some contracts will allow for royalties based on the dealer price or, alternatively, a lower royalty rate based on the higher retail price. Bear in mind that the record company is not in control of what actual retail prices are, and so it is often more accurate to account on a dealer price. Dealer prices vary between territories, and so royalty breaks may be used to reflect the current trends. In most contracts, the company includes a clause which reduces royalties to allow for a packaging allowance for the company.

It is always wise to have a contract looked over by a solicitor. Despite what some reports may claim, record companies are not full of sharks – but you should be clear as to your own position in order to avoid disappointments or misunderstandings in the future.

Above all, remember that making records is wonderful fun, and can be a great musical experience, but it is most successful when placed in the context of the artist's genuine *musical* aspirations.

170

THE PURCHASE OF FINE INSTRUMENTS

JULIA SEDDON

Julia Seddon works with the Cambridge-based firm, N W Brown and Company, where, together with the firm's senior partner, Nigel Brown, she establishes and runs schemes designed to raise finance for the purchase of fine stringed instruments for leading musicians. She has a degree in music from Cambridge University, having previously studied the piano at the Royal Northern College of Music.

You are probably reading this chapter in the full knowledge that you may be facing the prospect of buying something costing the best part of a year's earnings and perhaps more – and that is not your only problem. Finding and buying a house is child's play compared with choosing and financing any really decent instrument – the sort of instrument that gives you confidence and inspiration on the concert platform, and withstands hours of battering at home. But don't panic! There are ways and means of tackling what, at first sight, might seem an impossible task.

HOW MUCH DO I NEED TO PAY?

This is the first question you should ask yourself. To give a rough guide: pianists can expect to pay a minimum of £3,000–£4,000 for a new Japanese upright, £10,000 for a Japanese grand, and could easily be looking at a starting price of £17,000 for a 'West' German grand. Second-hand pianos are, of course, less expensive, but the decline in piano ownership since the war has meant that there are few good-quality instruments around.

Trumpeters and trombonists find it hard to spend more than £2,000, but for a professional quality tuba, you need to find about £5,000, and top quality horns retail at around £3,000. Second-hand brass instruments, however, can often be a third of the new price.

Prices of woodwind instruments are much more varied. A professional flautist might choose between an old French silver flute or a top-of-the-range Japanese instrument, both at around £6,000, and a gold flute with or without gold keywork at up to £40,000. A pair of new French clarinets or an oboe will probably cost £4,000–£5,000, but for a new Heckel bassoon you will need £15,000–£20,000 (after two years on their waiting list!). Fortunately, second-hand reed instruments change hands at around half the new price, but very few old instruments are acceptable today.

As for string players, the sky's the limit. It would be wrong to say that prodigious violinists such as Sarah Chang and Anne-Sophie Mutter have not

benefited enormously from playing on instruments worth several million pounds early on in their careers. However, this is only possible for the favoured few, and, for example, Guadagninis at around £250,000, Nicolo Amatis at £150,000–£200,000, or, in the case of cellists, Tecchlers at around £200,000 can make good solo instruments. Orchestral leaders and principals are often looking to spend from £80,000 to £150,000 on an Italian instrument, such as a Peter Guarneri, Gagliano or Rugeri. Of course, the much cheaper and often very acceptable option is to buy a modern instrument. Modern violins and violas range from £6,000 to £12,000, and cellos from £8,000 to £18,000.

A point to note is that auction houses levy a buyer's premium on top of the hammer price. This is typically calculated at 15% on the first £30,000 and 10% thereafter. Also, don't forget VAT, which may or may not be included in the price you are quoted.

Finally, remember that, in most cases, it is a buyer's market. Many dealers only just made it through the recession and, at this level, most prices are extremely negotiable.

HOW MUCH CAN I AFFORD?

Where the price range of possible instruments is broad, the question 'how much do I need to pay?' actually becomes 'how much can I afford?'. This, in turn, can be broken down into:

(a) your assets,
(b) borrowing money, and
(c) being given money.

Your assets

To work out how much of your own money you can put towards the purchase, you will probably get a valuation for your existing instrument. But don't forget that the price you get for a part-exchange will usually be less than you would get for sale on commission, which is normally in the region of 5%. Also, it is a good idea to warm up your banker before you start looking at instruments, as you may well need a bridging loan while your instrument is being sold.

Borrowing money

Banks and building societies There is a surprising number of different ways in which money can be borrowed for an instrument purchase. Unfortunately, it is very rare for a bank to give you a large personal loan for this purpose, but if you own property and if the value of your house has gone up, or if you have paid off some of the mortgage, you may be able to arrange a remortgage, second mortgage or mortgage top-up. But don't be taken in by the sales person who tries to sell you an unsuitable life assurance or mortgage indemnity product. Alternatively, a friend or family member could secure a loan for you by personal guarantee or by a remortgage of their property. Professional legal advice will be necessary in this case, however, as the liability for the loan is not yours.

Musical funds There are four major organisations which lend money for instrument purchases, and it is often better to approach these than a bank because they have lower interest rates and fewer charges. The Abbado European Young Musicians Trust, the Loan Fund for Musical Instruments and the Countess of Munster Musical Trust award interest-free or very low cost loans. Fine Instrument Finance is more commercial, and sets up hire-purchase arrangements, charging interest at typically 3%-5% over clearing bank base rate. However, as you will see from the table below, these bodies are by no means uniform in the way they make their loans. For example, the Loan Fund only considers instruments that will be used for public performance (not pianos, for example), and age limits range from twenty-seven (Countess of Munster) to sixty (Fine Instruments Finance). It is useful to know how long it will take from making an application to receiving the money. The Countess of Munster Trust only makes loans in September, and accepts applications between November and January, whereas the Loan Fund meets every three months. It is also common for there to be a maximum number of months within which you must take up the loan.

	Abbado EuropeanYoung Musicians Trust	Fine Instruments Finance	Loan Fund For Musical Instruments	Munster (Countess of) Musical Trust
Instruments	all	all	used for public performance	all
Age limit	30	60	25	27
Nationality	all	British	preferably British	British or Commonwealth
Interest rate	usually interest free	3-5% over bank clearing base rate	2% p.a.	interest free
Maximum duration of loan	5 years	5 years	5 years	8 years
Timescale from application to award	Trustees meet every 3-4 months	Awards made without delay	No delay	No delay. Applications Nov-Jan. Awards Sep.
Timescale for taking up offer	Within 1 month		Within 3 months	Within 6 months
Application for specific instrument?	yes	yes	yes	no

Patronage At the top end of the price range, Nigel Brown, senior partner of the Cambridge-based investment fund manager and financial services specialist, N W Brown and Company, has pioneered a very innovative scheme. For stringed instruments costing over £100,000, a syndicate of people is put together to own an instrument for your use for a set period of time (normally ten years). No interest is charged, but in order for you to end up as the owner, you must buy the syndicate members out during this time. However, stringed instruments in this price-range can appreciate substantially in value, and each year you have to pay the current market value for the syndicate members' 'shares'. Because this operation involves attracting the support of wealthy individual arts patrons, only musicians with impressive earnings potentials, or those with sufficient wealthy bona fide contacts are considered – but there is no age limit.

Orchestras If you play in a major orchestra, you should also enquire whether the orchestra might lend you money, or advance your salary, as many do.

Whatever the source of your finance, you should always ensure that the loan is set up in such a way that you can claim tax relief on the interest (for example, interest on personal overdrafts and credit card balances is never allowable). You should take professional advice about this, and also about any other business reliefs to which you may be entitled.

Being given money

There are many trusts which give small grants for instrument purchases. When deciding which to apply to, it is a good idea to find out which ones already support your orchestra (if appropriate) or region. Unfortunately, the gambling boom cannot be turned to your advantage – the Foundation for Sport and the Arts and the National Lottery do not give grants to individuals, but a number of orchestras and bands have made successful applications for money to buy instruments to be used by their members ...

If somebody offers to give you money, there are potential problems which can be avoided if proper documentation is drawn up by a solicitor or accountant. For example, if the donor dies within seven years of making a gift, the beneficiaries of the estate will be faced with an inheritance tax bill and may contest the gift. Also, the donor may try to change his or her mind, especially if, for instance, the demands of a divorce settlement have to be met.

Finally, the *British Music Yearbook*, the *Handbook of Music Awards and Scholarships* (produced by the Musicians Benevolent Fund) and *How To Get Your Hands on a First Rate Stringed Instrument* (produced by N W Brown and Company) are excellent sources of information on this subject.

CHOOSING AN INSTRUMENT

Assuming that you find an instrument you like, here are some of the other issues you should consider:

Authenticity

Since the prices of old and rare stringed instruments depend on their makers' names, and since labels are notoriously unreliable, all expensive instruments are sold with one or more letters of authenticity from dealers of repute. Only a handful of these are acceptable on an international basis, and you should not contemplate a large financial commitment without existing letters of authenticity, or even a new one, even though this may cost money. In the event of an insurance claim, these pieces of paper may save your life!

State of repair

Whether you are buying second-hand or new, the golden rule is to get the opinion of a trusted repairer/tuner. As well as being able to test the instrument properly, they are likely to know the foibles of different makes. For example, some makes of oboe are known to crack more easily than others, and some makes of piano sound fantastic in the showroom, but have been rushed through the manufacturing process and quickly go off. Pianos are affected by where they have been kept and how frequently they have been maintained, and you should ask about this. Stringed instruments are a particular minefield when it comes to defects being hidden, for example, by a new coat of varnish, and it is very important to get a second professional opinion.

Add-ons

Don't forget that the sound and action of an instrument can be dramatically changed by the extras that are part of it. For example, a different crook, mouthpiece, head joint, set-up, bow or lip-plate can make a big difference.

Teething problems

New and old instruments and their new owners can take time to get used to each other. Stringed instruments are notorious for sounding their best years after they are made, brand new grand pianos take a long time to play in and can often have mechanical teething problems as everything settles down, and woodwind instruments often have tuning and mechanical problems while they adapt to new handling. It is important to take these things into account when evaluating the potential of an instrument, but it is equally important not to be taken in by the 'it will improve' sales pitch.

THE DEAL

The best negotiator is an informed one, so here goes!

Auction houses

The big four auction houses – Sotheby's, Christies, Phillips and Bonhams – all have sales each March, June and November. However, it is worth asking at other times of the year whether they still have an instrument that did not sell, as deals can sometimes be struck. Trying an instrument in advance of the sale involves spending lots of time on the premises, as instruments cannot be lent out. Bids can be made in person or at least twenty-four hours in advance by telephone or fax. In the latter case, you will be asked to state your upper limit.

In order not be phased by the saleroom hype, it is a good idea to get your bearings by attending a couple of sales as an observer before the big day. Remember that an auctioneer's loyalty is to the vendor, and sales are one big performance. Most importantly, decide your price and stick to it!

Once you have made a purchase, you are immediately liable for the full amount, including buyer's premium and VAT (if applicable). In practice, this means that, if you do not pay within five days, interest will be charged, and you risk losing the deal. Also, remember that the instrument becomes your property the day the sale is made, and you should arrange insurance in good time, just in case you are successful.

Private deals

The most important thing to ensure with a private sale is that you get a watertight receipt. For a purchase of under approximately £100,000, it is probably not necessary to get a lawyer to draft a sale agreement, as long as your receipt includes the following:

- the price
- the date
- the name and address of the vendor
- the name and address of the purchaser
- a full and adequate description of the instrument which will include its dimensions, who the maker is considered to be, and its condition
- a statement that the vendor warrants that he or she is
- entitled to sell and transfer to the purchaser the full
- beneficial and legal ownership of the instrument

Incidentally, if you were selling the instrument, you should get the purchaser to confirm in the receipt that he or she is not relying on any representations made to him or her by the vendor.

Dealers

Nearly all dealers lend out their instruments to professionals on approval, but you will be expected to pay for the insurance. Some dealers on commission use this as a money-spinner, and will ask you for a full year's premium. It is possible to get temporary cover, and it can be worth getting a quote from a specialist musical insurance broker. Dealers very enormously when it comes to credit terms. Many offer deferred or spread payments over as much as three years, but the interest rate is likely to be a full commercial one.

Too many musicians struggle on with inferior equipment and fail to get where they should because they are daunted by the cost of the best instruments. I hope I have given some indication of how, by being imaginative and properly informed, the mountain can be climbed.

SECTION 3

SAFEGUARDING YOUR FUTURE

HEALTH PROBLEMS IN THE MUSICIAN

IAN JAMES

Ian James is a consultant physician at the Royal Free Hospital, and is married to a professional violinist. He is the founder of the British Performing Arts Medicine Trust and its affiliated body, the British Association for Performing Arts Medicine. He has undertaken research into the management of stage fright, overuse/misuse injuries in string players, and embouchure problems in brass players.

Musicians are just like sportsmen, in that they are prone to special occupational stresses, diseases and injuries which are specific to the profession. Unfortunately, if these problems are not recognised and tackled properly at an early stage they can lead not only to an inability to perform, with consequent loss of work, but also to permanent physical and psychological disability.

The Association of British Orchestras found some years ago that approximately 15% of players were off work for longer than a month because of occupation-related problems. Other surveys have shown that some 60% of musicians suffer from backache or one of the regional pain syndromes (pain in a shoulder or a pain in an upper limb) at some time during their professional life. The contracts of many brass players in their forties and fifties are prematurely terminated because of embouchure problems, and both wind and brass players can develop laryngocoeles and emphysema. Singers can all too easily damage their vocal cords, and develop other problems associated with voice strain which make them unemployable. Contact with instruments can cause skin problems, as witnessed by the necks of many violin and viola players.

It is a catastrophe when a career is halted in this way. Everybody thinks that 'It can't happen to me' but disaster does strike from time to time. What is not generally realised is that some of the problems encountered could have been prevented by a little common sense and a better understanding of common dangers.

Being aware of the dangers

In the first place, you should have a respect for your own body and realise its limitations. Ensuring good posture, having a sensible approach to rehearsal and your own practice, having a correct attitude to public performance, and especially avoiding excessive mental and muscular tension when you play or sing, are all essential if you want to stay healthy.

Second, all musicians should know very much more about the common occupational hazards and when to seek skilled help, be it medical or paramedical. It is essential, when you are in trouble, that you go to the right person: the doctor consulted should have the necessary knowledge and experience. However, not all doctors are equally knowledgeable in this area by any means. The British Performing Arts Medicine Trust (18 Ogle Street, London W1P 7LG) will supply the names of doctors and other health care professionals (including those from complementary disciplines) who have received special training in this branch of medicine.

It is conventional to divide up these occupation-related illnesses most commonly suffered by musicians into those which are psychological (for example, stage fright) and those which are physical (overuse/misuse injuries, repetitive strain injuries, etc). This is, however, very artificial, since many psychological problems related to excessive stress will masquerade as physical problems and, indeed, will turn into physical injury if not dealt with properly. Even a simple physical problem can provoke a serious mental reaction.

It is not possible in this chapter to give detailed advice on every possible illness which may befall the musician, but those most frequently affecting members of the profession are given brief coverage below.

Stage fright

One of the commonest medical problems to beset the performing artist is stage fright, and some of the very finest musicians have regarded stage fright as the price they had to pay for remaining in the profession.

True stage fright is not the mild apprehension which affects you when you first goes on stage and then evaporates; the term should be reserved for that condition which makes life a real misery for the sufferer. It is well known that a degree of apprehension is essential for a good performance, and the goal for the musician should be to experience the thrill of knowing the performance is going really well, yet remaining in complete and absolute control.

Musicians who have experienced the total disappearance of their voice, who have struggled to keep the bow somewhere near the string, who have felt that their hearts were going to explode through their chests at any second, will know what I mean by true stage fright. True stage fright has never improved anybody's performance.

Sometimes, lesser degrees of stage fright do not seriously affect the quality of performance itself, but have an adverse effect on the health of the individual instead. Self-help can play an important part here, and many musicians find the books *The Inner Game of Music* by Timothy Gallway (published by Pan Books) and *The Secrets of Musical Confidence* by Andrew Evans (published by Thorsons) extremely helpful. In anything but the most severe cases, there are a number of measures that one can take to make the occurence of stage fright less likely:

1 Make sure that what you have to perform is well within your competence.
2 Allow time for adequate rehearsal.
3 Plan a run-through prior to the performance with an audience of invited friends.

4 Employ relaxation techniques. There are many of these, and some suit certain individuals whilst some suit others. Relaxation techniques which can be performed at times of stress are particularly useful.
One of these is known as the 'quick response'. First, smile; second, take a slow, deep breath (count to 6); last, breathe out slowly at the same time as relaxing all your muscles.
5 Make sure you get to the concert hall in good time.
6 We all make mistakes, and the audience may not have noticed anyway

Two ways of reducing the effect of stage-fright should be avoided. Do *not* use alcohol to 'solve' the problem. This is the road to disaster (more of which later). Alcohol has destroyed the career of too many musicians. Also tranquillisers, such as the benzodiazepines, are ineffective, are addictive, and worsen performance. They should be avoided if at all possible. Their use in British orchestras is minimal and seems to be more common on the continent. When a musician suddenly starts to suffer stage-fright symptoms in the middle of a career, alcoholism and/or benzodiazepine dependence are commonly found to be the causes.

Certain drugs, on the other hand, can be helpful. It has been established, on numerous occasions, that the musical performance of players adversely affected by anxiety improves when they are given beta-blocking drugs. All the terrible symptoms associated with stage fright are abolished. Beta-blocking drugs can be recognised easily as their names tend to end in '-olol'. There are many different sorts, and they can only be obtained on a doctor's prescription.

Beta-blockers have few proven side-effects, although they can precipitate asthma in asthmatic patients, but the main risk associated with them is that, on rare occasions, their use prevents the real cause of the anxiety being addressed. When they are used in the correct way as a part of treatment, and under medical control, they are invaluable. However, the dose taken should be as low as possible and, in any event, it is essential to take the medication on a 'trial run' to be sure that it agrees with you. If the beta-blocking drug has an adverse effect then, obviously, alternative measures need to be employed. Medication should be combined with one of the many behavioural and/or counselling techniques available, since it is important to reinstil confidence and to give the individual a more positive approach to public performance. This combined treatment is particularly important in cases of repeated stage fright which, if experienced nightly, quickly leads to a state of severe depression which may require special treatment. In the presence of depression, beta-blockers alone are ineffective.

The magnitude of stress experienced by professional performing musicians is greatly underestimated by very many doctors who have never experienced stage fright for themselves. You learn how to experience stage fright in just the same way as you learn how to memorise a piece of music but, once learned, it then needs to be unlearned – which is more difficult! Beta-blocking drugs are useful in helping you to do this, and their use has saved many professional careers. If the event causing the acute anxiety is a single and rather unusual one, then the use of a beta-adrenoceptor blocking drug can be justified. Certainly they are far, far better than benzodiazepines or alcohol.

Depression

Whilst depression in the performing artist is often linked, or even provoked, by repeated attacks of severe stage fright, this is not the only cause. Frequently a competent musician suddenly seems no longer able to cope with simple problems, and becomes tearful. Many doctors believe that being depressed makes you more susceptible to overuse/misuse injuries. It is important to get correct treatment, which could be counselling or antidepressant medication, or both, as soon as possible. It is not all that easy to recognise depression in yourself, and you may be the last person to realise that you have it. Frequently, the illness is associated with disturbed sleep, where you keep waking at all hours of the night. Repeated early morning waking should be taken as a serious warning sign.

Alcohol-related problems

We all know of people who poison themselves daily with vast quantities of alcohol. Alcoholism can gradually catch up with you without your realising it. Remember the universally-accepted recommendations: if you are a man you should drink less than 21 units a week; if you are a woman, less than 14. (Most drinks count as one unit. One pint of beer counts as two units.) Alcohol is the too- easy answer to any problem, and alcohol itself can provoke anxiety the next day. Beware of the vicious circle where drinking leads to further anxiety which, in turn, leads to a further bout of drinking, and so on.

Overuse/misuse injuries

Pain in the shoulders, arms, elbow joints, forearms, wrists and hands following playing is the bane of many musicians' lives. These symptoms must be taken seriously. Some 60% of musicians experience this type of problem at one time or another during their career. The terms 'regional pain syndrome', 'repetitive strain injury', 'overuse syndrome' and 'misuse injury' tend to be used inter-changeably. It is most unlikely, however, that the pain has been provoked solely by overuse. Many experts in this field believe that increased muscular tension is a vitally important causative factor. Such increased tension can be due to bad technique, bad posture, or to excessive anxiety.

Whilst it may be essential to rest the limb initially, it is also very important that the period be kept as short as possible. Prolonged immobility, such as has sometimes been advised in the past by putting the limb in various kinds of splints, can lead to muscular atrophy with dreadful results. We now know that it is also very important to determine why problems arise when they do. There is always a provoking factor, and it is seldom the number of hours practised. Perhaps you are excessively worried about a performance, and are translating mental tension into muscular tension. Some people may tense their muscles during sleep if they are worried. Excessive anxiety and apprehension should not be ignored. The anxiety may not be simply performance-related, but can be due to other things such as marital problems or financial difficulties. Increased mental and muscular tension can also result from worry about the pain itself.

If increased muscular tension results from bad technique, advice from an experienced teacher is essential. If it is due to bad posture, sometimes due to an old injury or to congenital weakness, the Alexander Technique can play an important role. Backache, for example, is common in orchestral players. Some of this may be due to poor design of chairs, but a greater awareness of the benefits of techniques such as those of Alexander and Feldenkrais would be helpful.

Co-ordination problems

In recent years a strange new syndrome has been recognised. It is best described as being a painless lack of control. The term 'occupational palsy' has been used by some doctors, but it is important to emphasise that the problem is not a true palsy. Its exact incidence is unknown, but some 10% of American musicians who have to seek medical advice have this problem. Three stereotyped afflictions are described. The first involves a tendency of the fourth and fifth fingers of pianists to flex into the centre of the palm and a failure to extend properly. Secondly, guitarists have a tendency to flex the third finger of the right hand. The curling involves both the joints between the hand and fingers and also the finger joints. This disrupts fast tremolo passages which require rapid alternating flexion-extension movements of the third finger. The third involves oboists and clarinettists who experience third finger extension and fourth and fifth finger flexion during scale passages. Either hand can be involved, but it is commoner with the right. Co-ordination problems affecting the embouchure are also well known. The age at which this problem can first occur is anywhere between 17 and 70, with an average of 40. It is two-and-a-half times more common in men. Treatment is highly specialised and difficult. If you experience this problem, get the best advice as soon as possible. Feldenkrais has a role to play.

If the patient is also depressed, antidepressants may be tried. There are cases which have improved when the musician has been given antidepressant drugs, and others which have improved through the prescription of antiparkinsonian agents. It is again important that the best advice is obtained as soon as possible.

Problems with the voice

Just as instrumentalists can develop muscle and co-ordination problems, the singer or actor may develop hoarseness and loss of voice. Rest alone is sufficient in many instances. However, on occasions, an examination of the vocal cords by a specialist is necessary to determine the exact diagnosis. Cure is often effected by a good singing teacher or specially-trained voice therapist. As in the case of instrumentalists, excessive anxiety and stress may be largely, or at least partly, responsible. The voice may not return to normal until these problems are solved.

There is a long list of drugs which should be avoided if you are a singer, and this may be obtained from the British Performing Arts Medicine Trust by sending a stamped addressed envelope to their headquarters. The drugs include ones that dry the mouth and throat, such as certain antidepressants and antihistamines. Drugs given for pain, like aspirin and brufen, can dry the vocal cords. When you try to sing high notes after taking these drugs you may precipitate haemorrhage into the cords.

Drugs changing the timing of the menstrual cycle can also have an adverse effect on a woman's voice, and certain drugs taken for high blood pressure can cause coughs. Everybody knows that smoking can adversely effect the sinuses, but the same is true of alcohol. Certain local decongestants are bad since, while they will temporarily cause an improvement, they always cause rebound congestion.

If you are a professional musician, your technique is likely to be sound and your posture good. If you develop pain or any other problem when you play, get these things checked out. Avoid being excessively stressed when performing. Develop a relaxation technique that suits you. Be sensible about what you take on. Don't commit yourself to too much just because you need the money, but put your health first. If you develop a problem, seek competent, informed medical advice. Most orchestras in the UK now have their own medical adviser. The British Performing Arts Medicine Trust, with financial aid from the Musicians' Union and the Musicians Benevolent Fund, has opened an emergency telephone line (0171-636 61450) to give free advice and help to professional musicians and students in trouble. Most of the clinics set up in the last two years with the help of the MU and Equity are free. You don't have to spend a fortune to regain your health, but you would be best advised not to lose it in the first place. In all instances, prevention is better than cure.

INSURANCE

ALAN CLARKSON

Alan Clarkson is a Fellow of the Chartered Insurance Institute. In 1978 he joined the staff of the British Reserve Insurance Company Limited, and is now the Manager responsible for their Musical Instruments Insurance account. British Reserve is now a member of the Cornhill Insurance Group. He is also an amateur brass player and plays with local concert and brass bands.

I am usually disappointed to find that, when insurance people write on their subject, they fall into the error of assuming that everyone understands the technicalities and the 'lingo' we use amongst ourselves. I will try to avoid this pitfall by beginning this chapter with a brief outline of one or two of the basic principles on which the practice of insurance is founded, without recourse to everyday insurance jargon.

How often have you heard someone ask 'What's the use of insurance? I have paid premiums on my household policy for years and never got anything out of it'? They can only say this because they have not had the misfortune to suffer loss or damage to their property by fire, storm, burst pipes, theft, or one of the other perils which would have been covered by their policy. They have failed to understand that, when they enter into a contract of insurance of this type, they undertake to share in the losses of those other policyholders who have not been so fortunate.

Insurance is a matter of the losses of the minority of policyholders being paid for by the contributions *(premiums)* of the majority. The task of the insurer is to accumulate sufficient funds from the premiums paid to be able to pay for the insured losses or damage incurred, and to meet the cost of administration, together with setting up reserves for the very bad years. A reasonable return on the shareholders' capital must also be provided. The policyholder, for his part, undertakes to share in the loss or damage suffered by the other policyholders, secure in the knowledge that they will likewise share in his misfortune should the need arise. In a nutshell, everyone loses a little by paying premiums, but no-one suffers catastrophically as would be the case if, for example, they had to bear the entire cost of rebuilding their home following a fire.

Data collected over many years enables insurers to assess, with a reasonable degree of accuracy, the cost of claims for a future period. If unusual events occur, such as extremes of weather or an industrial disaster, the reserves referred to above, which have been built up over the years, help to even out unexpected demands on the fund.

Premiums are calculated by dividing the estimated cost of claims plus administration expenses, reserves and profit, by the number of units of risk. The most common unit of risk is the sum insured. Insurers can only get their arithmetic right, therefore, if sums insured represent the full cost of replacing the damaged property. This is why some policyholders find themselves penalised when they have not taken the trouble to ensure that the amounts for which they have asked to be insured are adequate. An inadequate sum insured means that the policyholder does not make a full contribution to the fund and, consequently, is not entitled to a full reimbursement of the loss.

A full sum insured is essential if a policyholder is to be fully indemnified. To *indemnify* means to place the policyholder in the same financial position after loss or damage has occurred as they were in immediately before it happened. This would normally mean that you could not replace new for old but, in recent years, this principal has been modified in some cases. It has, for example, become the practice to offer the alternative of household contents insurance on a new-for-old basis. Perhaps it has something to do with the fact that many items seem to have built-in obsolescense these days and it is easier to replace old with new. It does make the financial burden on the claimant less onerous: it would be very difficult, in many instances, to find a secondhand item in similar condition, thus necessitating laying out extra money for a new item were the claim settlement limited to the value of the item at the time the loss occurred. Where new-for-old cover is available, it is even more essential that the sum insured represents the full replacement cost as new, and that it is regularly updated to keep abreast of inflation.

We will now look at the particular insurance requirements of the professional performer, the private teacher and the administrator in turn.

The professional performer

The professional performer will be concerned with insurance under two main headings. First, the insurance of *property* and, second, the insurance of *income*. I have already made a brief mention of household insurance with which, together with motor insurance, most individuals are already familiar, and I will not take up valuable space by discussing them in detail.

Under the heading of property, I will restrict my remarks to the insurance of musical instruments. When considering this subject, the professional performer requires an insurance policy which will

    (a) offer cover in the most straightforward terms possible,
    (b) provide the widest cover available, and
    (c) apply anywhere in the world.

In order to meet the requirement in (a), the policy should be specifically designed to apply to musical instruments. Insurance policies are legal documents and must be capable of interpretation in a court of law should the need arise. This is why many insurers are reluctant to meet the demand for 'plain English' policies. If the policy has been specifically designed to apply to musical instruments, it will not contain unnecessary clauses which will make it more complicated than necessary. I have seen some attempts at adapting commercial policies containing pages of exclusions and conditions which are totally irrelevant and only serve to obscure those with which the policyholder is really concerned.

The best type of policy will usually be referred to as an *all risks* policy. The term 'all risks', however, only means all *insurable* risks, as some risks are simply not insurable. The cover should, therefore, be against accidental loss or damage to the property insured. The insurer should undertake at his own option to pay cash or to repair, replace or reinstate the lost or damaged instrument in the event of a claim.

You should make sure that the policy will apply whilst you are playing professionally anywhere in the world. Some policies only provide limited cover overseas. One policy I have in front of me, for example, only applies in the United Kingdom, Isle of Man, Channel Islands and Eire plus 14 days in the year anywhere in Europe. Another quotes different rates for various geographical limits. Professional musicians travel extensively nowadays, and it would be a nuisance to have to arrange for the policy to be extended each time you travel outside the limits, even if you always remembered to do so. In addition, you may end up paying a considerable amount of extra money by way of minimum additional premiums for these extensions of cover because of the extra administration costs incurred by the insurer. It is by far the best course to go for the widest cover at the outset.

Pay attention to the conditions and exclusions (sometimes called *exceptions*) printed in the policy, together with any additional clauses added by way of an endorsement slip. Read them carefully and make sure they do not have an adverse effect on the cover so far as you are concerned. If you do not understand anything in the policy, ask your broker or insurer to explain its meaning to you.

There is not enough space available here to discuss all the terms likely to be found in various policies, but you may find that losses from unattended motor vehicles are not covered by the basic policy. This cover can normally be added to the policy after payment of an extra premium and subject to certain conditions. In the case of orchestral instruments, it may only be necessary for all the doors and the boot to be locked and the windows securely closed. With electronic instruments, however, the terms may be more onerous and include the fitting of alarms and immobilisers to the vehicle.

I must return now to the subject of sums insured. Professional valuations, or a recent purchase receipt, are normally required for instruments worth £1,000 and over. The sum insured should represent the full cost of replacement. Proof of value and title will normally be required when making a claim, irrespective of the value. With new instruments this is straightforward enough but, where antique instruments are concerned, other factors come into play. Such instruments cannot normally be replaced by new ones and the cost of a similar antique instrument will be affected by supply and demand at the time. It is in the owner's interest to have instruments (especially stringed instruments) revalued every three or four years at the very least.

It is becoming common practice to *index-link* sums insured on house buildings and contents so that they are automatically increased with inflation. It is not possible to do this with musical instruments because of the various factors which affect the values of different types of instruments. Stringed instruments usually improve with age and their values increase, whereas brass instruments usually deteriorate.

It is important that the insurer understands the needs of the professional musician when loss or damage occurs. If your car is stolen, you will normally be required to wait six weeks or so before the claim is settled, to give the police a chance of finding it. If you have a series of concerts arranged and your instrument goes missing, you may need a replacement straight away. Your insurer should be prepared to pay for an immediate replacement and, if the instrument is subsequently recovered in good condition, should offer you the first option to buy it back if you wish. Immediate replacement of lost instruments is particularly important to the student or young musician who may not be able to afford a good second instrument, and to whom continuity of practice and performance is essential. It is also important that the insurer understands the complexities of instrument repair and has a good relationship with dealers and repairers based on mutual trust.

Members of the Musicians' Union have a limited amount of cover for instruments which are registered with the Union, as part of their membership benefits. This is an 'all risks' cover, limited to a total of £500 in all. It is on an indemnity basis (not new-for-old) and excludes losses of instruments left in unattended motor vehicles for more than thirty minutes during the hours of darkness. If subscriptions are not paid on time, however, this cover is forfeited. Some insurers are prepared to offer cover in excess of this £500 limit at special terms. Supplementary covers are available if the basic limits are inadequate. These limits change from time to time, so you should refer to the Union for up-to-date details.

I will turn now to the insurance of income which may be lost for various reasons. You may be unable to earn income as a result of temporary or permanent disability resulting from accident or illness. There is a class of insurance available known as *personal accident* and/or *sickness* insurance. These policies pay either a fixed sum in the event of death or permanent disability resulting from an accident, or weekly payments for temporary disablement resulting from accident or sickness. The weekly payments are normally only made for up to two years in the event of accidental injury and one year as a result of sickness. You are able to choose the amount of the payments subject to certain limitations, one of which is, obviously, the amount of premium you can afford to pay. Within the definition of permanent disability is included the loss of use of eyes, hands and feet, and there is a limited availability of cover where the loss of use is restricted to fingers – an important consideration for most musicians.

Nowadays, however, *permanent health* insurance is a far better form of protection. This type of policy does not make any payment in the event of death, but the payments for total disability will continue to be made for as long as the disability lasts, up to normal retirement age. If, after a period of total disability, a claimant is able to earn a limited income, the policy will make up the difference between the reduced income and the earnings prior to commencement of the disability.

Income might also be lost if you were to be sued for damages as a result of an accident caused by your negligence. Your motor policy will protect you in respect of accidents involving a car, but what would happen if you were accidentally to knock over a fellow musician's valuable violin or cello? Some years ago, a motor cyclist was awarded damages against a pedestrian who carelessly stepped off the kerb into his path with disastrous results. The pedestrian ended up paying about £2 a week for twenty or so years because she had no *personal liability* insurance. Nowadays, most household contents insurance policies include personal liability cover, but this excludes liability incurred in connection with the policyholder's business or profession. Various insurers place different interpretations on what constitutes 'business or profession' and, in the case of an orchestral musician, some might regard the accident described above as covered by the household policy extension. If your insurers would not, however, they might be prepared to extend the household policy for an additional premium, and this would normally be the cheapest way of obtaining cover. Otherwise, a separate public liability insurance will be required.

The private teacher

The subjects covered above will also apply to the private teacher. I would, however, emphasize the need for liability insurance. The household contents policy would apply to accidents happening to friends coming in for a musical evening (provided they could prove negligence) but not to accidents happening to fee-paying pupils. Here again, however, the household contents insurer may be prepared to extend the policy for an additional premium. If not, a separate public liability insurance is essential.

The administrator

The tasks of the administrator in the world of music are many and varied, and range from those of the college administrator to the duties of the concert promoter. I will concentrate on the needs of those involved with organising musical events.

First, it will be necessary to hire a venue in which the event can take place. This will involve signing a contract which will impose certain liabilities on the hirer. The terms of such contracts can be extremely onerous and not all of the liabilities imposed can be insured against. If the contract makes you responsible for damage to the venue resulting from your negligence, it is usually possible to extend an existing public liability policy if you have one, or to arrange a short term policy for the period of the hiring. If you are responsible for fire damage, you should try to arrange for the owner's fire insurers to note your interest by endorsement of the existing policy, in order to keep your costs to the minimum. These extensions of cover are necessary because standard public liability policies exclude damage to property in the policyholder's custody or control.

Public liability insurance has already been discussed, and this is essential for any business or other type of organisation, such as a voluntary or charitable body. If, however, you employ someone, then the law imposes very strict liabilities upon you in connection with accidental injury or illness associated with their employment. You are required to take out *employers' liability* insurance, and must display a certificate at each place of employment to show that you are correctly insured.

You will incur considerable expense in arranging any event, most of which would be lost if the event were to be cancelled for any reason. You will, therefore, require *cancellation and abandonment* insurance. Such policies can provide insurance against (a) accident or sickness of the performer or (b) any cause beyond the control of the policyholder or the performer. Such causes might include death of the monarch, war, strikes, destruction of the venue, bomb scares and epidemics.

The insurance will not apply to cancellation due to any pre-existing illness or condition of the performer. In some cases, medical evidence of good health may be required at the policyholder's expense. There will be a warranty as to the fitness of the performer at the time the insurance commences. It will also be a condition of the insurance that all financial arrangements will have been concluded prior to its commencement. Losses due to financial failures or lack of support will not be covered.

For open-air venues, insurance against cancellation due to heavy rainfall can be arranged. *Pluvious* insurance, as it is called, is arranged on the basis of an agreed sum insured being paid in the event of rainfall reaching an agreed level during set times on the day or days of the event.

In conclusion, a word or two concerning the best way to go about buying insurance. In the case of a simple musical instrument policy, it is possible to go direct to an insurance company. Many musical instrument dealers and repairers are able to recommend a suitable insurer; they know from experience in dealing with the replacement or repair of lost or damaged instruments which insurers provide the best and most sympathetic service when it comes to making a claim.

For the other classes of insurance, I would strongly recommend that you seek the services of an insurance broker. If you do not already know one in your area, the British Insurance Brokers Association will be able to put you in touch with one. I give this advice because the insurance requirements of each individual differ. Also, the attitudes and specialities of insurers vary, as do costs and availability of cover. The professional insurance broker knows the market, and should be able to find the insurer who can most economically meet your particular needs.

I know of two insurance brokers who are also professional musicians and, if you can find someone such as this who is experienced in both the world of music and the world of insurance, you will not do better.

It has not been possible to mention every aspect of insurance in this chapter or, indeed, to deal in very great detail with the subjects covered. I hope, however, that these few remarks will guide you in the right direction and enable you to seek out the protection you need.

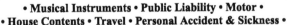

THE MUSICIANS' UNION

KEN CORDINGLEY

Ken Cordingley, like many brass players, started his playing in a brass band. He changed from trumpet to horn during his service in the artillery band in Woolwich. Two years at the Royal Shakespeare Theatre and a winter in the first UK tour of West Side Story *preceded seventeen years in the horn section of the City of Birmingham Symphony Orchestra, where his interest in orchestral politics was aroused. In 1979, he was appointed South West District Organiser for the Musicians' Union, moving to his current position as Assistant General Secretary in 1990.*

The Musicians' Union, with a membership of more than 33,000, is the largest single organisation for musicians in the world. The Union operates comprehensively in all areas of music, including performance, music writing and instrumental teaching. Its members benefit from belonging to a democratic organisation, run for musicians by musicians, and its structure seeks to serve musicians both geographically and in direct response to the specialist fields of music in which they might be involved.

In 1993, the Union celebrated its centenary, and Joe Williams, its founder, would be proud today of his creation. In the anonymous circular that he sent out to musicians inviting them to join together to form a union, he stated that a union was needed to 'protect us from amateurs, unscrupulous employers and, most importantly, from ourselves'. For certain, then as now, it was not amateurs who were the problem, but simply those who were paid for their talents but accepted considerably less than the accepted minimum. This is surely part of the 'ourselves' to whom Joe Williams was referring. His attempt at forming a union followed in the footsteps of many in the past seeking to band musicians together for protection. The difference for Joe Williams was that he succeeded in developing a truly democratic organisation which seeks to protect the rights and interests of musicians involved in each and every sphere of music.

Specialist section structure

Separate sections have been created to enable efficient and effective response to the particular problems associated with the specialist nature of their areas of work. Advisory and consultative committees have been elected from the Sections' membership in the following areas:

Session Section, covering musicians having a substantial involvement with media engagements (television, radio, gramophone recording, library music, jingles, feature films and videograms).

Theatre Section, covering musicians working in theatre productions of all types, both regional and in London's West End.

Freelance Orchestral Section, covering musicians working in the orchestral field in all areas as freelances, including early music and chamber, symphony, opera and ballet orchestras.

Music Writers' Section, covering composers, arrangers and music copyists.

Jazz Section, covering musicians who have a substantial involvement in the performance of jazz.

Teachers' Section, covering musicians who teach instruments in any capacity, whether it be in schools or privately.

The above committees have a direct input into the Union's Executive, the Union's highest policy making committee. They are joined by specialist occupational committees representing musicians in full-time employment from the Regional Orchestras, the BBC Orchestras, the opera orchestras and the ballet orchestras.

Agreements are reached with all major employers of musicians, covering the terms and conditions under which our members work. These include the Theatrical Management Association, the Society of London Theatre, the Association of British Orchestras, individual symphony, chamber, opera and ballet orchestras, the BBC (for both radio and television), the independent television companies (ITV), individual television and film producers (PACT), the British Phonographic Industry, the Institute of Practitioners in Advertising, holidays centres and shipping lines. In addition, the Union maintains a variety of national, district and branch agreements on rates, and continues to devolve negotiations, where appropriate, to branches and districts. In common with most other musicians' organisations throughout the world, media engagements are negotiated on a national basis, although the supervision and implementation of the Agreements is, to some extent, devolved. The Union has continued to keep under review developments in technology and the media that affect the negotiations and operation of Agreements. The trend over the past decade has been towards a wider range of uses for recorded performances, and our media Agreements reflect these changes. As a service to our members, the Union offers a wide range of standard contracts, ranging from the engagement of a band or group for a single casual gig engagement to private teaching, or for a season engagement at a holiday centre.

The policies adopted in reaching agreement with the major employers aim to improve the status and remuneration of musicians, and the Union seeks to involve its members throughout this process. The Union retains a constructive relationship with all those organisations and, almost without exception, they recommend that musicians should be in membership of the only organisation exclusively dealing with the problems besetting musicians across the spectrum. Having completed the negotiations and settled the terms and conditions, the

Union then goes on to seek to enforce the limitations of the Agreement, so that the employer or engager only secures those services which have been agreed within the terms of the Agreement and are commensurate with the level of remuneration offered. Musicians have to be protected from the notion that, having engaged the musician, their services can then be exploited in any way the engager thinks fit, maybe including broadcasting or recording the performance.

Not only does the Union seek to have all the current performers' protection under the law observed, as in the instance referred to above, but to extend that protection wherever possible. This is achieved by lobbying whoever is in government, and using whatever influence there is available through affiliation to the National Campaign for the Arts, and through joining together with the other unions in the entertainment field.

The Union is a leading member of the International Federation of Musicians, and plays a very active role on the international stage. It works closely with other musicians' unions across the world, seeking to protect musicians from those who would unscrupulously abuse their talents, particularly in the area of copyright and performers' protection. Constantly under review, both nationally and internationally, is the burgeoning of technology, providing, as it does, for the ever-widening possibilities of the abuse of musicians' performances.

The Union is becoming increasingly involved in the provision of other vital services, the most recent and significant example of which is its close relationship with the British Association for Performing Arts Medicine. A major part of this association's work is to provide medical services and advice to musicians who suffer disproportionately from ailments simply because of the nature of their work. The Union works closely with BAPAM and contributes a substantial amount of money to enable its work to continue and flourish. There is now a doctor (and, in most cases, more than one) attached to virtually every orchestra in the United Kingdom who provides a direct service to the musicians. Vital to the future of this service is the recognition by the musician that it is entirely confidential, and that nobody, not even the patient's closest colleagues, are aware that advice is being sought. A recent extension to this service is a telephone helpline through which all musicians in all areas of the profession can receive speedy and efficient medical advice in the same confidential way.

The Union has developed a wide range of additional services for members, including free public liability insurance, a sickness and accident benefit scheme, legal advice and assistance, specialist instrument and equipment insurance, a music business advisory service (particularly helpful for young rock and pop musicians in the areas of record publishing, management contracts, etc), personal financial advice schemes, and discounted rates for national breakdown, musical instruments, music and equipment purchases.

The Union is a Founder Trustee of the Loan Fund for Musical Instruments, from which hundreds of young musicians have benefited. The object of this fund is to enable young musicians who have launched themselves on a musical career to tackle the now almost insurmountable problem of providing themselves with a quality instrument which will not negate their talent. They do this by applying to the Fund for a loan, the terms of which, together with the long repayment schedule, are such that servicing the loan becomes a possibility within a relatively modest income.

A subcommittee of the Union's Executive is the Music Promotion Committee, which, under the ubiquitous slogan of 'Keep Music Live', has played a modest but well-targeted role in supplying funding for pump priming and sustaining music initiatives over a very long period and over the complete spectrum of musics. In addition, in the current stringent financial circumstances associated with the longest recession in recent times, the Union has been the last resort to which many of the major musical institutions have turned in order to forestall insolvency. The Union has been reluctant to take on this role, but when our much-loved centres of excellence, be they orchestras or jazz clubs, have been threatened in the way that they have, the Union has had little choice.

Like their sense of humour, musicians' concern for each other's welfare and their vulnerability in the profession is unique. Consequently, the Musicians' Union has a special affinity with all those complex things which go to make up a musician, regardless of the area of the profession in which they operate. With over a hundred years of experience looking after musicians' needs, the Union can rightly state that it is recognised to be the representative organisation for all musicians, not only by the employers of musicians but also by the politicians and the arts funders.

THE INCORPORATED SOCIETY OF MUSICIANS

NEIL HOYLE

Neil Hoyle studied music at Edinburgh University and at Corpus Christi College, Cambridge, before entering the Civil Service. His career at Whitehall included various postings as policy adviser and Private Secretary in the Departments of Transport and of the Environment, as well as the Treasury. During this time, he remained an enthusiastic musician: he plays the piano and horn, and sings (occasionally). He has been Chief Executive of the Incorporated Society of Musicians since January 1990.

The Incorporated Society of Musicians is the UK's professional association for all musicians. This chapter describes its history and current activities.

A little history

Britain in the late nineteenth century was hardly a 'land without music'. Far from it: there was an immense amount of music-making, both public and private. On one level, performers grappled with leviathan compositions for enormous forces; on another, every home which could afford it had a piano in the parlour. The Victorians – enthusiastic educators and classifiers, in music as elsewhere – set up institutions and systems to bring order into what they saw as an untidy world. By the middle years of the century, most of today's conservatoires had been established, and a network of private teachers stretched across the country.

Against this background, there was an obvious need for a strong professional association to protect musicians' interests and to speak publicly for them. In 1882, an organist called James Dawber organised a meeting in Manchester which launched the Society of Professional Musicians. This body saw its duty as representing its members and promoting music as a beneficial, cultural, educational and social influence (goals which still underlie the ISM's work). It also began to publish lists of bona fide qualified musicians, and to set examinations.

The new association grew quickly, changed its name to the National Society of Professional Musicians, and brought out a monthly journal. The first national conference was held in 1886, chaired by Ebenezer Prout and Frederick Cowen. International recognition quickly followed, and in 1892 the Society's constitutional position was established by law when it became the Incorporated Society of Musicians. All these things were not achieved without opposition: vested interests, then as now, resented the expansion of the Society's power and influence, and its efforts to flush out charlatans and bogus teaching diplomas provoked some hostility.

Like much else, the youthful Society was devastated by the First World War. Membership declined, and the Society's Benevolent Fund, created in 1917 to support members and their dependants who had fallen on hard times, was inundated with requests for help. New difficulties appeared on the horizon: broadcasting, recordings and player-pianos jeopardised performers' and composers' livelihoods and rights, while fewer people wanted to learn instruments.

The Society responded by changing its structure and its style. Over the years to 1930, under a succession of great Presidential names such as Sir Landon Ronald, Sir Donald Tovey and Sir Adrian Boult, it clarified its objectives, ceased its examining work, and created the first of its Specialist Sections, for solo performers. Amalgamation with the Union of Directors of Music in Secondary Schools (later the Music Masters' & Mistresses' Association) strengthened the influence of the school teaching profession within the Society. The subsequent decade saw figures such as Sir Edward Bairstow and Sir Thomas Beecham in the Presidential seat. To help cope with the ravages of the Depression, the ISM set up the National Federation of Music Societies in 1935, with the aim of encouraging and sponsoring concerts. The Society also lobbied successfully against what it saw as harmful pieces of legislation, and became a powerful voice for the profession in negotiations with the colossus of the BBC.

The years of the Second World War were traumatic, though the Society did its bit to help the national effort and to protect musicians' interests. In particular, it helped to set up CEMA – the Council for the Encouragement of Music and the Arts – which did much to keep music alive, and which was transformed into the Arts Council when peace returned. Further restructuring ensued, along with the formation of the Schools Music Section, which allowed the MMA to keep a separate yet federal existence (although some years later it seceded). Expansion continued up to the 1960s – during this period, the ISM more than doubled in size, to well over 6,000 members – and the Specialist Section for Private Teachers was set up in 1963.

The 1960s and 70s were a curious period for the profession, as they were for Britain generally. An illusory surge in prosperity had a profound effect on attitudes, both public and private. The prevailing climate of corporatism showed in the expansion of collective bargaining, the ascendancy of the closed shop, and the militancy of unions. None of this sat comfortably alongside the culture of the ISM, with its traditional respect for individual independence and personal responsibility. On the one hand, the Society achieved representation on a huge range of committees, an agreement reflecting the employment legislation of the time was signed with the Musicians' Union, and distinguished members such as Sir Charles Groves and Sir Geraint Evans picketed the BBC over plans for its orchestras. On the other, the ISM worked steadily – if less flamboyantly – to develop the concept of professionalism in music (by laying the ground for codes of ethics) and on improving the lot of the self-employed musician (by providing standard contracts, legal support, debt recovery services and promotional registers).

The 1980s saw a sharp dislocation in the economic and social patterns of the two preceding decades, setting the scene for the 1990s. Employment conditions in every sphere have now moved away from collective agreements towards individual arrangements, and the closed shop has, in effect, been abolished by law. Musicians have not been exempt from these changes. Nowadays, many more are working on a freelance basis, with individual contracts; they are also enjoying more varied patterns of work, from playing in symphony orchestras to private teaching. Since this reflects the ISM's ethos – that musicianship is diverse yet indivisible – the profession has begun to turn to the Society in increasing numbers. After shrinking slowly for twenty years, the ISM grew by around 25% between 1991 and 1995, with a particularly strong intake of young freelance musicians. This rate of growth seems set to continue.

The ISM today

The ISM in 1996 is, therefore, a dynamic and flourishing body, drawing its members from every corner of the musical world. It is run by a thirty-strong Council (chaired by the President and advised by an Executive Committee), most of whose members are elected to represent geographical districts. Three vigorous Specialist Sections – for Musicians in Education (mainly peripatetics, schoolteachers and lecturers), Performers and Composers (including soloists, chamber and orchestral musicians, conductors and organists, as well as writers of music), and Private Teachers (usually, those who work from home on a self-employed basis) – look after the development of policy in their areas of responsibility. A network of forty-seven local Centres, run by locally-elected committees of members, arranges programmes of events, ranging from lecture-recitals to social gatherings, all with the aim of improving musicians' professionalism and keeping them in touch with one another.

Special groupings for Associate (amateurs and music lovers), Student (under- and post-graduates) and Corporate members (businesses and institutions) lend valuable support to the ISM's work. In particular, the 150-strong corporate membership category helps to reinforce the Society's national role.

The ISM's fundamental aim remains 'to promote the art of music, and maintain the honour and interests of the musical profession'. Recent Presidents – who have included William Mathias, Lionel Dakers, Sir John Manduell, Gillian Weir, Jack Brymer, Philip Ledger and Emanuel Hurwitz – have each brought their own perspective to bear on this theme. For practical purposes, however, it is translated into three policy objectives: to protect and represent the interests of all those who work with music; to raise standards within all branches of the profession; and to offer the best possible quality and range of services to all its members. These points are worth examining in turn.

First, **Representing the Profession's Interests.** On the educational front, the ISM has been closely involved in formulating the National Music Curriculum. It has also been monitoring the evolution of local instrumental teaching services under the new legislative regime – an area which has seen a few unhappy developments, but many remarkable achievements. The ISM is frequently asked to advise on teachers' contracts; this is a field where a detailed yet pragmatic understanding of employment legislation is crucial. The Society serves private teachers by offering them professional development opportunities, as well as recommending minimum fees, resolving disputes and seeking redress from clients who refuse to pay bills. Performers – especially those following freelance careers – have been helped by the Society's contributions to national policy debates (for example, on the future of the BBC, on orchestras, and on legislation for performers' rights), as well as fee recommendations and contractual advice. The Society has recently published new terms and conditions for organists, and, with the aim of helping classical composers, has been discussing possible amendments to the Live Music Policy with the Performing Right Society. Broadly speaking, the ISM does not regard itself as a nannying bureaucracy; rather, it is an agent for empowering musicians to take control of their lives, and to cope with the consequences of change, whether vocational, economic or institutional.

Second, **Raising Standards in the Profession.** The ISM imposes stringent admission requirements, especially for entry to its Specialist Sections, so that the public can be sure of receiving a good service from its members. It has also published codes of ethics and good practice for different branches of the profession. To build on these foundations, the Society organises conferences, seminars and symposia, which aim not so much to increase technical proficiency as to raise the level of debate and discussion on issues affecting the profession. The Society is also leading the way in providing professional development schemes for musicians, such as the innovative Diploma Course in Music Teaching in Private Practice, run in conjunction with Reading University. Again, this is not a matter of merely improving existing skills; it involves helping musicians to ask fundamental questions about why they are doing what they are doing, and to appreciate the importance of their role in society – for, if they cannot fully understand it, they will never be able to do anything about it. Consequently, the Society aims to promote a wider cultural awareness – of other arts, of social, political and economic issues, and of philosophical and ethical questions – amongst musicians, and to help them work out their own solutions to problems, within a solid framework of professional values. In short, the ISM sees self-perception, self-assurance and self-control as the three keys which will enable musicians to take command of their careers and avert the notorious 'instrumental operative' syndrome.

Third, **Quality and Range of Professional Membership Services.** The ISM offers an immense variety of specialised services to its members. Legal and professional advice of all kinds – including debt recovery, tax and national insurance advice, and financial planning – is offered on an individual basis, as is a free 24-hour Legal Helpline covering any legal matter, whether professional or personal. Special insurance packages include free public liability cover (to £2½ million) and legal expenses, while large discounts are available on other exclusive insurance schemes, such as household, motor, musical instrument and loss of contracted earnings. ISM standard contracts have stood the test of the courts, and provide a high degree of security. The Society produces an immense range of publications, including the annual *Yearbook*, promotional registers for members of the Specialist Sections, *Careers with Music,* the monthly *ISM Music Journal,* and a battery of Information Sheets on professional matters ranging from employment issues to noise. ISM branded merchandise, such as memo pads, personal organisers, diaries, pencils, car stickers, pin badges and instrument case stickers, help to promote the Society while providing essential back-up for its members' business activities.

This, then, is the ISM today – a powerful association of dedicated professionals, committed to the professional values which underpin its constitution, and determined to provide the highest standards of service for its members and their clients. Its far-reaching cultural and artistic goals, allied to a painstaking attention to the needs of individual musicians, give it a unique position in the UK's musical life. And the Society is always ready to welcome new members who wish to subscribe to its goal of 'promoting the art of music, and maintaining the honour and interests of the musical profession'.

CHARITIES FOR PROFESSIONAL MUSICIANS AND THEIR DEPENDANTS

MAGGIE GIBB

Maggie Gibb is Secretary of The Royal Society of Musicians of Great Britain.

The working life of professional musicians is usually quite tough. Particularly in the freelance sector, they are responsible for generating all their own work, doing all the planning and organisation necessary for running a small business, budgeting for those times when work is slack, and trying not to overwork when the telephone seems, for a change, not to stop ringing. Most musicians cope admirably – until the unexpected comes in some form or another. A broken arm, a slipped disc, the death of a partner, a heart attack, the onset of arthritis, signs of mental stress: any of these, and more beside, can render the musician incapable of playing for many weeks or months. Not all musicians can afford to take out health insurance policies sufficient to cover every eventuality, and with no employer, and reduced or no entitlement to state schemes, to whom do musicians turn?

Fortunately, the music profession is supported by several well-established charities, whose purpose is to help musicians and members of their families who have fallen on hard times. Here is a brief outline of their aims and charitable objects (all contact names, addresses and telephone numbers can be found in *The British Music Yearbook,* published annually by Rhinegold Publishing).

The Royal Society of Musicians of Great Britain (RSM)

The Society was born in 1738, following a chance meeting outside the Orange Coffee House in London's Haymarket between Michael Festing, a violinist and composer, the flautist and oboist Charles Weideman, and a member of the Vincent family of instrumentalists. They spoke to two passing small boys and learned that they had been left destitute on the death of their father, Jean Christian Kytch, who had been a celebrated oboist but an improvident father.

The three musicians called other colleagues together, and drew up a Declaration of Trust which set out the rules for the Society of Musicians, to which over two hundred undertook to subscribe. It received a Royal Charter, and today, over 250 years later, Members of the Royal Society of Musicians continue to meet on the first Sunday of the month to procure help for colleagues or their families in distress because of accident, illness or old age. More immediate assistance can be, and is, given between Meetings.

The music grapevine must be one of the most effective communications systems: it is said that a sneeze in Sydney will be reported in London on the following day. Members, and indeed non-members, quickly advise the Society of those in need of financial help or specialist medical advice. The Society spends very little money on advertising, and can rely on its membership to tell it of those in need. In addition, the knowledgeable concern of colleagues is an important aspect of the Society's work.

Members may sometimes find it difficult to persuade those in distress to apply for help. The idea of seeking assistance from a charity, even in total confidence, can be psychologically distasteful to some, but experienced colleagues can help someone in need to overcome such diffidence.

Professional musicians now join the RSM only for altruistic reasons; the subscription is therefore low, although donations are always gratefully received. In its early years, membership of the Society and, similarly, of the Royal Theatrical Fund (founded in 1839 by Charles Dickens, for those within the theatrical profession) gave status within the professions. The membership subscription was, in effect, an insurance policy, and income from it was an important source of funding. The post-war implementation of Beveridge's proposals, however, led these charities to make changes to enable them to meet the changing needs of their professions. The granting of Supplemental Royal Charters permitted them to broaden their scope and assist colleagues who were not actually Members. Thus, it is now possible for any professional musician to seek help from the RSM.

Financial assistance for post-graduate studies in music is scarce at present, and not available from the Society. On the other hand, the Society (unlike the Musicians Benevolent Fund, mentioned below) may help music students suffering from accident or illness to obtain the necessary medical help, without which the completion of an academic year might be jeopardised. (The colleges of music also have financial resources for this purpose.)

In the early years of the Society, an important source of income was the proceeds from benefit concerts, for which Members were obliged to give their services. This may sometimes have been an onerous burden for the then relatively small number of London Members; those selected to perform who failed either to take part in person, or to pay for deputies, were liable to be expelled forthwith. No such draconian measure applies to the Royal Concert which, since its inception in 1951, has been held annually to raise funds and to celebrate the Festival of St Cecilia. All the musicians involved in the concerts and associated events give their services for the benefit of the various musical charities. The administration of the Royal Concert is undertaken by a subsidiary of the Musicians Benevolent Fund, Britain's largest charity for musicians.

Musicians Benevolent Fund (MBF)

Founded by Victor Beigel in 1921, in memory of the singer Gervase Elwes, the aims of the Musicians Benevolent Fund are similar to those of the RSM. In addition to providing financial assistance to beneficiaries, the Fund also maintains a residential home for musicians, and administers a holiday scheme. The Fund does not offer membership to individuals, but the Friends of the Musicians Benevolent Fund support its many endeavours.

The Fund's Visitors go to applicants' homes, and try to help with every kind of problem. This personal approach is considered by the Fund to be of great importance, a view shared by the Royal Society.

The MBF is not able to help student musicians suffering as a result of accident or illness, nor can it assist with grants for post-graduate study, but it can play a part in launching young musicians on their professional careers, through the publication of a *Handbook of Music Awards and Scholarships,* and through the administration of some awards. A recent new development for the Fund has been the provision of performance opportunities for young musicians.

British Performing Arts Medicine Trust

Together with the Musicians' Union and Equity Trust Fund, the MBF supported the setting up of the British Performing Arts Medicine Trust in 1984, for research and treatment in performing arts medicine. This Trust provides specialist medical help for all professionals in the world of entertainment. Its medical officers understand that while, for the general public, the loss of a tooth may be a cosmetic nuisance, for a freelance wind player it may be a catastrophe, leading to instant loss of livelihood.

Specialist knowledge is available to alleviate stress-related illness and injury, to which those in the performing arts are prone by the nature of their professions. A confidential helpline service is available to all performers, including students, for advice and help on performance-related medical and psychological issues.

Many of the Trust's honorary consultants are internationally recognised as specialists in their fields. Where possible, they work with the performers' own doctors to ensure that comprehensive treatment is available. Some clients may require ongoing therapy which may not always be available within the National Health Service; financial assistance towards the (generally modest) costs of such treatment, recommended by the Trust's advisers, may be sought from the charities already mentioned.

In addition, the Trust trains general practitioners, consultants, therapists, and para-medical staff in the specialist areas of performing arts medicine. It also undertakes research in this field, and co-ordinates the provision of its services throughout Great Britain and Northern Ireland.

The prevention of strain and stress is another important aspect of the Trust's work. This may range from encouraging managements to provide suitable chairs (which decrease the risk of physical strain), to advising performers on how to avoid occupational health problems. The music colleges, and specialist music and drama schools, have also recognised the importance of education and training in preventive measures.

Within the ambit of the Trust is the Association of Medical Advisers to British Orchestras. Increasing numbers of orchestras and opera and dance companies have their own benevolent funds.

Benevolent funds of professional organisations

Freelance musicians may, of course, belong to professional associations such as the Musicians' Union, British Actors' Equity Association, Incorporated Society of Musicians or Performing Right Society, all of which have benevolent funds whose benefits are restricted to members and their dependants. Contact names, addresses and telephone numbers of all these organisations, including the Musicians Social and Benevolent Council (set up by the Musicians' Union in 1939 with the purpose of being able to make quick charitable grants to its London District Members), are listed in the *British Music Yearbook*.

Organists' Benevolent League

There are also charities for specific branches of the profession, such as the Organists' Benevolent League, founded in 1909 by Sir Frederick Bridge when he was organist of Westminster Abbey. His successors have all been President of the League, which exists to provide assistance to organists or their dependants. The League is totally independent of any other organisation, and is nondenominational: in Bridge's words, 'the League extends to Anglican, Free Church, Roman Catholic and Cinema'. How many, these days, can remember the remarkable sight of the cinema organ?

General information

The two questions most often asked by people who are considering an application for assistance are *Should separate approaches be made to various charities?* and *Are there applications forms to be completed?*

You should always approach each charity individually as, whilst the aims of the charities for professional musicians and their families are similar, provision of assistance for various purposes differs. The inability of one charity to offer help may not mean that the application will be turned down by the others, but be aware that a charity may not feel it appropriate to offer money if it knows that another has already done so.

As to the necessity of filling in application forms, in this increasingly bureaucratic world where it seems mandatory to complete a form of application in triplicate for permission to breathe, the answer is, not unexpectedly, yes. However, charities recognise that, when a person is worried or ill, or concerned for others, and there is simply no time to write, action may have to be taken immediately. In such cases, an initial quick telephone call is sufficient to start the process: the paperwork can come later. Advice about completion of forms is always available from the charities' Visitors and staff.

The charities for those who work within the world of music, together with the associated medical trusts (such as the British Performing Arts Medicine Trust and the International Society for the Study of Tension in Performance), jointly endeavour to care for the welfare and health of active musicians, former musicians, their dependants, and students. There is very close co-operation between those already mentioned and the Guild of Aid for Gentlepeople, and the Professional Classes Aid Council, as well as the numerous charities associated with specific medical conditions.

In addition to the help and information provided by the Social Services and the Citizens' Advice Bureaux, the assistance of the charities, together with the specialist advice from honorary medical officers and from the financial advisers affiliated to professional organisations, provide a framework of comprehensive and immediate support to those whose music has enriched the lives of so many.

The practical expression of generosity of spirit, which has been the inspiration for countless charities, old and new, is a lasting tribute to their founders and their successors, to the many Members and Friends, to their honorary trustees who give so much of their time and experience, and who take responsibility for the sometimes difficult decisions in an increasingly regulatory complex world, and to those who also serve in honorary capacities as medical officers, financial advisers, and solicitors.

You can also help. Not only by your support of the charities mentioned above, but also by passing on information about these sources of help to the musicians who need it.

THE ART OF AUDITIONING

A Handbook for Singers, Accompanists and Coaches.

By Anthony Legge

£10.95 + £2.00 p+p in the UK

Order by post - simply send your cheque (made payable to Rhinegold Publishing Ltd) to: **Book Sales Dept, Rhinegold Publishing Ltd, 241 Shaftesbury Avenue, London WC2H 8EH.**

CREDIT CARD HOLDERS MAY TELEPHONE 0171-333 1721 DURING OFFICE HOURS

DISMISSAL, REDUNDANCY AND UNEMPLOYMENT

LAURENCE WATT

Since 1974, Laurence Watt has been a partner in the firm of Charles Russell in Lincoln's Inn. He acts for a number of professional musicians, including one of London's best known self-governed symphony orchestras, and two chamber orchestras. He was responsible for conducting the litigation which confirmed the freelance status of the members of the self-governed orchestras. He is a member of the London Philharmonic Trust, the Hanover Band Trust and the ABO Trust. He is also an amateur horn player.

Employment legislation has now been with us for about thirty years. The right to redundancy payments arose in 1965, and the right not to be unfairly dismissed arose in 1971. At its best, this legislation provides a framework in which genuine unfairness can be remedied, and out of which a measure of protection is given against the cessation of a particular job, or of the requirements of particular work, through redundancy. At its worst, it cuts across the traditional common law right of every individual or company to contract freely as to the terms, conditions and duration of employment. In addition, employment legislation, incorporating as it does so many protections and allowances in relation to union membership, has become a political football, resulting in increased complexity and constant change. The Employment Protection (Consolidation) Act of 1978 sought to bring all the legislation together into more or less intelligible form under one statute, although one or two stragglers have been enacted since.

Employed or self-employed?

Clearly, the difference between an employee and a self-employed person is of great importance, since only an employee will enjoy the protection of statutory employment rights.

The distinction between an employee and an independent contractor or consultant is a complex issue. The Courts will pay only limited regard to the labels used by the parties in their agreement, as these are often created to avoid the consequences of the legislation, but will look instead to the reality of the relationship. There is one fundamental prerequisite of a contract of employment: there must be mutual obligations on the employer to provide work for the employee and on the employee to perform work for the employer. If there are mutual obligations present, a Court or Tribunal will carry out a balancing exercise to establish the nature of the relationship, and will consider the following factors:

    (i)   Whether the individual works under the orders of another who controls not only what he must do, but also how and when he must do it. The Court of Appeal recently acknowledged that the control test was still important, and when an element of control was exercised it was likely that an individual was an employee. However, where skilled individuals were involved, then the control test may not be wholly relevant, and the test should be widened to 'whose business was it'. In other words, was the individual carrying out his own business, or was he carrying out that of his employer?

   (ii)   Whether the individual is employed as part of the business of the employer, and his work is done as an integral part of that business.

  (iii)   Whether the individual provides his own equipment.

  (iv)   Whether the individual hires his own helpers.

   (v)   Whether the individual takes a degree of financial risk.

  (vi)   Whether the individual has responsibility for investment and management.

 (vii)   How far the individual has the opportunity of profiting from sound management in performing his task.

Notice

Any person who is employed under a contract of service is entitled to minimum periods of notice laid down by statute. These apply regardless of any shorter period which the employee and his employer may have purported to have agreed.

    The periods laid down are as follows:

    (i)   Continuous employment for one month or over, but less than two years, will entitle an employee to a minimum of one week's notice.

   (ii)   Continuous employment for two years or more, but for less than twelve years, will entitle an employee to one week's notice for each year of continuous employment.

  (iii)   Continuous employment for twelve years or more will entitle the employee to not less than twelve weeks' notice.

An employee cannot agree to reduce his right to the statutory minimum period of notice.

Dismissal

Wrongful dismissal will always be unfair; unfair dismissal will not always be wrongful. This conundrum will perhaps better be understood by explaining that the word 'wrongful' should be read in the context of breach of contract, and the word 'unfair' in the statutory sense that dismissal, even if totally in accordance with the contract, can nevertheless give rise to an application to an industrial tribunal alleging unfairness, upon proof of which the complainant becomes entitled to compensation. Furthermore, the compensation awarded by an industrial tribunal bears little relationship to any damages that might otherwise have been awarded had there been a breach of contract. Indeed, in certain circumstances reinstatement or re-engagement orders can be made.

The other main difference of principle with which the musician is concerned is that, whereas wrongful dismissal can mean either termination of a contract for services or a contract of service (it simply involves breach of the terms of the contract under which the musician performs), unfair dismissal can only be claimed where a musician is employed under a contract of service.

For all practical purposes, to claim unfair dismissal an employee must have been in continuous employment for two years and be under retirement age. He must either (i) have been dismissed, or (ii) be working under a fixed-term contract which has expired without subsequently being renewed, or (iii) have terminated the contract himself under circumstances where his employer's conduct has forced him to do so (known as constructive dismissal).

The legislation lays down what are called acceptable reasons for dismissal, which cover misconduct, inability, ill-health, redundancy and illegality. An employer must establish one of these grounds, and then the tribunal will go on to consider the fairness of the dismissal, i.e. whether the reason given is justified, whether warnings have been given, and whether disciplinary procedures have been followed.

There are three reasons for dismissal which are automatically unfair. These are (i) trades union activity, (ii) pregnancy, and (iii) unfair selection for redundancy. The main remedies available from the tribunal are compensation and, much more rarely, orders for reinstatement or re-engagement.

Compensation is awarded in two layers:

(i) A basic award which follows more or less automatically on a finding of unfairness (although there can be reductions for contributory fault), and which is calculated precisely in the same way as redundancy payments (see below).

(ii) A compensation element up to a maximum of £11,300 which will, at the discretion of the tribunal, be reduced by any conduct by the musician contributing to his dismissal. The sanction for the refusal by an employer to re-engage or reinstate is an additional award which, depending upon the circumstances, can be between 13 and 52 weeks' pay, up to a maximum of £210 per week.

An application to an industrial tribunal alleging unfair dismissal must be made within three months of the termination of employment.

At the time of writing, the legislation states that an employee must have been employed for a continuous period of two full years before he is entitled to bring a claim for unfair dismissal. However, a recent Court of Appeal decision has cast doubt on this requirement, holding that a two-year qualifying period discriminates against women on the grounds of their sex, on the basis that it is more difficult for women to acquire two full years' service because women move in and out of the job market more frequently than men. The suggestion in the Court of Appeal decision is that a one-year qualifying period would not be discriminatory. However, there is much uncertainty surrounding the Court of Appeal's decision, and the Government plans to appeal against it to the

House of Lords. The uncertainty will remain until the Lords issue their final judgment.

Following the Part-Timer Regulations, issued in February 1995, part-time employees are entitled to the same employment protection rights as full-time employees. Accordingly, whereas previously an individual who worked more than eight but less than sixteen hours each week would not be entitled to bring a claim for unfair dismissal or redundancy unless he had completed five full years of service, he may now bring such claims after two full years of service (although see earlier comments on service). The Part-Timer Regulations swept away any hourly requirement of service, with the effect that all employees, irrespective of the number of hours worked each week (i.e. this can be less than eight), are entitled to the same rights as full-time employees in the same circumstances.

Redundancy

It is difficult to imagine circumstances where redundancy is likely to arise frequently for the employed orchestral musician. A symphony orchestra without its normal full complement of players would be like a spider with six legs – it would work, but would not be quite the same. Clearly it could happen, since the BBC could well, for instance, decide to disband one of its orchestras or, at any rate, cut down its string strength. Players so affected, and music teachers who find themselves the subject of financial stringency on the part of the educational establishment, will need the following requirements in order to come within the statutory protection provisions:

(i)   To have been dismissed;

(ii) To be 20 or over and below the age of 65;

(iii) To have been in continuous employment for a period of two years from the first day of employment. There are various events which, contrary to appearances, do not break continuity. The most pertinent of these are participation in a strike and, in certain rather complicated circumstances, where a business changes hands and the affected employee is offered the same job under the new ownership – for example, if the Western Orchestral Society were to take over the running of the BBC National Orchestra of Wales and keep on all the players.

(iv) To have been dismissed by reason of redundancy – in other words, for the reason that either the whole business in which the musician is engaged has either ceased or is about to cease, or the requirement for the particular work carried out by the musician has ceased or diminished or is expected so to do.

There are a number of exclusions from benefit, of which the three most important are:

(i)   employees dismissed for gross misconduct

(ii) employees who are offered suitable alternative employment or unreasonably refuse such an offer, and

(iii) employees under fixed-term contracts where rights to redundancy
have been excluded by agreement in writing.

Claims made outside a time limit of six months from dismissal will not qualify
unless within that time a claim in writing has been made to the employer direct
or by application to an industrial tribunal or, alternatively, payment has been
agreed or made. A claim for unfair dismissal within this period (noting as stated
above, that application for unfair dismissal has to be made within three months
of dismissal) will also suspend the six-month time limit.

The amount of the redundancy payment is calculated as follows:

(a) one-and-a-half week's pay for each year of employment during all of
which the employee is aged 41 or over,

(b) one week's pay for each year of employment during all of which the
employee is 22 or over, or

(c) half a week's pay for the years between 18 and 21 inclusive.

There is a maximum of 20 years that can count, working back on the above
scales, and the maximum weekly amount of pay for the purposes of the above
calculations is, in 1995, £210. During the final year before retirement age, any
redundancy payment is reduced by one-twelfth for each month by which the
gap closes to the 65th birthday.

An employer must always go about dealing with redundancy fairly,
whether he is making one person redundant or a hundred. There are, however,
recognised procedures that should be followed to ensure such fairness. Some
are obvious and some are less so. Here are the most important ones:

(i) Where there is a union, recognised by the employer, then the
employer must consult with that union before making anybody
redundant.

(ii) The employer must give as much warning as possible to the
employees concerned. Indeed, where there is a recognised union
and more than ten employees are likely to be made redundant
within 30 days, there must be a minimum of 30 days' consultation
before the dismissals take effect. Similarly, where 100 or more
employees are to be made redundant, the notice period is 90 days.

Unemployment

This subject by itself is huge, and this chapter can only hope to point musicians
in the appropriate direction and to endeavour to cut through the maze of
regulations to the most important points.

The benefits obtainable on being unemployed will depend largely on the
class of national insurance contributions being paid. However, Income Support
is not dependent on national insurance being paid at all – more on that later.
The employed musician who, together with his employer, should be paying
Class 1 contributions, will be entitled to the full benefits, including

Unemployment benefit
Incapacity benefit
Statutory Maternity Pay (SMP)/Maternity Allowance
Housing benefit/Council Tax benefit

Benefit for injuries suffered at work
Various types of pension payment
The Social Fund

The Benefits Agency provides, through all its local offices, a very comprehensive leaflet service, giving details of all the benefits available. It is wise to consult these, since the rules in relation to the payment of national insurance contributions and the entitlements to benefit are complex, littered with pitfalls for the unwary, and constantly changing. Alternatively, the Freeline Social Security may be contacted on 0800 666555 for further advice.

Self-employed or freelance musicians will usually be paying Class 2 contributions (and, in some cases, Class 4 contributions, although these by themselves confer no right to any benefit). Class 2 contributions entitle the musician to a number of benefits, the most important of which are:

Incapacity benefit
Statutory Maternity Pay (SMP)/Maternity Allowance
Housing Benefit/Council Tax benefit
Widows Allowance
(The Social Fund)

Separate from all the types of benefit referred to above is Income Support, to which I have already briefly alluded. Put in its simplest form, Income Support is available to all those people aged 18 or over whose income and capital are below a certain level and who are not working 16 hours a week or more. In special circumstances, Income Support may be paid to those aged between 16 and 17 years.

To claim Income Support, it is necessary to demonstrate that reasonable steps are being taken to find a job. Stringent income and capital limits are laid down, and the applicant must fall within such figures to be eligible for this benefit. However, once eligibility had been established, Income Support can prove to be a passport to other benefits, such as free NHS dental treatment.

SECTION 4

THE LEGAL SIDE

INCOME TAX AND NATIONAL INSURANCE

TREVOR FORD

Few accountants – even the good ones – would attempt to teach the violin in their spare time, and even fewer would inflict their teaching on members of their own family. Why is it, then, that hundreds of musicians still attempt to handle their own taxation affairs, blissfully ignorant of the fact that they may be paying thousands of pounds in unnecessary tax? The Inland Revenue is hardly likely to write with suggestions for successful tax avoidance, nor is the reading of this chapter going to provide a musician with all the expertise he or she needs to challenge dubious rulings by a local tax inspector. So why bother to print this chapter at all? The answer, of course, is that, by understanding the basic rules, a musician ought to be able to arrange his finances in such a way that major disasters are avoided. For those of you who still want to go it alone, what follows may help you to do it better, or may even discourage you from trying. And, if you are not sure that your accountant really understands how the music profession works, why not give him this chapter to read – it might plug a few holes in his knowledge.

Three warnings

It would be an understatement to say that most music students find tax an uninspiring subject. The number of final-year students who miss the opportunity of attending a specialist lecture is evidence of this – and these, of course, are the people who often get themselves into a dreadful mess two or three years later. Similarly, musicians who decide to freelance after a number of years in a contract orchestra or opera chorus rarely look upon sorting out their taxation arrangements as being the first priority. Unfortunately, the Inland Revenue isn't impressed by the excuse that 'I didn't get around to it', and automatic fines are being introduced for self-employed people whose accounts and tax returns are sent in late.

Rule No. 1: As boring as you may find the subject, if you are responsible for your own taxation affairs, do something about it immediately. Waiting until the Inland Revenue has contacted you is too late.

Having made contact with the local Inland Revenue office, you are then faced with the task of declaring your earnings and recording your expenses. The temptation, of course, is to conceal the former and to exaggerate the latter. Don't! Let's imagine that you have been paid in cash for a dozen engagements during the year, and that you have not declared them. Unbeknown to you, an

Inland Revenue inspector asks one of the promoters for a list of the musicians he has employed. Subsequently, you receive a letter from your own tax inspector, asking you for a breakdown of the figure you declared for earnings last year, showing the name of each engager and the amount received. This you supply. Your tax inspector discovers that the cash payment that he has been asked to check is not on your list. What does he do? What he *doesn't* do is write to you to point out that you have missed this particular engagement. Instead, he informs you that he has reason to believe that your earnings list is incomplete. Would you like to reconsider it? You now don't know if (a) he's bluffing, (b) he's discovered one cash date, or (c) he's found out about them all. You have no choice but to confess that you have under-declared your earnings – and the consequences aren't particularly pleasant.

The local tax office can ask for a list of your pupils – and will write to each of them to confirm that the number of lessons you say you have given them matches what is shown in their diaries, and that the amount you say you are charging corresponds with what they say they are paying. They can check your earnings against annual statements submitted by your various employers. They can ask to see your bank statements and your building society books; they know what sort of a car you have and what you paid for it; they know what your house cost and the amount of your mortgage. And, even if you successfully manage to conceal your cash earnings, your bank account will look a little odd if you never need to draw cash to pay for food and clothing.

Rule No. 2: Don't push your luck! Tax inspectors are not stupid, and they are paid specifically to track down people who are evading tax.

You will, sooner or later, meet the musician who has the perfect accountant. This musician never pays any tax, although he is earning twice as much as you are. Each year, this accountant proposes substantial – and unjustified – increases in the musician's expenses, which the Inland Revenue seems to accept without query. The accountant charges very high fees, but seems to be worth the money. Then, one day, our tax-free musician receives a letter saying that his accountant has retired and gone to live abroad. The following week, a letter arrives from the local tax office, informing the musician that the Inland Revenue has reason to doubt the information shown in his accounts for the past six years. And, of course, there is little point blaming the situation on the accountant: after all, as the Inland Revenue is always happy to point out, the responsibility for the accuracy of the accounts rests with the individual concerned, not with the professional adviser.

Rule No. 3: Beware of professional advisers who suggest that you should exaggerate your expenses or under-declare your earnings.

The real objective is to pay the minimum amount of income tax, using all the various methods of legal tax avoidance – rather than illegal tax evasion.

Allowances and expenses

There tends to be some confusion about the difference between allowances and expenses. Briefly, expenses are deductions made from an individual's gross earnings to arrive at his net income or profit. Expenses include, for example, instrument maintenance, travel costs and professional subscriptions. Allowances, on the other hand, are fixed by the Government, and are allowed in the tax year in which the income is taxed. Under this heading are found such items as personal allowance, married couple's allowance and age allowance; that is, items relating to personal circumstances, rather than to business activities. Pension contributions are also treated in this way.

There are considerable differences in the range of expenses which may be claimed by self-employed people (taxed under Schedule D) and employed people (taxed under Schedule E). The reason for this is to be found in the careful wording of the appropriate tax legislation. To be allowable, expenses claimed under Schedule E must be incurred 'wholly, exclusively and necessarily in the performance of [the taxpayer's duties]'. Expenses claimed under Schedule D, however, must be 'wholly and exclusively' for the purposes of the profession'. The matter hinges on the word *necessarily.* Whereas a self-employed musician who spent £100 on sheet music, £150 on a tape recorder to record her practice sessions, and £20 every two months on a haircut would have little difficulty in claiming these items as business expenses, the musician who is employed might well find that none of these items was considered to be necessary expenditure for the carrying on of her employment – in other words, she would still be able to perform her duties without them. Her claim could, in consequence, be rejected by the Inland Revenue.

The employed musician finds that there are very few expenses that may be successfully claimed. Those generally allowed include:

(a) *Instrument repairs and tuning* This includes reeds, strings and all usual maintenance. See also the section on *capital allowances* for relief of the cost of instruments.

(b) *Professional clothing* This will include dress suits,etc., but not ordinary clothing worn for professional work.

(c) *Travelling expenses* Only expenses incurred while working are allowable – not expenses in getting to the place of work. For example, a musician employed by a local authority to give school demonstration recitals will be able to claim the cost of transport between schools, if this is not reimbursed by the employer, but not the cost of getting to the first school from his home, nor the cost of returning home at the end of the day. It may, however, be possible to claim 'home to work' travelling if the musician has more than one source of income.

(d) *Subscriptions to professional associations*

(e) *Interest on loans* (but not on overdrafts or credit cards) for the purchase of instruments.

Occasionally, fixed expenses deductions are negotiated with the Inland Revenue for all members of a particular organisation (a contract orchestra or an opera chorus, for example). This makes life easier for all concerned and, as a concession, the deductions so negotiated tend to be on the generous side. Where no fixed deduction exists, the individual musician is left to negotiate with the Inland Revenue himself. Once agreed, expenses are usually allowed by an increase in the PAYE code number (see below), which instructs the employer to deduct less tax.

The self-employed musician finds himself in a position where negotiation with the tax inspector is more often necessary. The following expenses, however, are almost invariably allowed:

(a) Sheet music and books

(b) Recordings CDs and tapes may be claimed, for reasons of professional research: learning new repertoire, listening to other performers, and so on.

(c) *Instrument repairs and tuning*

(d) *Fees paid to other musicians* including accompanists' fees and deputies' fees.

(e) *Coaches' and repetiteurs' fees*

(f) *Travelling expenses* All expenses incurred inconnection with business activities will be allowed, including travelling to professional engagements, to rehearsals, to music shops, etc. Travel may be by public transport (including taxis), or by use of a private vehicle. If a car is used, it is usual to claim for all running expenses, including tax, insurance, repairs, petrol, parking, car washes and subscriptions to one of the motoring organisations, and to deduct an agreed percentage for private use.

(g) *Hotel expenses,* including breakfast when connected to an overnight stay, but not the cost of meals when away from home (although the Inland Revenue can often be lenient here), and not the cost of entertaining, even if involving an overseas client or promoter.

(h) *Professional clothing*

(i) *Dry cleaning and laundry,* where this relates to special clothing for professional use.

(j) *Hairdressing and cosmetics* for public performances.

(k) *Subscriptions to professional associations*

(l) *Telephone,* including regular domestic bills, phonecards or payphones, and the costs of a mobile telephone.
Fees paid to a diary service may also be claimed.

(m) *Postage and stationery*

(n) *Advertising and publicity,* including brochures, publicity photographs and advertisements in magazines and newspapers.

(o) *Agents' fees*

(p) *Instrument insurance,* and a percentage of your house contents insurance, insofar as it covers business items such as audio equipment, music, books, dress clothes, etc.

(q) *Professional magazines and newspapers*

(r) *Concert tickets,* to enable you to hear new repertoire, listen to other performers, and generally keep in touch with the development of the profession.

(s) *Interest on loans* (but not on overdrafts or credit cards) for the purchase of business equipment, including instruments and cars.

(t) *Accountant's fees*

(u) *Use of home as studio or office* If part of a private house is used for business purposes, a proportion of household expenses (i.e. heating and lighting, rent and Council Tax, insurance, decorations) may be claimed. However, if part of the house is used *exclusively* for business purposes, this may give rise to a liability for capital gains tax when the house is sold.

(v) *Salary paid to spouse* If a musician's wife or husband is either not working or does not have sufficient income to be liable for income tax, then it may be wise to pay them a salary for secretarial assistance. This may then be deducted from the profit in the normal way. However, certain important conditions must be observed: (i) the amount must actually be paid; (ii) the salary must be realistic for the work done; (iii) the annual total must be entered on the tax return as income of the recipient. Also, particularly where the spouse is a pianist, it may be possible to employ them in their professional capacity. For example, a clarinettist who taught privately at home was able to claim a salary paid to his wife as accompanist for his pupils during lessons and at examinations and competitions.

Contrary to common opinion, most medical fees may not be claimed. In *Prince v. Mapp,* a musician claimed £81 paid for an operation resulting from a cut finger. The expense was disallowed, the payment not being wholly and exclusively for the purpose of his profession. However, medical expenses which can be shown to be in connection with musical activities *only* may be worth negotiating: if playing the oboe causes your teeth to fall out, you may well be able to claim the cost of having the problem put right.

Capital allowances

The cost of purchasing instruments, equipment or cars is not an allowable expense under any of the above headings, but is treated separately. *Capital allowances* are granted, and these allow for the expenditure to be claimed over a period of time, rather than solely in the year in which the expenditure is incurred.

A *writing down allowance* of up to 25% of the cost may be claimed in the year in which the item is purchased and, in all subsequent years, a further 25% of the remaining balance may be deducted from profits. When the item is sold, an adjustment is made so that the total allowances granted over the years equal the difference between the purchase and the sale prices of the item. However, should the sale price exceed the purchase price, only the original cost need be declared – any profit is assessable separately under capital gains tax, and then only in the event that total capital gains in the current tax year exceed the lower level for assessment (£6,300 in 1996-97).

Expenditure on instruments and other equipment is pooled, and this simplifies matters considerably. For example, a musician buys a flute in 1996 for £3,200 and claims the 25% writing down allowance. In 1998 he buys another flute for £4,500, and sells the first one for £2,500. In 1999, he buys a piccolo for £1,250. Allowances will be as follows:

			Allowances
1996	Purchase of flute 1	3,200	
	Writing down allowance	800	£800
			===
		2,400	
1997	Writing down allowance	600	£600
			===
		1,800	
1998	Purchase of flute 2	4,500	
		6,300	
	Sale of flute 1	2,500	
		3,800	
	Writing down allowance	950	£950
			===
		2,850	
1999	Purchase of piccolo	1,250	
		4,100	
	Writing down allowance	1,025	£1,025
			=====
	Carried forward	3,075	

Cars costing over £12,000 are subject to slightly different rules, the maximum claim for any year being restricted to £3,000.

If a musician has owned an instrument or other item of equipment before becoming self-employed (for example, as a student), and subsequently brings the instrument into use professionally, he is considered to have incurred expenditure equal to the market value of the instrument on the day on which the instrument is first used in the business. This is of vital importance to students, who can claim the value of their instruments at the start of their professional careers against future tax liabilities. Valuations of all their instruments made by a recognised dealer when they leave college will prevent any dispute, although the Inland Revenue only rarely disagrees with valuations provided by the musicians themselves. Instruments received as gifts from generous friends or relatives may also be treated as though purchased by the musician on the day they are received, and the full cost of an instrument which has been purchased with the help of funds provided by a charity will usually be allowed.

Purchasing instruments, equipment and cars near the beginning of the accounting year should be avoided. By buying the item a few days earlier, capital allowances may be claimed against an earlier year's earnings. For example: a musician who makes his accounts up to 30th September 1997 buys a new instrument on 3rd October 1997. He will not be entitled to claim capital allowances until the tax year 1998-99. Had he purchased the instrument three days earlier, the expenditure would have fallen in an earlier accounting period, and the first 25% of the cost would have been claimable in 1997-98.

Capital allowances do not *have* to be claimed, and there is no point claiming in a year when you have no tax liability anyway. if your earnings are just over the tax limit, you can claim only a part of your entitlement to capital allowances – just enough to eliminate your potential tax bill – leaving the rest of the cost of your instruments and equipment available for claiming in future years.

The computation of income tax

The rules for the computation of income tax are divided up into various classifications, known as *schedules,* and subdivided into *cases,* according to the type of income being assessed. For example, Schedule A deals with profits arising from rents from land or property in the UK. The schedules that the musician is most likely to encounter are (i) Schedule E Case I, dealing with income from employment, and (ii) Schedule D Case II, dealing with income arising from the following of a profession or vocation on a self-employed basis. It is quite possible, and indeed common, to be assessed under both Schedules D and E simultaneously: a musician who is employed as a full-time instrumental teacher by a local authority will almost inevitably be taxed under Schedule E; if she also undertakes a certain amount of freelance work and private teaching, this will be assessed separately under Schedule D.

There are many advantages in having your income assessed under Schedule D, and a considerable amount of confusion exists as to which income may correctly be classed as arising from self-employment. Thus, a freelance musician who is engaged as a part-time professor at a music college may well find that his tax inspector will classify the fees received as income from employment, and will instruct the college to deduct tax, even though the musician is taxed as self-employed for all his other work. However, it is sometimes possible to have a decision such as this reversed, and the intervention of a good accountant is invaluable here.

The rules for the taxation of income from employment are less complicated than those for income assessable to Schedule D, and so these will be dealt with first.

Schedule E

Usually, the employer will operate the *Pay As You Earn* method of tax collection, whereby income tax is deducted at source and paid over to the Inland Revenue by the employer. As explained above, every taxpayer is entitled to certain statutory allowances which are deducted from his earnings before tax is calculated. The amount of the allowances to which an employee is entitled is worked out by the employer after referring to the *tax code* allocated to the employee by the Inland Revenue. This is established by adding together all the allowances and expenses to which the taxpayer is entitled for the year, and removing the final digit. Thus, if the entitlement is to allowances of £3,765, the code number will be 376. The number is usually followed by a letter, H or L for example, indicating whether the employee qualifies for the higher or lower rate of personal allowance. This makes it easier to change code numbers in general should there be an increase in allowances during the course of the tax year, following a Budget or other economic statement by the Government.

On each pay day, the employer will deduct the appropriate proportion of the year's allowances from the employee's earnings (one twelfth if the employee is paid monthly, or one fifty-second if weekly), and tax will be calculated on the balance. At the end of the year, any necessary adjustment will be made by the Inland Revenue.

If the musician has more than one employer, allowances and expenses will usually be allocated to one of them, and the others will operate code BR, indicating that tax at the *basic rate* is to be deducted from all income, thus making sure that there is no chance of the allowances being given twice.

Schedule D

Self-employed musicians are assessed under the rules of Schedule D Case II, which deals with earnings arising from the following of a profession or vocation. The musician will have to prepare annual accounts, and the tax due will be calculated with reference to the profit shown. These accounts may be made up to any date which the musician chooses.

The advantages of being assessed under Schedule D are obvious. First, the musician receives his fees in full and has the use of the money until the tax on it becomes due – this may be almost three years later. Second, the value of the money with which the tax is paid will depreciate in the period between earning it and paying the tax – a £2,000 tax bill may seem a lot to pay in 1997 but may feel a little less like the end of the world by 1999 – and the money saved to pay the tax bill can be invested in the intervening period. Finally, as has already been explained, the expenses which may be claimed under the rules of Schedule D are far more wide-ranging than those which are allowed under Schedule E.

Self-assessment In the year 1996-97, the new self-assessment scheme is introduced, and this fundamentally changes the way in which income tax is calculated, and when it becomes payable. The rest of this section explains the law as it will be under the new regime. The system is quite complex, and may not, at first, be easy to understand. If what follows seems to make little sense, please ask your accountant to explain it to you. If you have no interest in how the sums are worked out, feel free to skip to the next section.

The first tax returns under the new system will be issued in April 1997, and will relate to the year ending 5th April 1997. These returns must be filed with the Inland Revenue by 31st January 1998, together with information taken from the accounts for the year ending in the fiscal year 1996-97: in other words, all accounts running to a date between 6th April 1996 and 5th April 1997 will have to be submitted with the 1997 tax return by the end of January 1998. This pattern will be repeated in all future years. If your accounting year ends on 30th April, you have 21 months to prepare your figures; if your accounts run to 31st March, you have only 10 months.

The tax payable is also due on 31st January. There will be no tax assessments: all the calculations under the new system will be made by the taxpayer or by his or her accountant. Alternatively, it is possible to ask the Inland Revenue to make your tax calculations for you, but in this case the return has to be filed four months earlier, by 30th September. Tax returns submitted late automatically incur a penalty of £100.

Interim payments In most cases, payments on account (interim payments) will be due on the preceding 31st January and 31st July, based on the tax liability for the previous year – the amount of each interim payment is half the previous year's tax liability. Interim payments are not required where the previous year's tax bill was very small, and the interim payments will be reduced to half the actual liability where it can be shown that the normal interim payments would be excessive.

The following table shows how to calculate the year of assessment and the due dates for payment of tax from the date of the accounts.

Accounts made up to any date between	Year of assessment will be	Interim payments due 31 January & 31 July	Final payment due 31 January
6.4.96 and 5.4.97	1996-97	1997	1998
6.4.97 and 5.4.98	1997-98	1998	1999
6.4.98 and 5.4.99	1998-99	1999	2000
6.4.99 and 5.4.00	1999-2000	2000	2001

There will normally be two payments due on 31st January each year, therefore: the final, top-up payment of the previous year's liability, and the first interim payment on account of the current year's liability.

Let's take a practical example: A musician makes his accounts up to 31st December each year. His 1997 accounts produce a tax liability of £6,666, and his 1998 accounts result in a liability of £8,000. The 1997 accounts fall within the year of assessment 1997-98, and the final tax payment will be due on 31st January 1999. The 1998 accounts fall within the year of assessment 1998-99, and the final tax payment will be due on 31st January 2000. On 31st January 1999, he will have to pay the full liability for 1997-98, which is £6,666 (assuming, for the sake of argument, that there were no interim payments in 1998). At the same time, the first interim for 1998-99 will be due, and this will be half the liability for 1997-98, or £3,333. The total payment due on 31st January will be £9,999, therefore. On 31st July 1999, the second interim for 1998-99 will be due, also for £3,333. On 31st January 2000, the tax on the profits for the accounting year ending 31st December 1998 will be payable, after deducting the two interims, and the sum of £8,000 – £6,666 = £1,334 will be due. On the same date, the first interim for 1999-2000 will have to be paid, based on half the liability for 1998-99, resulting in a further payment of £4,000, and making a total payment of £5,334. The second interim, due on 31st July 2000, will be for £4,000. On 31st January 2001, the tax based on the accounts for the year ending 31st December 1999 will be payable, after deducting the interim payments of £8,000 made in the year 2000.

The transitional year The year 1996-97 is a transitional year. Tax payments due on 1st January and 1st July 1996 will have been paid, under the old system, on profits based on accounting years ending between 6th April 1994 and 5th April 1995. The first set of interim payments, due on 31st January and 31st July 1997, will, in most circumstances, be the same as the payments made in 1996. The profits of the two accounting years ending between 6th April 1995 and 5th April 1997 will then be averaged to produce the assessable tax liability for 1996-97 under the new system.

Returning to the previous example, the musician making his accounts up to 31st December 1994 will pay tax in equal instalments on 1st January and 1st July 1996 under the old system. On 31st January and 31st July 1997, he will pay the same amounts again. His profits for the years ending 31st December 1995 and 1996 will then be averaged to produce the final liability for 1996-97, and the tax will be due on 31st January 1998, less the two interim payments already made in 1997.

Copyright royalties

Royalties received by composers and other musicians are normally treated as income under Schedule D Case II. If the composer has spent more than 12 months in writing the composition, special rules apply to enable the tax to be spread over a number of years:

    (a) *Lump sums received on assignment of copyright about time of first publication,* and

    (b) *sums receivable within two years of first publication other than lump sums* If the period of work has not exceeded 24 months, one-half of the payment is treated as being received on the actual date of receipt, and the other half is treated as having been received 12 months earlier. If the period of work exceeded 24 months, one-third is treated as being received on the actual date of receipt, one-third as having been received 12 months earlier, and the remaining one-third has having been received 24 months earlier.

(c) *Lump sums received ten or more years after first publication* If the assignment is for a period of at least two, but less than six, years, the payment may be spread by equal annual instalments from the date on which the payment became due, the number of instalments being equal to the number of years of the period. If the assignment is for six years or more, the payment may be spread in a similar way over six years.

Overseas earnings

Special provisions relate to earnings from engagements overseas. These are complicated, and only the broad details are given below.

If a musician who takes up foreign employment is absent from the UK for a continuous period of 365 days or more, no liability for UK income tax will arise on his earnings overseas. He is allowed to spend in the UK (a) up to 62 consecutive days or (b) up to one-sixth of the total number of days spent abroad, without affecting his entitlement to this relief.

Self-employed musicians who accept freelance engagements abroad must declare their overseas earnings in the usual way, converting their fees to sterling using the appropriate rate of exchange. Of course, all expenses incurred in carrying out the engagement are allowed as deductions, including the cost of travel where this is not provided by the engager. If the fee received has foreign tax deducted from it, it is almost always possible to have this tax set against the UK income tax bill, so that the amount of tax paid is no more than it would have been if the engagement had been in the UK. It is extremely important to obtain some sort of payslip or tax deduction certificate as proof of the overseas tax, showing the gross amount of the fee, the tax deducted, and the net amount paid.

Keeping records

Musicians are notoriously bad at keeping records, and this partly accounts for the fact that many members of the profession pay too much tax.

Well-kept records have three advantages. First, the preparation of accurate end-of-year accounts, either by an accountant or by the musician himself, will be made much easier. The musician who has to rely on memory when listing his past year's expenses will inevitably forget some items, and these may mount up over a period of years to a considerable sum. Second, should a dispute arise with the Inspector of Taxes, the musician who can produce documentary evidence in support of his figures is in a far better bargaining position than the person who only produces an untidy diary and a shoe-box full of payslips. Third, accountants do not enjoy sifting through heaps of screwed-up petrol bills, credit card vouchers and till receipts, and consequently charge high fees when obliged to do so. Musicians who are registered for VAT, and who have thus been

		RECEIPTS					PAYMENTS			
1996						1996				
Feb	16	AB Orchestra	12	150	00	Feb	16	Petrol	10	17	50
	17	Teaching fees		15	00			Reeds	11	8	00
	18	BBC	16	25	50		17	Insurance	13	105	00
	21	XY School – fee	20	65	00			Taxi fare		5	50
		– expenses		5	50		18	Accountancy	14	264	38
	23	Sale of oboe		850	00			Dress shirt	15	24	99
	24	CD Orchestra	23	90	00			Concert ticket		6	50
								Bus fares			75
							19	Telephone	17	80	70
								Music	18	10	50
							21	Petrol	19	17	00
							22	Hotel Bill	21	35	00
							23	Brochure printing	22	75	00
								Fares		1	30
								Postage			88
							25	Gas bill	24	89	50

forced to keep legible records, have often found that both their tax bill and their accountant's bill have been reduced.

In their simplest form, a musician's records may consist of a small book with income entered on the left hand pages and expenditure on the right, and a file in which payslips, receipts and bills are kept in corresponding order. Suitable account books, known technically as *cash* or *single-cash* books, may be purchased from any stationer, and it is a good idea to buy two so that records can still be kept while the accountant is preparing the annual accounts. A typical account book might look like the table above.

The space next to the figures column is for reference numbers, and this may be used to cross-reference entries in the book to the relevant payslips and receipts; if you have just spent three hours putting your receipts in order when the cat knocks the whole lot off the kitchen table, you may well regret not having numbered them in the first place.

In-depth investigations and back duty

If the Inland Revenue suspects you of evading tax, your tax inspector will usually start his enquiries by asking you or your accountant a few searching questions about the figures you have sent him. He may also propose disallowing some of your expenses. The next stage will involve a request to see your records, your bank statements, your building society accounts, and so on. Your inspector is looking for evidence either that you have received money which you have not declared, or that you are claiming expenses which you have not actually incurred or which you should not be claiming. If you find yourself becoming involved in what is known as an 'in-depth investigation', make sure that you have an accountant to represent you – if you subsequently end up being invited to your local tax office to meet your inspector, and you decide to go alone, you may well find yourself in a very difficult position, having to cope with questions which, had you had time to consider, you might have answered differently. However, if you are confident that you have behaved honestly, don't be tempted to admit to a few fictitious misdemeanours, just to get the inspector off your back – it doesn't work.

If you have been evading tax on a large scale for some years, and the Revenue finds out, you may find yourself the subject of a major investigation. These 'back-duty investigations', which can last for years and may go back to the commencement of business, are extremely unpleasant and almost invariably result in the payment of large amounts of extra tax, interest, and a fine. Should you find yourself the subject of such an investigation, the only sensible thing is to be completely honest and to co-operate with the Inland Revenue as far as possible. Any further attempts at concealment will result in very heavy penalties.

National insurance contributions

No-one, not even the Department of Social Security, seems to understand the national insurance rules as they apply to musicians. The problems arise because so many musicians are simultaneously employed and self-employed, while others, who are treated by the Inland Revenue as fully self-employed for tax purposes, still find national insurance deducted from their pay cheques. A brief description of the four types of national insurance contribution follows:

Class 1 contributions These are calculated as a percentage of gross earnings and are deducted at source by employers under the PAYE scheme. As a general rule, Class 1 is only payable by employed people, but certain orchestras and opera and ballet companies, together with many educational establishments, deduct Class 1 contributions from everyone who works for them.

Class 2 contributions are payable by self-employed people, either quarterly in arrears, or by monthly direct debit from a bank account. If earnings are below a certain limit, the DSS will issue a small earnings exception certificate, and contributions do not then have to be paid.

Class 3 contributions are voluntary, and may be paid by people who would not otherwise be making regular contributions, to enable them to qualify for certain Social Security benefits.

Class 4 contributions These are extra, earnings-related contributions payable by self-employed people, and are assessed as a percentage of profits above a certain limit. For example, for 1996-97, Class 4 contributions are charged at 6% on profits between £6,860 and £23,660.

It is quite possible, and indeed common, to pay Class 1, Class 2 and Class 4 contributions all within the same year, and this is why so much confusion arises. The Government, via the DSS, sets maximum contribution levels and, if an individual's total contributions exceed this maximum, he will be entitled to a refund. This is usually dealt with automatically by the DSS when only Class 1 contributions are involved. However, the situation is far more complex for self-employed people, and many musicians actually end up paying more than they should.

What, then, can you do to ensure that the DSS does not end up with more money than it is entitled to? The following advice should be helpful:

1 Make sure that anyone who deducts national insurance from you has your correct national insurance number, otherwise the contributions will not be credited to your account.

2 If you are self-employed and do not qualify for small earnings exception, pay your Class 2 contributions on time. It is not always possible to pay late contributions at the rate which was in force when they should have been paid, and you may well find yourself paying old contributions at the current year's rate.

3 If Class 1 contributions have been deducted from occasional earnings which you have included in your self-employed accounts, *and* you have been assessed for Class 4 payments on those accounts, you can apply for a refund of Class 4 contributions to compensate for the fact that you have been charged on the same earnings twice.

4 If you regularly pay Class 1 contributions on Schedule D (self-employed) income, you should apply for *deferment.* To avoid the lengthy process of first paying too much and then having to apply for a refund, the DSS will defer charging *any* Class 4 contributions until your correct liability has been ascertained. If your Class 1/Schedule D income is substantial, deferment may also be granted for Class 2 contributions. Should you be awarded Class 2 and Class 4 deferment, deduction of Class 1 contributions will continue as usual, but you will not be expected to pay Class 2 contributions, neither will you be assessed for Class 4 payments. As before, the DSS will wait until all Class 1 contributions have been credited to your account and will then calculate any additional amount due from you.

To apply for deferment, it is necessary to fill in a simple form (a CF359), and leaflet NP18, obtainable from most post offices, includes this form. Alternatively, contact Deferment Group, DSS, Newcastle upon Tyne, NE98 1YX, who will also deal with applications for the refund of overpayments in previous years.

THE MUSICIAN AND VAT

TREVOR FORD

Comparatively few musicians are registered for VAT these days, registration now being compulsory only for persons with an annual 'taxable turnover' of over £47,000, following the 1995 Budget. However, a good number of musicians have retained their registration from the days when the compulsory registration limit was far lower, and others have registered voluntarily. In certain respects, being VAT-registered can have considerable advantages for the musician, and some who deregistered when the registration limit was increased are now finding themselves financially less well off. How, then, can HM Customs & Excise help a musician towards a rather healthier bank balance (or smaller overdraft) than he might otherwise have? This chapter explains the workings of VAT, and sets out the benefits which may result from either compulsory or voluntary registration.

What is Value Added Tax?

Value Added Tax is, as the name suggests, a tax on the value of goods or services. The tax is 'value added' in that the amount of the tax increases as the goods gain in value. This, coupled with the fact that registered persons or businesses are able to claim back the tax which they have paid, ensures that only the ultimate consumer actually pays any tax. Take the following illustration:

Choppit & Co (Timber Merchants) come across a piece of wood which they think would be suitable for making a viola. They value the wood at £100 and agree to sell it to Norman Guarneri & Co (Viola Makers). However, being VAT-registered, Choppit's charge Guarneri's an extra 17½%, and Guarneri's thus pay a total of £117.50. At the end of their next VAT period, Choppit's will have to pay £17.50 to HM Customs & Excise.

Meanwhile, Mr Guarneri discovers that the piece of wood is too good for him, and arranges to sell it to his friend, Neville Stradivari, who has a reputation as a craftsman. Since Guarneri's have spent some time cleaning the wood up and investigating the beauty of the grain, they sell it at a profit, charging Stradivari £150. Being VAT-registered, however, they have to add an extra 17½%, and so they receive a cheque from Mr Stradivari for £176.25. Guarneri & Co must then pay HM Customs & Excise the £26.25 tax which they have charged, but first they can deduct the £17.50 which they paid to Choppit & Co.

Neville Stradivari, who is also VAT-registered, spends a few hours producing a rather splendid viola, and eventually sells it to Fiddlers (Dealers in Fine Instruments). He feels that it is worth £1,000, charges 17½% VAT, and collects his cheque for £1,175. Later, he will pay HM Customs & Excise the £175 VAT charged to Fiddlers, less the £26.25 paid to Guarneri & Co.

Fiddlers put the instrument in their shop window in Soho with a price tag stating that the viola can be purchased for £5,875, this being £5,000 plus VAT at 17½%. In comes Michael Loadzakidz, credit card at the ready, and walks out of the shop with his new instrument and a fingering chart. Fiddlers pay HM Customs & Excise the £875 charged to Mr Loadzakidz, less the £175 paid to Neville Stradivari, and there the story ends: Loadzakidz is not VAT-registered and, therefore, cannot reclaim the tax paid.

The result of all this is that the VAT office is better off to the tune of £875, all of which has been paid by the ultimate purchaser. None of the firms involved with increasing the value of the instrument has been financially affected by the tax, having paid over everything that they have charged and reclaimed everything they have paid, and the amount of tax has been calculated on the maximum value of the goods.

Of course, had our violist been earning enough to take him above the limit for compulsory registration or, indeed, had he registered voluntarily, he would have been able to reclaim the £875 tax charged on his new instrument.

This example illustrates, in the simplest possible way, the workings of VAT. Of course, it is highly unlikely that any registered person or company would be involved in only a single transaction in any tax period, and so the amounts paid to, or claimed back from, HM Customs & Excise at the end of each quarter usually represent the total of VAT charged to customers (called output tax) less the total VAT paid to suppliers (called input tax).

Rates of tax

There are currently (in 1996) three rates of Value Added Tax: the standard rate (17½%), the home fuel rate (8%), and the zero rate. The way the standard rate works is illustrated in the example above, and it is this rate that the musician will most often encounter. Zero-rating is explained in the next section, which should be read in conjunction with the section that deals with exempt supplies.

Zero-rating

Tax is not charged on zero-rated goods, but the manufacturer is allowed to reclaim input tax paid to suppliers, even if this results in his total tax on purchases regularly exceeding his total tax on sales – in which case a refund will be due from Customs & Excise at the end of each VAT period. Among goods and services which are zero-rated are the following:

(a) Most food (but not catering)
(b) Books, printed music, brochures and leaflets (but not stationery or manuscript paper)
(c) The construction of dwellings
(d) Most forms of public transport
(e) Drugs and medicines
(f) Exports of goods outside the European Community
(g) Children's clothing

Exempt supplies

Exempt supplies are often confused with zero-rated supplies because VAT does not have to be charged on either. However, the difference is of considerable importance. Whereas, as was explained in the previous section, making zero-rated supplies does not affect the right to reclaim input tax, making exempt supplies can mean that the registered person may not be able to recover some of the VAT that he has paid out. If this sounds confusing, the following example should help:

A musician who spends two days each week teaching at home will find that he will no longer be permitted to claim back all the VAT that he has paid on his expenses. This is because 'education' appears on the list of exempt supplies. He is thus not required to charge VAT to his pupils, but neither will he be allowed to reclaim any VAT that he has paid on any expenses connected with his work as a private teacher.

A similar problem will arise if a musician is engaged under a contract of employment on a part-time basis. It will not be possible to claim back VAT paid on expenses which relate to the employment, since work undertaken as an employee is outside the scope of VAT.

Items treated as exempt include the following:

(a) The grant of an interest in land (including the sale of private houses and offices, but not including hotel accommodation, holiday lettings and parking facilities)

(b) Insurance

(c) Postal services supplied by the Post Office

(d) Betting, gaming and lotteries

(e) The provision of credit (including hire-purchase and credit sale agreements)

(f) Education provided by schools, universities or colleges, and private tuition by an individual teacher in subjects ordinarily taught in schools, universities or colleges

(g) Services of doctors, dentists, opticians, etc (but not of certain practitioners, including osteopaths and psychoanalysts)

(h) Membership fees to trade unions and professional bodies

(i) Fund-raising events organised by charities, trade unions or professional bodies

Compulsory registration

Following the 1995 Budget, registration for VAT is compulsory for all persons whose taxable supplies have exceeded £47,000 during the previous twelve months – unless they can show that their turnover for the following twelve months will be below the deregistration limit (currently £45,000). The first important consideration is that it is the person, not the business, who is registered. A musician who earns £40,000 in a year from performing, but who increases his earnings by, let us say, working as an accountant in his spare time, is liable for registration if his income thus exceeds £47,000 in total. VAT would then be chargeable on all his business activities, provided they are not zero-rated or exempt. 'Person' may include an individual, a partnership (a string quartet, for example, where this is treated as a business for tax purposes), a limited company, an association or a charity.

Registration is thus compulsory if, at the end of any month, taxable turnover during the past year has exceeded £47,000. If this is the case, you must notify the VAT office within thirty days of the end of the month, and your VAT registration will come into effect on the first day of the second month after your turnover went above the limit. For example, if annual earnings to 31st March exceeded £47,000, the VAT office would have to be notified by 30th April, and VAT registration would come into effect on 1st May.

Details of the current registration limit may be obtained from any VAT office (listed under 'Customs & Excise' in the telephone directory), and the leaflet 'Should I be registered for VAT?' is worth getting if you are likely to have to register compulsorily.

It is extremely important that 'taxable turnover' is calculated accurately. It should include income from all business activities, including amounts received as expenses, any sideline activities (letting a holiday caravan, for example), and any amounts 'passing through' which may not initially appear to be part of one's own income. If a cheque is received for an engagement undertaken by an ensemble, paid into an individual's bank account and subsequently partly paid out to the ensemble's other members, the total amount of the cheque may count towards the taxable turnover of the individual musician. (If you do not wish to register for VAT, open a separate bank account for ensembles or groups, and ensure that cheques are made payable to the ensemble, and not to an individual member.) However, sales of capital assets (instruments, for example) may be ignored when working out whether or not the registration limit has been reached.

The calculation of taxable turnover should not include exempt supplies and, therefore, sums received for private teaching need not be taken into account; it should, however, include items which are zero-rated (in the unlikely event that you are supplying goods or services on the zero-rated list). Any earnings received under a contract of employment (usually suffering income tax or class 1 national insurance deductions at source) should also be disregarded.

If a person fails to register, he will be treated as though he had been registered from the date on which registration should have taken place. VAT will, therefore, have to be accounted for, even though it has not been charged. This can prove very expensive, and it is consequently advisable to register on time. Attempts to avoid registration altogether are doomed to failure, since the VAT authorities can ascertain taxable turnover easily by asking to see the accounts which have been submitted to the Inland Revenue. There are also substantial fines for evading registration.

Voluntary registration

If total taxable turnover is below the compulsory registration limit, it is still possible to apply to be VAT-registered if it can be shown that the business would suffer if registration was not allowed. Voluntary registration is worth considering if you are planning to spend large sums of money on instruments or equipment on which VAT will be charged, or even if your bills for, say, car repairs or advertising are high. However, once registered, it is not possible to cancel the registration for two years.

Charging VAT on earnings

It is compulsory to begin keeping VAT records (see below) and to charge VAT as soon as registration becomes legally necessary. This might well be before a VAT number has been allocated by the VAT office, in which case VAT should be added to invoices for work done (although it must not be shown separately). Proper receipted VAT invoices must then be sent out for this work after the registration number has been notified.

Once you are fully registered, you must issue tax invoices to all other registered persons or organisations. These invoices have to show:
  (a) an identifying number,
  (b) the tax point (usually the date of the engagement or, if the invoice is for more than one engagement, the date of the invoice or the date of payment, whichever is the earlier),
  (c) your name, address and VAT number,
  (d) the customer's name and address,
  (e) a description of the work (e.g. concert 26th June 1996),
  (f) the fee for the work,
  (g) the rate of tax charged, and
  (h) the total tax payable.
It is not necessary to issue full VAT invoices to persons who are not themselves registered for VAT, although they may ask for them.

Some organisations, including many orchestras, operate 'self-billing'. Under these arrangements, the employer prepares a remittance advice and sends it to the musician with the payment for the work carried out. The employer retains a copy of the remittance advice, and this replaces the VAT invoice which would normally be required from the musician. This saves the employer the job of subsequently collecting VAT invoices from numbers of people with whom it may not be in regular contact. If a self-billing system is in operation, you must *not* make out another tax invoice and send it to the employer concerned: the self-billing invoice is sufficient and it should not be duplicated.

Finally, as was mentioned earlier, any earnings received under a contract of employment are outside the scope of VAT. This means that VAT does not have to be charged on income assessable to schedule E income tax. In general, if income tax or class 1 national insurance contributions are being deducted at source, VAT should not be charged. Do, however, bear in mind that your right to claim VAT on your expenses may well be restricted in these circumstances.

VAT for composers

The rules for composers are no different from those for other musicians, but problems often arise with commission fees, due to misunderstandings of the system. A grant for a commission, paid to an orchestra or ensemble by, for example, a Regional Arts Board, is outside the scope of the VAT regulations – the ensemble has not 'earned' the money (there has been no service or supply of goods), therefore VAT is not applicable. If the Melodious Quartet is paid £1,000 by its RAB for a work by Sally Brown, then the quartet pays the £1,000 straight out again to the composer; the commission money does *not* count as part of the quartet's 'taxable turnover'. Sally Brown, on the other hand, has worked for the money (she has supplied 'goods' to the ensemble) so, if she is VAT-registered, she must charge VAT on top of the £1,000. If the quartet is registered there is no problem: she will invoice them for the VAT (£175 while the rate of VAT is 17½%), and they can claim it back from HM Customs and Excise. If the Melodious Quartet is not registered, Sally Brown may be reluctant to ask them for the VAT, since they will then make a loss on the commission, but the VAT office will then assume that the £1,000 she has earned is inclusive of VAT. She will therefore have to pay £148.94 to Customs and Excise, and put up with a reduced commission fee as a consequence.

Further complications arise when the person paying for the commission in the first place is a business rather than a grant-giving body. In such instances, the ensemble itself may have to 'earn' the commission money by, for example, making free tickets available to the business. The commission now begins to resemble sponsorship, and this might well alter the VAT position: if the commission money is earned by an ensemble that is registered for VAT, it may have to charge VAT to the sponsor – who may not, of course, be registered, and who may not be able to claim it back. It would be best to consult a reputable accountant at the outset to avoid losing part of your commission money unnecessarily.

Sales of second-hand instruments and equipment

There are special rules which may be used when selling second-hand goods, and these can help to avoid substantial tax bills when expensive instruments are sold by VAT-registered musicians to other musicians who are not themselves registered.

In normal circumstances, VAT must be charged on all sales of goods and services, and this means that VAT at the standard rate has to be added to the price of an instrument which is for sale. This is all very well if the purchaser is also registered: the seller will give the purchaser a VAT invoice, and the purchaser will claim back the VAT at the end of the next VAT quarter.

However, the addition of an extra 17½% on to the usual price of the instrument may well be enough to persuade all non-registered purchasers to stay clear, in which case the only solution is to reduce the price to what it would be without the VAT, and then to suffer the tax as a reduction in the profit on the sale.

Under the second-hand goods scheme, VAT has to be charged only on the profit being made on the equipment, rather than on the full selling price. The conditions are (i) that VAT was not claimed when the item was purchased, and (ii) that no VAT invoice is issued when the item is sold.

Here are some illustrations of the various ways in which this can all work, using the example of an instrument which originally cost £8,000 and which is now being sold for £10,000.

First of all, in cases where the purchaser is VAT-registered, there is no point in using the scheme. The price of the item is agreed (£10,000 in this example), VAT is added (£1,750) by the seller, who issues a VAT invoice, and the tax is claimed back by the purchaser. Whether or not the seller paid and reclaimed VAT when the instrument was purchased makes no difference.

In the second illustration, the purchaser is not registered for VAT. The seller bought the instrument for £8,000 plus VAT, and reclaimed VAT of £1,400 at the time. The second-hand goods scheme cannot be used. The purchaser is not prepared to pay more than £10,000, and the seller has to work out the VAT sums on the basis that VAT is already included in this figure. The net sale price is effectively reduced to £8,511, with VAT at 17½% on this (£1,489) taking the total price to £10,000. The seller will have to pay the VAT to the VAT office.

In the third example, the purchaser is not VAT-registered, but the seller did not claim VAT on the original purchase. The second-hand goods scheme can be used, therefore, and VAT is only chargeable on the profit, which is £2,000. The VAT is therefore £350, making the total price £10,350. If the purchaser still will not pay more than £10,000 altogether, the profit is reduced further, the sale price becomes £9,702, the VAT on the profit (£9,702 – £8,000 = £1,702 x 17½%) is £298, and this is the figure that has to be paid to the VAT office – rather less than the £1,489 in the second example.

In cases where the second-hand item is sold at a loss, there is no VAT to be charged at all – provided, of course, that the two conditions for using the scheme are still satisfied.

Claiming VAT on expenses

Once registered, VAT may be reclaimed on all business expenses – but only, of course, where VAT has actually been charged. Items which are either zero-rated or exempt will not include VAT, and neither will goods supplied by traders who are not themselves VAT-registered. So, for example, there is no VAT included in car insurance or in music books in any circumstances, and charges made by a local dry cleaners may well not include VAT if the turnover of the shop is too small to be registered.

To be able to reclaim VAT, invoices must be obtained for all business-related expenses. Purchase invoices should be full tax invoices, unless the total VAT-inclusive amount does not exceed £100, in which case a less detailed invoice is sufficient, such as is issued by many garages for petrol. Tax invoices are not needed for expenditure below £25 on telephone calls from public or private telephones, for purchases from coin-operated machines, or for car park charges.

At the time of registration, VAT paid on equipment purchased prior to registration can be reclaimed, provided the equipment concerned is still being used for business purposes. This enables VAT paid on instruments to be claimed back, even if the instruments were purchased before an application to register was made. A full VAT invoice will be needed, as proof of the VAT paid, however. There is no time limit on this claim: the VAT paid on an item purchased in 1973, when VAT was first introduced, could be reclaimed in 1997, provided the necessary conditions were fulfilled.

Where items are used partly for private purposes, the VAT office will allow only a partial claim of the VAT paid. This will affect such regular expenses as telephone bills. In normal circumstances, the simplest solution is to claim the same percentage as is claimed for income tax purposes, so if 85% of your telephone bill is work-related, only 85% of the VAT on each bill can be claimed.

A proportion of the VAT charged on domestic fuel can also be reclaimed, where a percentage of gas and electricity bills is being set against tax. The calculations are similar to those illustrated for telephone bills, although it is important to remember that VAT is charged at a lower rate on domestic fuel.

As a general rule, VAT paid on the purchase of a car cannot be reclaimed.

Petrol scale charges

Until 1987, VAT on petrol could be reclaimed in the same way as VAT paid on anything else used within a business. If petrol was occasionally used for private motoring, then it was usual to deduct a percentage of the VAT to take this into account. Since April 1987, however, a system has been in force which has probably resulted in more disputes with VAT inspectors than any other single piece of VAT legislation.

To compensate HM Customs & Excise for businesses claiming VAT on petrol used for non-business mileage, a set of scale charges was introduced, replacing the old percentage deductions agreed by individuals with their VAT offices, and effectively disallowing a fixed amount of the petrol claimed each quarter. The scale charges are based primarily on the size of the car's engine and, for example, assume that petrol to the value of £151 is used for private purposes every quarter by a car with an engine of between 1,401 and 2,000cc.

Thus, a musician owning an average-sized car who spends £175 on petrol in a three-month period is allowed to claim back the VAT on petrol to the value of only £24, even if practically all his mileage has been in connection with his business. If the cost of petrol during the quarter has been less than £151, there is no benefit in his claiming back the VAT at all (although he won't be expected to pay the scale charge if he has not claimed for VAT on petrol).

Whilst the scale charges may not be unreasonable for companies whose employees are given free petrol (and, of course, it is the company, not the employee, who pays the scale charge), the charges are extremely unfair for most self-employed people. There is, however, a way round them, although the paperwork involved tends to make many musicians feel that it is really not worth the trouble.

If it can be shown that no petrol used for non-business purposes has been included in the VAT records, then the scale charges do not apply. The only practical way to prove this is to keep detailed records of all business and private mileage, and then to work out the precise percentage of car mileage for each VAT quarter which is not allowable. If this percentage of the VAT on petrol is then deducted from the VAT account for the quarter, no VAT inspector can insist that the scale charges apply. If you decide to adopt this method, you will need to note your car's total mileage on the first and last day of each quarter, and to work out from this the total number of miles you have covered during the three months. If you have kept accurate records of all business and private mileage during the quarter, it should then be quite an easy matter to calculate how much VAT is not claimable.

To give an example: if your total mileage on 1st January is 45,000 and on 31st March is 49,000, you have covered 4,000 miles during the quarter. If your records show that you have driven 3,000 miles on business and 1,000 miles on private motoring, you will not be allowed to claim one-quarter of the VAT on your petrol for the quarter. If you have spent a total of £250 on petrol, which includes VAT of £37.23, you will have to deduct one-quarter of £37.23, or £9.30, from your VAT claim for that quarter. This is far better than the scale charge, which would mean a disallowance of £22.48 for an average car.

Imports and exports

The subject of VAT on imports and exports is appallingly complicated, and there is only room here to look at a few specific situations where some knowledge is needed. If in doubt, consult an accountant or call your local VAT office – although, in the latter case, you will probably get a different answer every time you telephone.

Let's look at the situation relating to imports first. Inevitably, the rules are different, depending on whether the goods are despatched from outside or from within the European Community. Goods arriving from outside the EC will be taxed by Customs on arrival in the UK, and the VAT charged can be reclaimed by a VAT-registered person in the usual way. Goods arriving from another country within the EC will normally arrive with VAT charged by the supplier, unless the purchaser has notified the supplier in advance that he is also registered. In these circumstances, the goods imported into the UK are taxed in the country to which they are sent, rather than in the country from which they originated. If this sounds confusing, then you are right – it is: a musician who is VAT-registered will be required to charge himself the VAT on the goods received, and then to claim it back again! But first, he must make sure that the supplier in the EC country from whom the item is being purchased knows that he is registered in the UK, and that he has his VAT number. As usual, an example should help:

Nick Messifield, an oboist, intends buying a supply of cane, costing the equivalent of £100, from a shop in the south of France. In normal circumstances, VAT would be charged, but Nick is VAT-registered. He therefore notifies his supplier of this fact, and gives him his UK VAT number. The supplier must then supply the goods without French VAT being charged, showing both his own VAT number, and also Nick's VAT number, on the invoice. When the invoice arrives, Nick works out the VAT that should be charged, at the UK standard rate. This is £17.50. At the end of the quarter, this figure is added to the VAT that he has charged on his earnings and on any other sales during the period, and the same amount is also reclaimable as VAT paid. Effectively, whilst both VAT totals for the quarter have been increased by £17.50, no tax has actually changed hands.

The situation for exports is similar. Goods going outside the EC are zero-rated, and so VAT does not have to be charged, but proof of the export must be obtained – usually a Parcel Force customs pack, or an airfreight waybill. VAT must, however, be charged on goods sent to another EC country, unless the purchaser supplies a valid VAT registration number. If the purchaser can prove that he is registered in his own EC country, the sale becomes zero-rated, but the purchaser's VAT number must be shown on the invoice for the goods. Once again, an example should help:

Ifor Tuckbusch arranges to sell a horn to a colleague in Germany for £2,500. In normal circumstances, he would have to charge VAT of £437.50, but the purchaser notifies him of his German VAT number. Ifor is therefore able to sell the horn without VAT, but he must show both his own UK VAT registration number, and also the purchaser's German VAT number, on the invoice.

In simple terms, therefore, VAT should not be charged on goods going outside the EC, or on items going to EC purchasers who are themselves registered for VAT. VAT must be charged on goods sold to non-registered persons in other EC countries.

Goods received from outside the EC will be taxed by Customs on arrival, and this VAT can be reclaimed. Goods received from other EC countries will include VAT, unless you have notified the supplier in advance that you are VAT-registered.

The cash accounting scheme

In the early days of VAT, all calculations were based on something called the tax-point. This is, quite simply, a date – usually the date on the VAT invoice – when the VAT is considered to come into existence. When completing the quarterly VAT return, VAT to be paid or reclaimed was not the tax actually received from engagers or paid to suppliers, but rather the VAT invoiced by, or charged to, the musician, whether or not payment had actually taken place.

For example, a musician working for the Orchestra of St Luke's might invoice the orchestra for some work done on 15th February. If that musician's VAT quarter ended on 31st March, he would have to pay the VAT to HM Customs & Excise, even if he had not been paid by the orchestra, thus being out of pocket until the orchestra actually paid up. On the other side, if the musician had been sent a bill for some equipment before the end of the quarter, the VAT would be reclaimable within that quarter, even if the musician had not actually paid the bill.

This system caused numerous problems for registered individuals. The Government eventually came to recognise this, and introduced the cash accounting scheme for smaller traders. Under the scheme, anyone with a taxable turnover of less than £350,000 can apply to their local VAT office for permission to base their VAT records on payments made and received, rather than on invoice dates. Thus, VAT only becomes payable to HM Customs & Excise when it is actually received from the engager.

The advantages of the scheme are so great that, under almost all circumstances, it is worth joining it immediately on registration. The application form is very straightforward, and membership of the scheme can save considerable amounts of money when confronted by late payers or, of course, non payers.

Records

If a musician is keeping correct records, as described in the chapter **Income Tax and National Insurance**, few modifications will be necessary to take into account the requirements of VAT law. Details of all taxable and exempt supplies must be kept, such as will enable the amount of VAT charged to be calculated easily, as must details of all input tax paid on expenses. This may be achieved by using an account book with three columns on both the receipts and the payments sides: the first column will show the total amount paid or received, the second will be used for VAT, and the third will be the net amount exclusive of VAT (that is, the difference between column one and column two).

Copies of all tax invoices issued must be kept, together with invoices received for purchases.

Every three months, a VAT return must be submitted within four weeks of the end of the tax period. Initially, the VAT office will decide the dates on which your quarterly returns are due, but these can be changed if, for example, it would be more convenient to have one quarter coinciding with the end of your accounting year. Completion of the return involves summarising VAT records for the quarter in question in a special book, or on a special page within the tax records, known as the VAT account. This must show:

    (a) the total of tax charged,

    (b) the total of tax paid, and

    (c) the net amount payable or repayable.

These amounts are entered on the VAT return and the difference between (a) and (b) paid to HM Customs & Excise. If the total input tax exceeds the total output tax, a refund will be paid. The return also has to show certain statistical information – usually just totals of earnings and expenses exclusive of VAT – for each quarter.

A visit from a VAT inspector usually follows some nine months or so after registration to check that correct records are being kept. These visits tend to continue at varying intervals throughout the registration.

Cancellation of registration

If, for any reason, taxable supplies cease, then registration must be cancelled. Registration may also be cancelled voluntarily if annual taxable turnover falls below a certain level (following the 1995 Budget, this is £45,000), but Customs and Excise cannot insist on deregistration simply because earnings are under the current registration limit.

However, if registration is cancelled, the VAT office can assume that all instruments and equipment owned by the musician are sold on the day that the cancellation takes effect (provided that VAT was claimed when the equipment was purchased), and tax must be paid accordingly, unless the total amount involved is below £250.

For example, if Mr Loadzakidz had been registered at the time that he purchased his new viola, he would, as shown above, have been able to reclaim the VAT paid to the shop. If he subsequently applied for his registration to be cancelled, he would have to account for VAT at the rate of 17½% on the value of the instrument at the date that the deregistration came into effect. This can be costly, and it is often worth remaining registered, even after it has become possible to cancel the registration, just to avoid this unexpected tax liability.

The advantages of being registered for VAT are obvious: tax is collected from employers at no cost to the musician, who is then able to claim back the VAT paid on all business expenses. The better records that he will be obliged to keep will make the preparation of his annual accounts easier and these, in turn, will be more accurate, resulting in lower accountants' bills and smaller income tax demands. However, the administration and paperwork involved is, at best, inconvenient, and the temptation to spend the VAT collected from employers before it becomes payable to the VAT office is almost irresistible.

If you are well-organised, able to keep your accounting records up to date, good at putting money aside for future bills, and confident that you can deal with the administration yourself, then voluntary registration may be well worth considering. If, however, you hate paperwork, never know how much is in your bank account, and can't cope with form-filling, stay well clear until your earnings are above the compulsory registration limit – by which time you ought to be able to afford to pay someone else to look after the whole thing for you.

THE LAW OF CONTRACT

LAURENCE WATT

Since 1974, Laurence Watt has been a partner in the firm of Charles Russell in Lincoln's Inn. He acts for a number of professional musicians, including one of London's best-known, self-governed symphony orchestras, and two chamber orchestras. He was responsible for conducting the litigation which confirmed the freelance status of the members of the self-governed orchestras. He is a member of the London Philharmonic Trust, the Hanover Band Trust and the ABO Trust. He is also an amateur horn player.

The law of contract is such that encyclopaedias are barely sufficient to encompass in-depth analysis of its all embracing principles. None can escape its tentacles; the musician who wants nothing more out of life than to make music, still needs to eat and sleep and, accordingly, will need cash to pay for it. He, therefore, has to persuade an audience to pay him money in return for his ability to transport them into his own particular harmonious brand of heaven.

OFFER, CONSIDERATION AND ACCEPTANCE

At the simplest level, the musician makes his services available and the public offers money for him to play. The essence of the contract which is thus formed is the *offer,* the mutual *consideration* (this being the performance in return for either an agreed sum of money or an equivalent benefit), and its *acceptance.* Without these three elements in some form, a contract cannot exist. However, life is never as simple as it appears and, if the law of contract were as straightforward as this, there would be no need for this chapter.

The regulation of the complex web of legal relationships that exists between the musician and his audience devolves down to these three fundamentals, and an understanding of them is, therefore, of prime importance.

Offer

The advertising of a musician's services, in whatever form, is a simple indication to the profession and the world at large of his availability to perform. The first stage in the contractual process is when an offer is made to engage that musician's services. The offer can be in writing, it can be verbal, directly or over the telephone, or it can be inferred from conduct. It must, however, be more than an indication of intent. 'I am planning a performance of *The Pines of Rome,* and I intend to offer you the part of the nightingale' will not, by itself, constitute an offer by a promoter which is capable of acceptance, even though that musician may hold himself available for the performance.

Consideration

Consideration is basically the legal requirement for something of value, not necessarily money, to pass between one person giving and another receiving a 'promise', to make that promise legally enforceable. It is essential that it is reciprocal, but it must also be understood that the law does not require that the thing of value necessarily be adequate. One might make a good deal or a bad one, and the fact that the apparent benefit derived by one party might be hugely greater than that enjoyed by the other is not, in the absence of fraud or misrepresentation, something in which the courts will usually be interested. A member of the public who decided to purchase a ticket to hear Florence Foster Jenkins, expecting an enlightening operatic experience, would have been in for a rude shock, but would not have been able to claim back the price of the ticket.

Acceptance

The offer having been made, and the terms of that offer having been ascertained, the contract is concluded by its unqualified and final acceptance. As with the offer, an expression of intent to accept is not sufficient. A response to the *Pines* invitation above, along the lines 'I intend to accept if my dentist agrees' would not bind the promoter to engage him if the dentist gave him the all clear. Unless the person making an offer has stipulated that acceptance must be in a particular form, it can be verbal (including by telephone), in writing, by post, telex or otherwise. It can also be by conduct: if our colleague turns up for the first rehearsal of *The Pines* (the offer not having been withdrawn) but misses the performance, it will not usually suffice for him to say 'I could not find my teeth but, in any event, you never confirmed acceptance' (but see *frustration* below).

Postal acceptance can be tricky. A decision to use the post must be reasonable according to the circumstances, but if it *is* reasonable, then the acceptance operates from the moment of posting. Furthermore, if that postal acceptance is not received, the contract will still be complete, such that if the date is then offered by the promoter or engager to someone else, then that promoter or engager will still be bound by his contract with the first person. In practice, it would always be sensible in such situations to keep proof of postage, even though 'post' means in the ordinary course of the post. It should be noted that, whilst this rule applies to telegrams, it does not apply to telexes or faxes, where actual communication must be proved.

An offer can be withdrawn at any time prior to its final and unqualified acceptance, although such withdrawal must be communicated to the person to whom the offer was made. This seems an obvious statement perhaps; but a note of caution where acceptance has been by post: in view of the rule that acceptance takes place at the moment of posting, a withdrawal of an offer which is posted *before* the acceptance was posted, but which arrives afterwards, will be too late and the contract will be binding, regardless of that withdrawal.

Finally, in whatever manner they are made, both offer and acceptance must be clear enough to be capable of enforcement.

RULES CONCERNING CONTRACTS IN WRITING

There is a common misapprehension that, to be enforceable, a contract needs to be in writing. As can be seen from the above, a contract, subject to the exceptions mentioned later, can be in any form which will satisfy the basic rules described.

However, there are a number of legal exceptions. The important ones are as follows, where the contracts must be in writing, or evidenced in writing, signed by both parties and where, in some cases, special rules are rigorously applied:

1 *Contracts relating to the disposition of land or an interest in land*
2 *Employment contracts under the employment legislation* Where there exists an employer/employee relationship, it is a requirement of that legislation
   that a written statement of the terms of employment be given to an employee within 13 weeks of employment being taken up. Such a statement does not of itself form the contract; it simply records, and is evidence of, the contract terms.
3 *Consumer credit agreements* There are very strict rules imposed by the consumer credit legislation which regulate comprehensively the supply of credit to individuals. The all-embracing Consumer Credit Act was passed in 1974, covering the ground previously occupied by a jumble of legislation, including the 1965 Hire Purchase Act. Consumer credit agreements are very strictly controlled and have to be in writing. There is, normally, a ceiling of £15,000, but one section of the Act specifically deals with extortionate credit bargains where there is no upper limit on the amounts involved. The rules, insofar as they relate to the lender/hirer, are extraordinarily complicated, very strict and cover such things as –
   (a) cash loans and any form of financial accommodation, which will range from a standard bank overdraft to a mortgage,
   (b) credit sales in relation to goods,
   (c) the supply of services on credit, including cheque cards and credit cards and
   (d) consumer hire agreements, which could include the hire of anything from a bombardon to a video recorder.
   The important facts in relation to these rules as they apply to the musician are:
   (i) such agreements must conform to the particular type of agreement
      they purport to be and which are defined in the Act,
   (ii) they must be signed in the manner prescribed in the Act,
   (iii) they must set out all the terms of the agreement and, as such, be legible. Furthermore,
   (iv) there are detailed provisions for withdrawal and cancellation under particular circumstances – a defined cooling-off period is

provided for, within which a hirer or buyer under a hire purchase, credit sale or conditional sale agreement can cancel that agreement.

4 *Contracts for insurance*

5 *Assignments of copyright* on whatever grounds, and whether in whole or in part, must be in writing and signed by the person doing the assigning.

PARTICULAR TYPES OF CONTRACT

Agency contracts

An agency contract is one where the musician or ensemble (the principal) requests or authorises another (the agent) to act on his behalf, and that other person agrees and acts accordingly. The agent is thereby empowered, within the ambit of his instructions, to enter into a contract on behalf of his principal, and to perform, to compose or to conduct as if he were the principal. It is particularly important to delineate very carefully the actual authority being given to the agent, the type of work to be undertaken, the fee scales to be applied, the agent's own commission, and the limits of authority within which the agent can operate.

There is implied in any general agency agreement (where not dealt with expressly) a power for the agent to incur reasonable expenses to carry out his duties. In the absence of any contrary agreement, there is a duty on the agent to keep a separate account of all money received and expenses disbursed on behalf of his principal (the performer) and to make payment promptly, and there is a duty on the principal to make prompt payment of any commissions due to the agent.

Agents come in various shapes and sizes, ranging from those catering for many musicians, to telephone or diary agents, who keep a diary for orchestral and other musicians and who are thus always available for consultation. Their authority will depend upon what is agreed but, within that authority, a date made for a musician will be binding. Since the very nature of the agency relationship is a personal one, the performer will always be dealing with an individual, whatever the size of the company. The agent's authority will be governed by contractual principles; any arrangements made by an agent on behalf of his principal can be subject to confirmation by the principal only if that is what is agreed at the outset.

Often, an agent will issue a note of confirmation of a date arranged between the agent on behalf of his artist (the principal) and a promoter or engager. There is occasionally argument as to the contractual status of such notes. Unless it is signed by both parties (unlikely), it will simply serve as evidence of a fixture already verbally agreed between the agent and the promoter which, depending on the agent's authority, will bind his client.

An agent will not be liable to the musician in respect of any problems arising between the musician and the engager providing:

(a) he has used proper care and skill in arranging the contract.

Any breach of such a duty of care will potentially render him liable to the musician for any pecuniary loss suffered, and

(b) that it is clear to the promoter that he is contracting with the agent as an agent and not as a principal.

The operations of agencies are restricted by virtue of the provisions of the Employment Agencies Act of 1973 which, whilst not altering the basic agency law, made obligatory as from the 1st July 1976:

(a) the registration of employment agencies and businesses, together with detailed particulars of their operation and affairs. The relevant class of employment listed in relation to musicians is for *performers and other occupations in the entertainment industry*,

(b) the provision by the agency to its clients of a written statement of the current terms under which the business is conducted.

Auctions

Musical instruments, particularly ones of high value, frequently change hands as a result of an auction sale. The contractual principles governing an auction sale are as already set out above. It is important to note that the auctioneer's request for bids is only the 'invitation to treat', and it is the actual bid which constitutes the offer. The formality of acceptance is specifically provided for by statute (Sale of Goods Act 1979 Section 57), which states that a sale by auction is complete on the fall of the hammer – assuming it has not been dropped accidentally. Up to that point, a bid may be withdrawn. A seller at an auction is entitled to fix a reserve price which, if not met, will terminate the sale. It should be noted that, if the auctioneer makes a mistake and purports to accept a bid below the reserved price, he can still withdraw the item from sale. The auctioneer is also entitled to bid himself, providing the right to do so has been expressly reserved; otherwise, any sale where this happens may be treated as fraudulent by the buyer, entitling him to repudiate his acceptance of the bid and thus his contract.

Freelance contracts and contracts of service

The real distinction is between a contract *for services* and a contract *of service*. The former category governs the relationship that exists between players and, for example, the four self-governed symphony orchestras in London, and *ad hoc* orchestras and smaller ensembles across the country. The fact that such players are not employed in the statutory sense of the word, does not mean that they are not working under a contract. An engagement for a single session is as binding as for a series of engagements. A common practice is to present a schedule of firm dates to the players for a forthcoming period. This constitutes the offer for those dates which apply to the particular player. The acceptance of all, or (with the agreement of the promoter) a proportion of, the dates for the relevant fee and conditions will represent the conclusion of the contract. If a player, having confirmed his availability, fails or refuses to turn up to a particular session in such a list, he will be in breach of contract.

Contracts with persons under a disability

English law defines four groups which come within this heading:

1 Minors
2 Drunken persons
3 Married women
4 Mentally disordered persons

Since married women are now largely emancipated from their traditional restrictions, their position is not of concern in relation to the subject matter of this article. Furthermore, whilst mental disorder may well be a matter of subjective and strongly-held opinion from person to person, the clinical state to which this category refers again takes us away from practical realities for our purposes. This leaves us with categories 1 and 2.

Drunken persons It cannot be a frequent occurrence that a contract is purported to be concluded when one or both parties are in a state of complete intoxication. If it is, the courts will say of the affected party that he is 'of no agreeing mind' and that the contract is void accordingly – unless later ratified when sober.

Minors In view of the prodigious musical talents of mere babes in arms that one from time to time comes across, it is necessary to consider the validity of contracts sought and made with persons under the age of 18. The general rule is that no contract made with a minor is absolutely binding, except a contract for what are termed *necessaries*. Necessaries are defined as being things 'necessary and suitable for the condition and life of the infant'. For example, contracts for the repayment of money by a minor and contracts for goods supplied are regarded as absolutely void unless they are necessaries. Necessaries can, under certain circumstances, include legal or medical services.

A logical extension of this principle is that a minor can bind himself to contracts of apprenticeship, education and instruction which must be beneficial to him. Whilst some, especially the minor, might dispute what a court would regard as being fair and beneficial, such a contract has to be so regarded in relation to the minor when he enters into it. For a musician, the purchase of an instrument, subject only to the reasonableness of the terms of that purchase, would probably be regarded as coming within the category of necessaries.

There are categories of contract which a minor can enter into which, whilst strictly invalid, can be ratified and confirmed within a reasonable time of the minor achieving majority. These relate to land, marriage, partnership and share purchase.

PERFORMANCE, VARIATION, TERMINATION AND REMEDIES

Performance and breach

A contract having been entered into, all the parties concerned must perform that which they have undertaken to do at the appropriate time and in the manner intended. Frequently, a contract may provide for flexibility in performance. A promoter engaging an orchestra to perform *The Pines of Rome* may reserve the right to substitute an alternative work of equivalent orchestration (difficult!). If he substitutes a Haydn symphony, he will be in breach of his contract and will be liable to pay for any loss and expenses incurred by the orchestra as a result of the change. The orchestra will have included the larger work in its schedule and, assuming all those regular players and any extras have accepted the date, would in turn be bound by those individual contracts – our nightingale's peculiar talents make him quite unsuitable for anything else other than Leopold Mozart's Toy Symphony, and he would have to be compensated accordingly.

Contract terms are either fundamental (as above) or of less significance in relation to the whole performance of a contract. In a contract to perform, clearly the time of attendance for rehearsal and performance is vital. Failure by a player to attend a rehearsal would entitle the promoter, be he the orchestra itself or an independent entrepreneur, to treat the contract as at an end and to employ a substitute player. An alteration of the dress requirements or the venue for a performance is unlikely to be fundamental, and would only entitle a performer, inconvenienced by such change, to compensation for any extra costs he might incur as a result of the change.

Variation

A contract can always be varied in its terms (whether such a variation is fundamental or otherwise) by agreement between all parties. If there is a unilateral variation, such as a change of date by a promoter or the cancellation by a record company of a recording session, this will represent a breach of contract with the performer. A lawful variation can only be by mutual agreement within the contract.

If a performer or ensemble refuses or fails to perform a contract, thus repudiating it or being in fundamental breach, the courts in this country will not insist that the contract is carried out. They will only compensate the aggrieved party with damages for any loss and expense arising since, as a matter of principle, the courts will only enforce a contract for services under the most exceptional circumstances. It is arguable whether this would be extended to forcing an orchestra to comply with its contractual obligations to play at a particular place and time. The resolution of that argument may well depend on the make-up of the orchestra itself; the position with one of the freelance self-governed orchestras may be very different to that of an employed orchestra, such as those coming under the auspices of the BBC. So far as I know, the position of an orchestra in such a situation has never been tested.

Frustration and force majeure

This might, under different circumstances, be regarded as a definition of a subject more appropriate to a criminal text book. However, a contract may be terminated by fundamental circumstances beyond the control of either the musician or the promoter or agent. Strike, civil war, riot, tempest, flood, sickness are all typical conditions referred to by lawyers as *force majeure*, or simply *frustration*. In 1956, the following legal test was formulated by the House of Lords: 'frustration occurs whenever the law recognises that, without default of either party, a contractual obligation has become incapable of being performed because the circumstances in which performance is called for would render it a thing radically different from that which was undertaken by the contract.'

The contract itself terminates on the occurrence of the frustrating event. The legal consequence of such a situation used to be that the loss lay where it fell; payments advanced were irrecoverable, as were payments due. In 1943, a law was passed to remedy the patent unfairness of this situation. Although a contract can, and frequently does, provide for what is to happen upon frustration, the law now requires that, unless otherwise provided for, all sums paid or payable shall respectively be repayable or cease otherwise to be payable. There is an exception, however, that where reasonable expenses have been incurred, a contracting party can keep or recover compensation accordingly. It is worth noting that, if a contract is frustrated at a point (and for different reasons) *after* a breach has already taken place, the party responsible for the breach may still be liable in damages.

The importance of this aspect of law to the musical profession comes into particular prominence

(a) where a performer is sick or otherwise incapacitated from performing for reasons demonstrably beyond his control, and

(b) when considering some of the overwhelming problems that can occur with foreign tours by artists and orchestras. It is, however, important to ensure that any contract for such a tour is governed by English law, otherwise the statute referred above will not apply. This is fine if all fees and expenses have been paid in advance, but potentially disastrous otherwise.

MISTAKE, MISREPRESENTATION AND FRAUD

Mistake

A contract entered into as a result of a mistake will be void. Such a situation is very rare, since the word 'mistake' is so narrowly defined. A mistake must be mutual and go to the very root of a contract and, in any event, must be one of fact rather than law. It must be much more fundamental than a situation where, for example, our nightingale discovers that it is not intended that he should use his peculiar personal talents, but simply press the button on a tape recorder. The only circumstance where this would not be correct would be where the performer of the nightingale had become so famous, or notorious as the case may be, for his talents that the audience were coming to hear *him* as opposed to *The Pines of Rome*. In that event, the following two headings could have some relevance.

Misrepresentation

This is a subject governed by the common law and statute, and basically means what it says. If a person is induced to enter into contract as a result of a misrepresentation of fact by the other party, whether fraudulent or innocent, express or implied, then he will be entitled to reject the contract. To that extent it will be void. He may, however, affirm it after discovery of the true facts and, if he does so, the contract will be valid and enforceable. As with most other areas of contract law, it has convolutions (convulsions even) and intricacies of interpretation which are beyond the scope of this article.

Fraud

A contract induced by the fraud of one party will, as with misrepresentation, be voidable. In other words, it can be rejected by the aggrieved party unless he chooses to affirm it. If the audience turning up to hear Florence Foster Jenkins had been induced to attend by extravagant comments concerning her prowess as a coloratura soprano, there will certainly have been a misrepresentation, possibly even a fraud – but I don't think anyone would have minded ...

A PRACTICAL GUIDE TO COPYRIGHT LAW

RUTH ORCHARD

Ruth Orchard qualified as a solicitor in private practice in 1977. After a period of general experience in the law, she began to specialise in commercial litigation and became a partner in a firm in Chancery Lane. She then joined the Performing Right Society in October 1983 and, until 1991, held the position of Company Secretary with responsibility for the overall legal protection of members' interests. She has now returned to private practice.

This chapter will be of use to those who need a working knowledge of copyright law, both as creators and as users of music. It will also explain some of the main points to be considered by anyone who wishes to perform or otherwise use copyright music and associated lyrics or to offer his own works to others for publication, performance, recording or broadcasting.

In practice, there are problems for copyright owners in trying to enforce their rights, and for music users in ensuring that these rights are respected. Unlike a manufacturer of goods, a composer of music cannot withhold supply of his work as a way of negotiating better terms once it has been made available to the public and, indeed, his livelihood depends upon the widest possible exposure. Music is particularly difficult to protect, both by its very nature, and also given the technological advances which have provided sophisticated methods for its widespread reproduction and dissemination. For example, the legal implications of the use of music on the Internet have yet to be resolved! There is an ever-increasing risk of piracy, such as recordings of high quality being made of a live concert which are then readily marketable without payment of royalties to the composers and/or publishers of the music, out of whose talent and investment the profit will be made (the *Live Aid* piracy problem is but one example). Unauthorised 'sampling' of existing recordings (to produce a work in recorded form consisting of drumbeats from one, guitar riffs from another, with a monotonous vocal 'rap' added on top) is no longer the problem it was. It is established practice now for samplers to seek the necessary permissions. However, many ordinary people may inadvertently break the law through ignorance, and deprive composers of income, for example, by making photocopies of musical scores for the church choir, or by taping from the radio for use as background music to a theatrical production. No actual profit may be made in such circumstances, and the unauthorised use of the music in each case may not be widespread, but eventually such consistent lack of reward for those whose works are being freely used would have consequences no music-lover would wish to see. With little or no incentive, new works would cease to be created, concert promoters, publishers, broadcasters and record companies would go out of business for lack of musical talent, and in the long term the nation's culture would suffer. It is, therefore, very much in the interests of everyone involved in the music world to be aware of his own legal rights, and to respect the rights of his fellows.

THE NATURE OF COPYRIGHT

First, a word of warning: copyright is a complex area of law, and legal advice should be sought if there are any doubts about rights or obligations in a particular situation. The legal principles discussed here are embodied in the Copyright, Designs and Patents Act 1988. The Act governs copyright law in the United Kingdom which has evolved during a period which, significantly for the musician or composer, has seen the invention of the gramophone record, radio and television, cable and satellite transmissions, tape recorders, computers, and DAT and photocopying machines.

Historically, the first right which was recognised by law for a creator was the right to prevent others from copying his work without his permission, hence the term *copyright*. However, given all the developments which have occurred since that right was first legally recognised, the copyright in a work now embraces several different rights, including the exclusive right to perform the work in public, to broadcast it, or to publish it.

Copyright is a right of ownership, and the owner can license, assign or bequeath copyright in his works, wholly or in part, much as he might lease, sell or bequeath all or part of a piece of land. In effect, the owner of the copyright, usually at first the creator of the work, has the exclusive right to do and to prevent anyone else from doing those things without seeking and obtaining his permission, for which, in turn, the copyright owner is entitled to negotiate terms as to payment.

DURATION OF COPYRIGHT

Until 1995, copyright protection in the United Kingdom lasted for the lifetime of the creator and for fifty years after the end of the calendar year in which he died. Any work in copyright in the European Union on 1st July 1995 will be protected in all EU territories for seventy years after the end of the year in which the author died. At the time of going to press, it is understood that the European directive embodying this harmonisation of the period of copyright protection will not come into effect by enactment in the UK until at least November 1995. Works, the copyright in which has expired between these dates, will therefore come back into copyright in the UK on the November date.

There are additional provisions in UK copyright legislation relating to duration of copyright in works of joint authorship, anonymous works and posthumous works (i.e. those unpublished or unperformed until after the creator's death). If a work was in copyright before the 1988 Act came into force, there are also various transitional provisions which apply to the copyright period. Even if the work itself is no longer protected by copyright, a publisher may still own the copyright in the typography and layout. This protection lasts for twenty-five years from the date of first publication. Therefore, it is always important to check this aspect thoroughly when planning to perform or otherwise exploit a work; for example, even if the original work is no longer protected by copyright law, a later arrangement of it may still be in copyright.

COPYRIGHT PROTECTION

Copyright arises automatically when a work is recorded, in writing or otherwise, such as a manuscript score or a tape recording. There is no copyright in an idea, in a title as such, or in a tune which someone whistles in the street. However, no actual formalities are required in order for copyright to subsist once a work is 'recorded' and fulfils the other conditions in the Act to qualify for copyright protection (see below). It is common practice, however, to use the symbol © with the name of the copyright owner beside it on, for example, printed scores of the work, which will indicate the person (or company) from whom permission must be sought. It can also be important to prove the date on which copyright protection commenced. There are several methods by which this can be done (see *Conclusion* below).

The Act defines a 'musical work' for the first time (previous legislation did not); to paraphrase, it is 'a work consisting of music, exclusive of any words or action intended to be sung, spoken or performed with the music'. The words and music in a song are therefore protected as two separate copyrights, the lyrics being a 'literary' work and the music being a 'musical' work.

In order to be protected, the work must also be produced by a *qualifying person,* someone who is a citizen of, or resident in, the United Kingdom or another appropriate country, or it must have been first published in such a country. In practice, 'appropriate country' means one which, like the United Kingdom, is a party to one or both of the multilateral treaties governing international copyright protection, namely, the Berne Convention and the Universal Copyright Convention. Of all the major powers, only China belongs to neither, though its first copyright law came into force on 1st June 1991, protecting Chinese works for the first time, in China.

The work must also be *original,* which is not defined in the Act, but it has been established in practice that the work must not be directly derived from the efforts of others, and must involve some skill and labour. This means that a new arrangement of existing music can, in certain circumstances, acquire its own separate copyright in law, and the arranger is then in the position of original composer as regards the arrangement, with the exclusive rights mentioned above (and detailed later in this chapter). This is so, even if the existing music is no longer protected by copyright at the time of the arrangement; for example, a piano arrangement of a Beethoven orchestral work. If the existing music is in copyright, however, permission must be sought of the copyright owner before the arrangement is made, otherwise it will infringe that copyright, and the arrangement must be of considerable originality before it will qualify for separate copyright (though this is a matter of fact in each case).

OWNERSHIP OF COPYRIGHT, ASSIGNMENTS AND LICENCES

The Act uses the term *first owner* of the copyright, and this is normally the composer in the case of musical works, or the author in the case of lyrics (literary works). It is only by express agreement to the contrary that someone other than a composer or author can claim first ownership; for example, his employer, by a contract of service under which the composer is creating music in the course of his employment. This, in turn, is strictly interpreted in law, with a distinction between *contract of service* and *contract for services;* as an example of the latter, when a composer is commissioned to write a specific musical work by the BBC, it would be the composer who is the first owner unless otherwise agreed in writing. An *assignment* of copyright, which passes ownership of the copyright, similarly takes effect only by express agreement in writing, and must be distinguished from a *licence,* which is the term used to describe the form of permission given by the copyright owner to others to perform, publish or broadcast the work in return for payment.

As we have already seen, copyright is a collection of different, separate rights and it is possible in theory to assign or licence each right individually to separate persons. In practice, however, the entire copyright in a musical work is usually assigned by the composer as first owner to his publisher in return for a share of royalties on sales of sheet music, performances and so on. The publisher is then the copyright owner, and permission must be sought from him by anyone else wishing to use the music. The length of the period of ownership granted to the publisher will vary, but it is usually for several years, and such assignments tend to be renewable in any case. Publishers can then assign copyrights to other publishers at will, and this can sometimes create complicated chains of ownership, or 'title'. There is another complication here, because many composers are members of the *Performing Right Society* (PRS), and will already have assigned certain rights to the Society under their terms of membership. This enables the PRS to administer these rights on their behalf by granting licences giving the necessary permission to music users (for example, to the BBC) to broadcast its members' music, and collecting royalties paid in return for such use, which are then distributed to those members whose works are used in this way. The assignment of copyright to a publisher by a composer who is already a PRS member at the time of the assignment is always subject to the rights already assigned to the PRS.

ELEMENTS OF COPYRIGHT – PRIMARY RIGHTS

As stated above, copyright embraces different and separate rights. The effect of vesting these rights in the composer as first owner is to enable him to restrict others by imposing terms for giving his permission for exercising those rights, or doing specified acts. The elements of copyright are accordingly known as *restricted acts* and are as follows:

(a) copying the work
(b) issuing copies of it to the public
(c) performing, showing or playing the work in public

(d) broadcasting the work, or including it in a cable programme service

(e) adapting the work

(f) doing, in relation to an adaptation of the work, any of the acts specified in (a) to (d) above

Items (c) and (d) together make up the *performing right,* which is controlled by the Performing Right Society on behalf of its members. Those rights, together with the copying right, are likely to be of most interest to the readers of this chapter, and will be discussed in some detail below. At this stage, however, it may be helpful first to explain that a further and separate copyright also arises, for example, where a musical work is broadcast by the BBC. The copyright in the music itself may be owned by the composer or publisher, but a separate copyright also arises in the broadcast, of which the music is only a part, and the BBC owns that copyright. Similarly, there is separate copyright in a sound recording which, when first embodied in a gramophone record, cassette tape or compact disc, gives rise to rights for the company or persons first producing the record, cassette or disc. The broadcast use of a copyright recording must be separately authorised by the owner of that copyright. Thus, although a broadcast or recording is really serving as a medium for conveying the music to the public, the law has nevertheless conferred separate copyright protection which is additional to and independent of the copyright in the music, even though without it the recording or broadcast would not exist.

In general, failure to obtain the necessary permissions from all copyright owners involved would infringe the copyright in the work, in the recording or in the broadcast (and sometimes in all three), and would give rise to remedies for the copyright owner in each case (for example, a claim for damages). It is, therefore, important for readers to appreciate the implications of these technicalities, and the practical consequences of failing to observe them.

COPYING THE WORK

This means reproducing the work in any material form. For musical works, the commonest means of reproduction are (a) photocopying the score and (b) making a recording from a live performance or taping from a broadcast record.

Photocopying

In theory, permission for taking even one copy of the score of a copyright musical work, or any substantial extract from it, must be obtained from the copyright owner, who is usually the publisher. There are exceptions to this requirement, including copying for research or private study, criticism or review, provided that it is accompanied by sufficient acknowledgement which identifies the work by its title or other description and names the composer. Copying for the purpose of judicial proceedings also does not require permission. Section 32 of the Act also provides a number of exceptions for educational purposes. Copying by certain libraries and museums for specified purposes is also exempt.

A *Code of Fair Practice* for copying musical works has been agreed between representative organisations for the composer and publisher and a wide range of bodies which use music, including schools and amateur orchestras. The extent of copying is still limited to specific circumstances in which the copyright owners have agreed that they will not claim for infringement, and does not include the taking of copies to avoid the cost of hiring or buying the score. Copies of the Code are available from the Music Publishers Association, the Incorporated Society of Musicians, the National Federation of Music Societies and the Standing Conference for Amateur Music.

Recording a musical work

The first aspect to consider here is when a musical work is performed live and a recording is made of that performance. The recording right is controlled by the owner of the copyright in the musical work and is known as the mechanical right. This right is administered on behalf of its members by the *Mechanical-Copyright Protection Society* (MCPS), and their licence must be sought before a recording of any kind is made of a live performance. The performer of the music could not give the required permission, and should never attempt to do so. A second right arises in any recording of a musical work, and the lyrics associated therewith (if any). If, for example, a private individual tapes a friend's gramophone record to save the cost of buying the record himself, he is infringing the copyright of the person or company which first made the record, as well as the copyright of the composer and/or publisher of the music. The right to perform or broadcast recordings is controlled on behalf of the record industry by *Phonographic Performance Limited* (PPL). A broadcaster or dance hall which uses a gramophone record must, therefore, obtain PPL's permission before doing so. An affiliated body, Video Performance Limited (VPL), collectively administers the rights in music videos.

If it is purely for private and domestic use, a tape of a radio or television broadcast does not infringe the copyright of the broadcaster in that broadcast. However, it would still infringe the record company's copyright if a record was being broadcast, and also the copyright in the music itself. It is important to note that, even if the music itself is no longer protected by copyright, the gramophone record will probably still be protected, the duration of copyright protection for recordings being fifty years from the end of the year in which the first recording was made. Broadcasts are similarly protected.

Private recording

The MCPS used to operate a scheme whereby, for a modest fee, the individual user could obtain a licence to make private recordings for domestic use. However, audio and video taping has reached such proportions that it has become impossible to administer such a scheme. Instead, copyright interests have been pressing for legislation which would impose a levy on blank tapes at the point of sale. A royalty is already payable as a percentage of the sale price of pre-recorded gramophone records and cassettes, which is passed on to the owner of the copyright in the music and in the recordings; sheet music sales also contain an element of reward for the copyright owner. The blank tape levy is intended to extend this principle, to compensate for the loss of income caused by the effect of home taping on record sales. It would reward copyright owners for the use of their works by the millions of domestic users of taping equipment. Such a system is already operating in France, Germany, Austria, Hungary, the USA and Australia, and is still under consideration by the European Commission, which has recommended a levy in all EC territories as part of the drive to harmonise copyright legislation in the Community.

Until adequate legislation is passed in the UK, music users must continue to obtain the necessary permissions from the owners of all copyrights involved which, as we have seen, can mean approaching several different persons or companies.

PERFORMING, SHOWING OR PLAYING THE WORK IN PUBLIC

A public performance is not defined in the Act, but the concept has been considered often by the courts, and various decisions have established that even a performance in a private club, or the playing of a radio in a garage for employees' benefit, constitutes public performance. It can be confusing to realise that a television set can also give a public performance if it is situated in a hotel lobby, and that the hotel premises must obtain a licence for that use, even though the hotel is not responsible for the broadcast itself. The broadcaster, on the other hand, is also not responsible if the hotel fails to obtain the necessary licence.

The public performance, broadcasting and cable rights in paragraphs (c) and (d) of Section 16(i) of the Act (as set out above) are all administered on behalf of its composer, author and publisher members by the PRS; control is worldwide, through the international network of similar societies in most other countries, so that an American work performed here will be credited in the same way as a British work, and the American society to which the composer/publisher belongs will be paid the appropriate royalty for onward remission to its member.

For the live public performance of copyright works in its repertoire, blanket licences are issued by the PRS to premises where such performances take place, giving permission for the performance of all or any works in the PRS repertoire. Performers or concert promoters should always first approach the PRS to establish whether a licence is already in force which will cover the performance in question. Concerts promoted by music societies or clubs affiliated to the National Federation of Music Societies are automatically covered by a special agreement with the PRS, even if the premises do not have a blanket licence. However, care should be taken to ensure that details of works performed are still sent to the PRS so that the composers, authors and publishers can be paid royalties to which they are entitled.

There are several kinds of public performance which are commonly and mistakenly believed to be exempt from the licensing requirements; for example, in a church, for charity, where an unpublished manuscript is used, and where the composer has already been paid a commissioning fee. There are also certain kinds of performance not covered by the PRS blanket licence for which an individual licence would have to be negotiated; for example, choral works, or excerpts therefrom, lasting more than twenty minutes. It can easily be ascertained from the PRS whether a blanket licence is in force and, if so, whether it excludes any kinds of music or performances for that particular premises. The licence fees are fixed by reference to standard tariffs agreed between the Society and representative bodies of music users. The PRS does not set its own licence fees and, if a music user considers a fee unreasonable, the matter can be referred to a special arbitration tribunal set up under the Act called the *Copyright Tribunal*, which is empowered to hear both sides of the case and to make an order setting the terms and level of tariff for the particular category of use.

The Society does not administer the performing right in dramatic performances of musical plays, operas, operettas or ballets, for which a licence must be obtained direct from the copyright owner (usually the publisher). It is relatively simple for the parties concerned to identify and to negotiate with each other, hence the Society's non-involvement. However, the PRS does control *excerpts* from such works in many cases, and also controls concert performances.

For the sake of clarity, it should be emphasised that a PRS licence permitting public performance in a premises does not give anyone the right to make a recording of that performance, and the performers of the work are in no position to give that separate permission: an MCPS licence is needed. Furthermore, a public performance which uses a gramophone record requires two permissions: from the PRS for the performance of the music itself, and from PPL for the performance of the recording.

PERFORMERS' RIGHTS

Not to be confused with the right of public performance in copyright works, the rights of singers, musicians, actors or dancers are protected by a new code in Part II of the 1988 Act, replacing the Performers Protection Acts (1958-72). Protection has been extended beyond performers, to persons who have 'recording rights in relation to the performance' who will be mainly film and record producers.

The rights given under the new law are not assignable, unlike copyright, being civil rights of legal action, which may be brought when live performances are used in various ways without the performers' or producer's consent. Injunctions or damages can be awarded to the performer or producer, and fines can be imposed on the offender, as the new code preserves provisions making criminal penalties for certain offences. Importing, or trading in, an unauthorised recording is also an offence. Thus, if a member of the audience tapes a concert without the orchestra's written permission, that person is guilty of an offence, quite apart from the question of infringement of the copyright in the material being performed. It is also a separate offence to use the recording to manufacture 'bootleg' gramophone records or tape cassettes for sale to the public, or to broadcast the live performance without the consent of the performers concerned. These offences are committed whether or not the works performed are protected by copyright law, but there is no copyright for the performer to own in his performance as such.

BROADCASTING THE WORK OR INCLUDING IT IN A CABLE PROGRAMME

These rights include satellite transmissions, and are administered by the PRS by issuing blanket licences, for example, to the BBC, or to the Independent Television Commission, the Cable Television Authority and the Association of Independent Radio Contractors, as the representative bodies for commercial broadcasting and cable companies, and to BSkyB, the one satellite operation in the UK. The terms for these licences are either negotiated or, failing agreement, are determined by the Copyright Tribunal.

A composer who is a member of the PRS does not, therefore, have to negotiate the terms on which his works are to be broadcast or cabled, but he is still in a position to require a commissioning fee if the work is to be specially written, for example, as the theme for a television series or for an advertisement. Payment of the commissioning fee accordingly does not relieve the broadcaster or cabler of his obligations to the PRS, as is often mistakenly supposed, nor can the broadcaster or cabler purchase the performing right from the composer under such an agreement if he is already a PRS member, as he will have already assigned the performing right to the PRS on his admission to membership.

MUSIC IN FILMS

Under the 1988 Act, a film is defined as a recording on any medium from which a moving image may by any means be produced. The soundtrack is separately protected as a 'sound recording'. (Under previous legislation the soundtrack was part of the film.) In practice, the maker of the film is often the maker of the soundtrack, and will own both copyrights. Where a recording of an existing musical work already protected by copyright is subsequently used in a film soundtrack, the owner of the copyright in the soundtrack does not acquire the copyright in the original recording, but he does have the right to prevent anyone else from using the soundtrack incorporating that recording.

It is common nowadays for records and tapes to be issued of a film soundtrack to promote the film and to provide an additional source of income. The owner of the copyright in the soundtrack must give permission before anyone else can issue such a record or tape which is directly derived from the soundtrack itself. Separate copyright in the gramophone record or tape then arises; if a broadcast or public performance takes place of the recording, it will not infringe the copyright in the *film,* provided the permission of the copyright owner of the record or tape has been obtained.

Commissioning agreements

When music is specially written for a film soundtrack, the terms of the agreement will first depend on the type of music to be commissioned, from background links to full score. Although such agreements tend to be in fairly standard form, care must be taken in defining the extent of the composer's services, establishing who will own the copyright in the music, and negotiating the terms of payment. For example, the composer often does not simply write the music – he can be involved throughout the making of the soundtrack and the film, re-writing, advising generally, and participating in the recording. The basic rule as regards copyright ownership is that the composer is first owner of the copyright in the music, but it is not unusual for the film company to take an assignment of that copyright in return for royalty payments to the composer, or to agree that the composer's publisher takes the copyright. However, the right to the soundtrack as a whole (of which the music forms part) may well belong to the film company, as we have seen above.

This is an area in which the composer must take separate legal advice; often a substantial lump sum is offered, as well as future royalties, but where, for example, the music is of fundamental importance (as in a film of an opera), the composer should negotiate for a share of the profits as well. The composer may also conduct the performance of the music for the soundtrack and be paid an additional fee for that, together with an increased share of royalties on the sale of the gramophone record of the soundtrack (if one is made) to acknowledge his services both as conductor and as performer.

CONCLUSION

To summarise the most important practical points, here are two checklists for the copyright owner and for the music user respectively, to ensure that the owner protects his rights and that the user does not infringe them.

The composer as copyright owner

(a) The work must be 'recorded', in writing or otherwise, in a material form, and it is important to sign and date the manuscript or tape which first embodies the work.

(b) *Duration of Copyright* To establish the date whenprotection commences, send the manuscript or tape to yourself by recorded delivery post, or deposit a copy, signed and dated, in a bank vault. It is also possible to register a work at Stationers' Hall for a fee. This could be crucial evidence if an infringing work subsequently appears. If the work remains in manuscript or on tape, but is not performed or published in your lifetime, copyright will last from the date of first performance or publication until the end of the year 2039, being the fiftieth anniversary of the end of the year in which the 1988 Act came into force (1989). The 1988 Act effectively phases out posthumous protection in this way. (There is no extension to the period of posthumous protection to seventy years under the EC directive.)

(c) *Arrangements* Always be sure to trace the copyright owner of the music to be arranged, and obtain permission before making the arrangement. Even if the copyright period has expired on the original work, there may be another arrangement already in existence, and you may risk infringing that copyright.

(d) Assignment This should always be in writing, dated and signed. Legal advice should be sought for entering into an agreement with a publisher, but the standard form usually assigns the whole copyright to the publisher (subject to PRS rights) in return for a share of royalties and a percentage on the sales of sheet music and records. The *British Academy of Songwriters, Composers and Authors* (BASCA) can offer some guidance here, and can also recommend expert lawyers.

The music user

(a) *Photocopying* Consult the *Code of Fair Practice* if in doubt, depending upon the purpose for which the copying is made. If it is not covered, seek the permission of the copyright owner as indicated on the document to be copied.

(b) *Recording*
(i) From a record, tape or compact disc: consult the MCPS
(ii) From a broadcast: no permission is needed from the broadcaster if it is purely for private domestic use, but you will infringe the copyright in the music itself, and in the recording if it is a gramophone record, unless permission is obtained. However, it may be that, depending on the purpose of the copying of recording, a free or nominal licence will be granted by the copyright owner or by the appropriate organisation on his behalf.

(c) *Public Performance*
(i) For live performances, always check with the PRS regarding the licence for premises, type of performance, etc.
(ii) Always check with the PRS for performances of records, tapes and compact discs, and with PPL, as their licence is also required.

(d) *Broadcast/Cable* A PRS licence is required. If you wish to record before broadcasting, a licence from the MCPS is also required. If broadcasting a grammophone record, a PPL licence is needed as well.

FORMING A REGISTERED CHARITY

RUTH MEYER

Ruth Meyer worked for many years as a solicitor in London, and has been responsible for the charity registration of various arts organisations, including the National Youth Wind Orchestra.

Should my ensemble, orchestra, or choir register as a charity? Many musicians consider applying for charitable status at one time or another, often after hearing of similar groups which have successfully done so. Certainly, there are advantages to be had from forming a charity, but it should be remembered that there are also constraints and some costs involved. Before going ahead, you will need to be sure that, in your particular case, the benefits will outweigh the expense, the effort, and, in some cases, the inconvenience.

What benefits can charitable status bring? There is no doubt that it is much easier for charities to obtain funding and support, both from grant-giving bodies (some of which may be prevented by their own internal rules from helping non- charitable organisations) and also from the public at large. This is for many the principal reason for seeking charitable status. Registering your organisation as a charity will give it some degree of permanence independent of you, the founder. There are also certain tax advantages, notably the freedom from income tax on investment income and from capital gains tax on capital profits. Trading profits, or profits from running a business, are, however, taxable. There are also tax laws designed to encourage charitable giving which increase the value of donations from the public. Obviously, the value of these tax advantages depends very much on your organisation's finances. If you do not have, and cannot reasonably hope to have, much income or capital, then the fact that these may be tax free is largely academic.

These advantages carry with them some constraints. In particular, those running the charity will find themselves answerable to the Charity Commissioners and/or the Inland Revenue. You will therefore find your activities limited to those agreed with the Charity Commission, and your actions subject to some controls. It is a basic principle of charity law (to which you will be subject if you register a charity) that those who run charitable organisations may not take any financial advantage from the charity. In practice, this means that you must not be paid at all if you wish to be involved in the management of the charity. You may be employed by the charity and receive fees or a salary, but in this case you may not take any part in the running of the organisation. Many musicians find that this rule, which is strictly applied by the Charity Commissioners in all but the most exceptional cases, is a stumbling block. Often they are already putting in unpaid extra hours, and are simply not in a position to work without pay, but are unable, or in some cases unwilling, to find others to run their organisation on a voluntary basis.

If you do decide to go ahead and form a charity, you will, in practice, need to register with the Charity Commissioners (in England and Wales. In Scotland registration is dealt with by the Inland Revenue.) There is no reason why you should not do this yourself, although professional advice may be needed, and an accountant or solicitor who is experienced in the field should be able to speed things up. It is worth asking others who have successfully registered charities for recommendations. Insist on being told at the outset the basis on which you will be charged and the likely cost of such professional advice! Many find it is money well spent in terms of time and trouble saved, but if yours is a small operation on a tight budget, you may be able to deal with the matter on your own. In this case, you should try to get advice from fellow musicians who have already gone down the charitable path. Such help is especially valuable when it comes to wording the documents and filling in the forms to be approved by the Commissioners.

Some form of document will have to be submitted for approval and registration. This will be the constitution or governing deed for your charity. The type of document you submit for approval will depend on the structure you choose for your charity – in practice, either a company or a trust. Although legally very different entities, either is suitable. The most obvious practical differences are that a company will have to follow certain rules and procedures applicable to all companies. In particular, accounts will have to be submitted to the Companies Registry. However, these may take a simplified form for small organisations, and the work is not likely to be much greater than that involved in preparing the financial records which all charities (trusts or companies) will have to keep to satisfy the Charity Commissioners. On the other hand, one of the perceived advantages of a company – the ability to take on a lease or loan in the name of the company – may be illusory. Although the company can act in its own name (whereas those running a trust will have to take on the responsibility themselves), in the case of a small company with limited assets the directors may well be asked to give personal guarantees.

Particular attention must be given to the wording of the documentation, in particular to that part which sets out in detail what the charity is established for and what it may do. The charity is limited in its activities to those set out in the documentation agreed and registered with the Charity Commission, and so these need to be wide enough to cover all its proposed activities. However, the Commissioners are always reluctant to allow wide or loose wording, as they will want to be sure that the proposed activities are exclusively charitable.

Surprisingly, there is no all-embracing definition of what activities are charitable. However, education and recreation are considered charitable when there is some element of benefit to the public (as opposed to a purely private benefit – say, an ensemble whose sole purpose was to give private concerts to a rich man). Most performers and music schools will fall within the definition. In this area above all, it is helpful to have help in drafting your documentation, either from an experienced professional or from an existing charity which has similar activities to your own.

NOISE NUISANCE

NIGEL HOUSEGO

Nigel Housego, Barrister at Law, is a property law specialist employed by Hambro Legal Protection Limited on their 24-hour telephone legal advisory service.

> How sweet the moonlight sleeps upon this bank!
> Here will we sit, and let the sounds of music
> Creep in our ears; soft stillness and the night
> Become the touches of sweet harmony.
> (Shakespeare)

While music is undoubtedly the food of love, it can in certain circumstances have just the opposite effect. The purpose of this chapter is to explain how the law seeks to balance the interests of musicians and the public at large.

In general terms, we are free to do as we please on our own land, but when our activities unreasonably interfere with the use and enjoyment of another person's property, a legal nuisance may exist, and steps can be taken to prevent it from recurring. We are concerned here specifically with noise nuisance and the rights and duties of individuals affected by it.

In assessing whether a legal nuisance exists, the law takes into account not only the level of the noise but also its duration, the locality in which it takes place, and the conduct of the parties concerned. So, while a one-off party is unlikely to create a legal nuisance, regularly playing a trumpet late at night in a residential area is! Furthermore, while somebody with undue sensitivity to 'noise' may not have any redress, the fact that a nuisance may have existed prior to a new neighbour moving in does not prevent that person from pursuing a claim.

The noisy neighbour

In the event that you feel that a nuisance exists, a number of options are available to you, namely:

- To complain directly to the person causing the disruption in the hope of resolving the matter amicably. This course of action is to be recommended certainly in the first instance, and will, it is hoped, prevent the matter escalating further. Failing this:

- To report the matter to the local Environmental Health Department who, being satisfied that a 'Statutory Nuisance' exists, will serve a Noise Abatement Notice on the person concerned. A statutory nuisance is defined to include a 'noise emitted from premises so as to be prejudicial to health or a nuisance', and also covers the situation where loud music is being played in the street. Failure to comply with the notice is an offence, and upon conviction will render the person liable to a fine – currently up to £5,000. In addition, for each day that the nuisance continues after the conviction, a fine – currently up to £500 – is imposed.

This option has a number of advantages, not least being able to discuss your problem with somebody who can offer useful help and guidance and assess the merits of your complaint. It also means that responsibility for dealing with the nuisance will be taken over by the local authority.

- To apply in person to the Magistrates under Section 82 of the Environmental Protection Act 1990 for an order requiring the defendant to abate the nuisance, and/or prohibiting its recurrence. In the case of a noise nuisance, not less than three days' notice of intention to bring proceedings must be given to the defendant beforehand, specifying the matter complained of. If satisfied that a nuisance exists, the Magistrates may, in addition to making an order, impose a fine – currently up to £5,000. There are also penalties for failing to comply with the order itself.

  The Magistrates have the power to make an order for costs in the applicant's favour, and may also, in appropriate circumstances, make an award of compensation (which always tends to be on the low side).

- To issue proceedings in the County Court for damages and/or an injunction, the major disadvantages here being delay and the financial outlay involved.

In certain cases, other remedies may be available: for example, if a tenant is acting in contravention of a lease, a complaint may be made to the landlord who may be prepared to take action against the offending tenant. You may, however, be required to indemnify the landlord for any costs incurred in this respect, particularly where you are a tenant of the same landlord. It is also important to bear in mind that a landlord is not generally liable for the behaviour of his or her tenants, although he may be liable for his own acts or omissions.

Clearly, in order to succeed in a claim for nuisance, whether it be before the Magistrates or a County Court Judge, evidence will be required to prove your case. It is important to keep a record of the incidents giving rise to the claim – for example, a diary of times and dates can be extremely valuable when it comes to establishing the nature and extent of the alleged nuisance. It may also be necessary to obtain the opinion of an expert such as a sound specialist to confirm that a given noise is more than 10 decibels above normal background noise (a useful guide for determining the existence of a nuisance), or medical evidence where the noise is alleged to have been prejudicial to health. It will also be beneficial to obtain written statements from any independent witnesses who are prepared to support your claim.

The noisy musician

We now need to consider the position where the boot is on the other foot, so to speak, and you are the one being accused of creating the nuisance.

First, try and resolve the matter amicably and, if at all possible, attempt to agree a compromise. If this fails, you may receive a visit from an Environmental Health Officer as a prelude to the steps referred to above, in which case co-operation can go a long way to avoiding any further problems. In the event that a notice is served or proceedings are issued or threatened, legal advice must be sought as a matter of urgency to ensure that your position is protected: for example, there may be grounds for appealing against a Noise Abatement Notice, and strict time limits need to be observed.

By following a few simple rules, it should be possible to eliminate, or at least greatly reduce, the chances of a claim being brought against you for nuisance. Prevention is, after all, always better than cure!

- When planning your activities, have consideration for others and particularly for your neighbours.

- Before buying or leasing accommodation, check to see whether there are any restrictions imposed which could affect the use to which you intend to put it. Frequently in residential accommodation, you will find that you will not be allowed to carry on a trade or business (a term which has been very widely defined by the Courts) from the premises, and this may be reinforced by a requirement not to cause a nuisance or annoyance to your neighbours. It goes without saying that what you might regard as being reasonable your neighbours may not, and this is particularly important where you share a building with others, as is frequently the case with rented accommodation. Flats are notorious trouble-spots in this respect, and it is well worth checking to see if your flat is properly sound insulated. If it is not, you should take such steps as are necessary to reduce noise transmission to a minimum.

- Problems very rarely go away by themselves, and where it has not been possible to settle a matter amicably, advice should be sought at the earliest opportunity with a view to determining what steps need to be taken to prevent things from getting out of hand. This is particularly important where, as a tenant or lodger, you have been threatened with eviction.

Whilst bearing these things in mind, you should not be afraid to blow your own trumpet!

SECTION 5

A BUYER'S GUIDE TO FINANCIAL SERVICES

SAVINGS AND INVESTMENT

CHRISTINE NORMAN

Christine Norman is employed by Friends Provident as a Senior Financial Consultant. She has worked in the financial services industry since 1984, developing an enjoyable and successful career. She is married, and lives in Hertfordshire. Her leisure pursuits include needlework, travel in France, cookery, reading and music.

Like it or not, financial survival is one of life's necessities. Whatever the level of your income and savings, it is vital that you make sure that your money is being used to your greatest advantage. And yet it is surprising that, while many people will make some sort of an attempt at organising their finances, very few consider and plan for the future, let alone review their decisions regularly. They do not create a flexible, long-term 'master-plan' to achieve their eventual objectives, but merely make decisions based on what they want and can afford now. This, of course, is better than nothing at all, but it is far more sensible to assess what you need and can achieve now in relation to what you will need and would like to achieve in the future. By creating your master-plan, you are going a long way towards ensuring that you will always be able to survive financially, even when income falls – or stops – or when one of life's periodic catastrophes creeps up on you. This chapter will show you how to survive, how to plan, and how to identify your needs.

Identifying your needs

Identifying your needs and objectives involves assessing your lifestyle, your income and your taxation, and deciding if you are vulnerable in any respect should circumstances change. You must therefore ask yourself some searching questions:

(a) Are you paying more in taxes than is necessary? Perhaps some small changes could increase your disposable income by reducing taxation.

(b) Do you have capital sitting idly in your current account 'in case you need it'?

(c) Were you to die tomorrow, could your dependants survive without your income? Would they have to sell your home? Would your spouse be forced to earn a living while the children are young? Would the private school fees which you can afford today be paid next term?

(d) How would your partner's death affect your ability to work or to continue in your profession?

   (e) If you were to become disabled, could you still play your instrument? Could you still transport yourself?

   (f) If illness stopped you working, could you survive for more than a month or so?

   (g) What is the state pension today? Could you live on it tomorrow?

   (h) Do you want to continue to live in your present property, or would you like something better one day?

   (i) Are you likely to inherit money in the future?

These questions, and many more, should be answered now if you are to achieve that 'financial security' referred to – the peace of mind that comes from knowing that, while you may not yet have everything right, you have an idea of what gaps need to be filled.

Having asked and answered your questions, perhaps with help from a professional adviser, you can now begin to look at them in terms of what must, or should, be done quickly, what can wait for a while, and what is least important of all. Obviously, actions which cost nothing, such as investigating the tax efficiency of income and capital investments, should be dealt with immediately, regardless of their personal importance to you – savings made in this way could provide the funds needed to achieve other objectives. Thought should also be given to long-term goals which, if they are to be achievable, need fairly immediate action – retirement planning is a prime example of this.

What is your income? How much of this can you divert towards achieving your goals? Based on past income and your own potential success, by what percentage is your income likely to increase next year? How much of that will you decide to use to achieve your next objective? In this way you will create your master-plan and, if you are going to plan your financial future effectively, you will treat it with the same respect as any other important document, referring to it and reviewing it at least once a year to make sure it remains a valid reflection of your aims and objectives. Your circumstances will change, economies will change, many things will change, and for this reason your plan must be flexible. It will never become a definitive document, but it will always serve as a guide, a reminder of your intention to plug the gaps that deny true financial stability.

What do you want from your savings and investments?

In the not-so-distant past, it was fairly easy to decide where to invest your money. You simply put it in your local building society, bank or Post Office account where it would earn some interest. Nowadays, we are plagued with a plethora of advice, through our letter-boxes, on the television and in the press, all claiming to offer the best return for our hard-earned money. So, how do we decide what is not only best but also right for our own particular little nest egg? Much will depend on how accessible the capital must be, and much should depend on how the investment will be taxed.

Before deciding which of the many investment areas you should be using, there are, once again, a few questions which you should answer:

(a) how much of your income can you save?
(b) how much risk are you prepared to take?
(c) will you want access to the funds in the immediate future?
(d) will the investment you are considering keep up with inflation?

If the answer to (a) is 'not much', you should be aiming to keep your lump sum or regular payment safe, while at the same time earning some interest. The gains you make may not be spectacular, but your savings will not be under any risk. In other circumstances, it could make more sense to create a 'portfolio' which will spread your money between different types of investment, vary the degree of risk and take advantage of any available tax savings. Naturally, you should monitor them to ensure that they continue to meet the criteria you have chosen. Finally, you should always have an emergency fund upon which you can draw immediately in case of unexpected needs.

NOTE: Throughout this chapter you should bear in mind that any reference made to taxation is based on current understanding and is subject to change in the future.

National Savings schemes

These are forms of investment provided by the Government. There are several schemes available, and they can be purchased through the Post Office. Most require a five-year term to be really effective methods for creating capital appreciation. They carry no risk, and your money is always accessible if you are prepared for what might be viewed as a dramatically reduced return. While they might certainly form part of a wide philosophy for investment, as an individual's only investment they are rarely a good idea.

(a) Index-linked Savings Certificates provide a fixed investment return over and above the rate of inflation. If the certificates are not held for the full five-year term, the percentage return is reduced. There is no tax payable on the interest.

(b) Fixed Rate Savings Certificates also run for a five-year term. Interest is tax free, but is reduced if the certificates are not held for the full five years. No interest is paid at all if the certificates are repaid in the first year, unless they are reinvested certificates from earlier issues.

(c) A Capital Bond pays a higher rate of interest than Savings Certificates although, again, the rate is reduced if you keep the Bond for less than five years. Interest is credited gross but is taxable and must be declared on your tax return.

(d) Income Bonds pay monthly interest and your money can be repaid to you with three months' notice, but if you request a repayment in the first year you lose half the interest on the amount withdrawn. Again, interest is paid gross but is taxable and must be declared.

(e) National Savings Investment Accounts are, in some ways, similar to some deposit and building society accounts. The interest is variable, and a higher rate is paid for higher amounts invested. Withdrawals require one month's notice and interest, which is taxable, is credited annually and paid gross.

(f) An Ordinary Account has the lowest interest rate of all, with an additional percentage being paid if certain minimum criteria are met. An element of the annual interest is free of tax, and no notice is required for defined withdrawal amounts. Higher withdrawals require a few days' notice.

Building society and bank deposit accounts

These offer various forms of savings. Although banks tend to stay very much in line with each other, building societies will vary according to their strengths and the type of accounts offered.

In general, banks and building societies are viewed as a 'safe' home for savings. Interest will be accumulated either at a fixed or a variable rate, and will often depend upon the amount of capital in the account or the notice period required to withdraw money. For example, an amount of capital in excess of £2,500 on a 90-day notice account will usually attract a higher rate of interest than will £500 in an instant access account. Interest arising on these accounts is usually taxable. Basic-rate income tax will be deducted from the interest before it is credited to your account and, if you are a higher-rate taxpayer, you will be liable for extra tax when you have sent in your tax return. However, if you are a non-taxpayer, you are entitled to have the interest credited gross. In order to do this, you will be required to complete a certificate which gives the bank or building society the authority to pay interest without deduction of tax.

Building society and bank deposit accounts are not speculative. They may yield less than other, more adventurous, investments, but they are generally considered to be a suitable home for funds upon which you may need to call at relatively short notice, and with the guaranteed return of, at the very least, your original capital. As such, they are an essential part of any investor's portfolio. This is particularly true if you are not a tax payer, and are eligible for interest to be credited gross. Those approaching the higher-rate tax threshold should be careful that interest from this type of savings account does not push their taxable earnings over the limit, thus creating a higher-rate tax liability.

Tax Exempt Special Savings Accounts (TESSAs)

These are operated by banks and building societies. They were introduced in the 1990 Budget, and investment levels are restricted. An individual may have only one account, and joint accounts are not permitted. Up to £9,000 may be invested over a five-year period, the maximum for the first year being £3,000. However, it is possible to invest the total maximum amount with the TESSA provider in the first year. It will then be held by them as an ordinary account, generating taxable interest, but they will make a payment from that account to the TESSA each year.

Interest is usually at a variable rate, although there remain one or two providers who continue to offer a fixed rate throughout the five-year term. When TESSAs were originally introduced, interest rates were exceptionally high, and investors who managed to obtain fixed rates then will soon be reaping rich rewards. A fixed rate is not necessarily a good idea, though, when rates are low and likely to rise during the five-year period of the investment.

Provided you do not withdraw the capital within the five- year term, the interest is free of tax. You can, however, withdraw the interest at any time provided you withdraw only the net amount: in other words, the amount that would have been paid if tax had been deducted. All undrawn interest can be withdrawn free of tax at the end of the term. It is important to exercise care in making withdrawals during the term of the TESSA because if, even unwittingly, you withdraw any part of the capital or too much interest the TESSA automatically closes, and all interest earned will become liable to tax.

After five years, the account automatically ceases to be exempt from tax. However, in the 1994 budget the Chancellor announced proposals which will enable investors to transfer to a new TESSA the full amount of the capital (up to a maximum of £9,000) on the maturity of their existing TESSA.

TESSAs can be transferred from one provider to another, but this may result in a loss of bonuses or incur transfer penalties. Not all providers will accept transfers.

TESSAs represent an excellent opportunity for taxpayers, particularly those who are chargeable at the higher rate, to accumulate tax-free savings over a five-year period, and also to obtain a little income, if needed, during the term.

Equities

Essentially these are shares: when you buy an equity, you are buying a share in a company. Recent years have seen the privatisation of many major companies, such as British Gas, British Telecom and the electricity and water companies. As a result, there has been an increased interest in share purchasing among investors who might not have previously considered shares as a means of investment. It must be said, however, that small share purchases are generally not a good idea since the charges involved in buying and selling can outweigh the profits. It is also a complicated business and, unless you are prepared to study the stock market and undertake thorough research, you should seek professional advice. Because the value of shares can fluctuate significantly on a day-to-day basis, you should consider carefully whether you can afford to be without that capital being available, possibly for a long while, should the value of your shares fall below what you originally paid for them. Nevertheless, they can be sold at any time, so they do represent reasonably accessible capital.

If you hold shares over a period of time, it is likely that the company will pay you a dividend. When a dividend is paid to an investor, he also receives a 'tax credit' equal to 25% of the dividend actually paid – thus, there is effectively a 20% tax deduction on the gross amount of the dividend. There is no further tax to pay if the recipient of the dividend is a basic-rate taxpayer, but an additional 20% is payable by higher-rate taxpayers. A voucher is issued with the dividend cheque which confirms the amount of the tax credit. The dividend must be declared on your tax return, even if there is no further tax liability.

Should you be fortunate enough to sell your shares at a profit, that profit may be liable to capital gains tax. It will be added to any other gains you have made during the year and, if the total gains exceed the Capital Gains Tax exemption limit, a tax charge related to the rate at which you pay income tax will be made.

Broadly speaking, shares should be used for money which you do not require in the short term. You should be able to wait for their value to increase in order to sell them, rather than being forced to sell for emergency expenditure. The exception to this would be individuals who know enough about the stock market to buy and sell on an informed basis, perhaps on the advice of a stockbroker, or by using a management service and allowing the broker to deal on your behalf. This will not protect you, though, from unexpected stock market falls.

Direct investment of large sums of money into shares is really not for the faint-hearted, nor for those who seek security and/or immediate access to their capital.

Unit Trusts

Unit trusts provide a way into the stock market for investors who might otherwise have insufficient capital to make such investments worth while, or who do not have the expertise to make direct investments in shares. They provide a method of investing in equities (shares) while spreading the risk. Unit trust managers invest your money across a wide range of shares which they manage for you. In effect, you are buying into a 'pool' of money which is then used by the fund managers to purchase investments on behalf of their collective investors. In this way, a more cost-effective and professional management of your capital can be achieved, combined with a wider spread of risk than your own limited capital can provide. For example, if you invest £1,000 in the shares of one company, you are vulnerable to the fortunes, good or bad, of that one company; the same amount invested into unit trusts could be spread over hundreds of companies and, as a result, your exposure to risk is considerably reduced.

Like share prices, unit trust values can go up or down. It therefore follows that they should not be used for short-term savings which may be required for a known purpose at a specific time – for example, next year's holiday or next term's school fees.

The taxation of income arising on unit trusts is similar to that of income arising on shares. Dividends arise from the investments made by the fund managers. These can either be paid to you (distributed) with a 20% tax credit, or they can be credited (reinvested) to your unit trust investment or savings plan, again with a 20% tax credit. You will be issued with proof of the tax credit, and a further liability will arise only if you are a higher-rate taxpayer. When you sell your units, any profit is added to your other gains during the year and a capital gains tax liability may arise.

Generally, it is possible to invest on a regular basis with small sums of money, as well as investing larger, single capital payments. Unit trusts can thus be considered as a suitable alternative to interest-bearing savings accounts. However, although the funds accumulated in this way remain almost instantly accessible, they should be viewed on a longer-term basis than, say, a building society savings account. This is because, like equities, they are subject to variations in value, and there is no guarantee that your capital will be returned. It is not considered sensible to invest capital which you know you will need to withdraw within a two- or three-year period.

It is possible to arrange for your capital to be managed across a wide range of funds, using professional managers to buy and sell units on your behalf as and when investment conditions are appropriate. This creates a portfolio of unit trusts which is managed for you. As with most unit trust investments, an annual management charge is made, usually by deduction from your investment, but you are relieved of the decision-making and the paperwork. The portfolio can be structured according to individual capital and income needs, and it is a particularly suitable investment for individuals who have capital to invest but who do not want the hassle of administering it – or who do not have the expertise to do so.

Personal Equity Plans (PEPs)

These were introduced in the 1986 Budget to encourage individuals to invest in the UK stock market. Investors must be over the age of eighteen, and must be resident or ordinarily resident in the UK. A new plan can be commenced each year, or it is possible to effect a 'continuing' plan with regular contributions over a longer period of time. Two types of Personal Equity Plan are available, and an individual may have either or both. The annual investment limit has always been restricted and, for 1995-96, £6,000 may be invested into a General PEP and £3,000 into a Single Company PEP.

There is no liability for income or capital gains tax on PEP investments, and any tax paid on interest arising on cash deposits can be reclaimed by the PEP manager.

General PEP

An individual may hold only *one* provider's PEP in any one tax year. Plans must be administered by a manager authorised under the Financial Services Act 1986, and must be registered with the Inland Revenue. The PEP may be invested into investment trusts or authorised unit trusts which are at least 50% invested in UK and EU equities. With the advent of the single European market, PEP rules are about to be changed to allow for investment of up to £6,000 in equities of EU companies. A PEP can also hold cash.

Single company PEP

Since January 1992, it has been possible also to invest up to £3,000 in a single company PEP. This must be issued either by a listed UK company, using shares only in that company, or by a recognised Plan Manager, in which case switches between shares of differing companies are allowed. Many people use shares from new issues, particularly privatisations, which can be transferred into a PEP within forty-two days of the announcement of an allocation and an issue price.

In general terms, PEPs represent an extremely tax-efficient way of saving into the equity market, particularly for those who are liable to higher-rate tax. For basic-rate taxpayers and those who have no liability at all to income tax, the rewards are less exciting, particularly if the provider's charges are high. The return on a PEP is not guaranteed – like other unit trust or equity investments, the value of the investment can fall as well as rise. They should be viewed as long-term investments, in which case they can represent a useful part of the overall investment strategy.

Of particular note in recent years has been the use of PEPs in conjunction with mortgages, a point which will be expanded upon in another chapter. PEPs also feature in the section relating to pension planning where, again, they can provide a useful tool for tax efficiency, accessibility, and funding beyond the Inland Revenue limits imposed on pensions.

Offshore investments

A surprising number of people remain unaware of the fact that investments held offshore are no longer free of UK taxation. If you are resident in the UK, you must declare your worldwide investments for income and capital gains tax purposes in the UK. There are certain agreements which prevent you from being taxed twice – but you must declare *all* income, wherever it arises.

Creating your master-plan

So, now you know a bit about investment, a bit about what is available, a bit about whether it is taxable or not, long-term or not, speculative or not, restricted or not. How are you going to tie it all together to create your master- plan?

If your income is below your personal allowance for tax purposes, your first consideration should be those investments which create income or interest which is taxable. Until that interest or income brings your total income up to your personal allowance limit it is effectively tax free. Building societies, deposit accounts, unit trusts and some National Savings investments will do this. Your next objective should be to use the tax-free limit for capital gains. Once this is fully utilised, you should be looking for investments which carry no tax liability at all. If you are married, and particularly if your spouse has no taxable earnings, remember that he or she also has the same allowances as you. Careful planning by both of you can avoid a great deal of tax.

It is rather pointless to reduce or eliminate your tax liability on investments, and then find that money you urgently need is tied up for months or years at a time. For example, suppose that last year you invested £3,000 in a TESSA and last month you invested £6,000 in unit trusts. Last night, most of your roof blew off in a gale. You can't get at the TESSA without paying tax on the interest, and the unit trusts are worth less than you put in. Disaster! Plan your investments so that some money is instantly available without penalty or loss, whilst other funds are accessible over varying periods of time.

What are your real objectives? Do you want to create an income, or are you looking for longer-term capital appreciation – or do you want a mixture of both? If you attempt to supplement your present income, make sure that the provision of that income does not erode your capital. Be aware of how much income a given amount of capital is likely, realistically, to provide.

Capital appreciation rarely happens overnight, so be prepared to wait. Be sufficiently aware of your investments to make necessary adjustments from time to time, but don't make the mistake of valuing them daily – that little exercise can be very depressing!

In essence, if you define your investment and savings objectives as being (i) specific or non-specific, (ii) long or short term, and (iii) speculative or risk free, it becomes a simple process to eliminate those investments which are unsuitable. It is also important to identify your 'risk threshold': if you cannot bear the pain of watching your speculative investment fluctuate in value, then you will probably feel happier with a low, but guaranteed, return, even if it is taxable and/or inaccessible. If a speculative investment fulfils all your other criteria, use it whilst remembering that you don't actually lose money unless you sell the investment, just as you don't really make a profit until the investment is sold: until then, the gain or the loss is all 'on paper' only.

The above paragraphs describe some of the more common types of investment. Those that have been mentioned are suitable for large and small investors alike. They are the simpler and more readily-available schemes most often used by the average investor. Depending upon taxation, accessibility, income and growth needs, a personal investment strategy should be created using a carefully planned combination of all or some of them.

Volumes have been, and will be, written which delve into the technical background and suitability of many more investments than are listed here. If you are considering more unusual investments, you really should consult a professional adviser. Many investments can sound exciting, but they often carry a substantial degree of risk.

LIFE ASSURANCE, INCOME PROTECTION AND MEDICAL INSURANCE

CHRISTINE NORMAN

Note: Throughout this chapter you should bear in mind that any reference to taxation is based on current legislation, and is subject to change in the future.

When we talk about protection, we are talking not about stopping something happening, like vaccinating our children to avoid measles, but about protecting ourselves against the results of something which will, or may, happen in the future.

Life assurance is probably the single most widely used and discussed form of protection. There is, though, a range of eventualities which can have a devastating financial effect upon an individual or a family, and provision for these should not be forgotten. For example, the death of a breadwinner, provided he or she is covered by life assurance, need not necessarily create financial hardship. However, if the person is seriously injured or too ill to work for several months or years, perhaps permanently, the financial impact can be appalling. Similarly, a critical or terminal illness can lead not only to lost earnings but also to an increased need for money. These possibilities can now be provided for, often quite inexpensively, thus removing financial problems at a time when the emotional ones alone are hard enough to bear.

Many people, particularly those who are self-employed, would like to be able to choose a convenient time to go into hospital for treatment, or choose the location of the hospital and the consultant who will treat them. Private health insurance schemes now enable us to do this, and so plan our working lives to adapt to a temporary absence, rather than leaving everything in chaos when the NHS letter drops through the letter-box giving two days' notice of surgery for which we have waited months. We can also be treated more speedily than might be possible under the NHS – and what conductor needing a hip replacement wants to put up with eighteen months of pain while waiting to have that done?

LIFE ASSURANCE

Life assurance is designed to provide a specified, minimum amount of money upon the death of an individual – the life assured. The policy may last for the rest of the individual's life, or for a period of time agreed at the outset. The premiums paid for the policy will be determined by several factors:

    (a) the amount of benefit to be paid on death,

(b) the number of years the policy is intended to last,

(c) the age and sex of the individual, and

(d) the individual's medical history, lifestyle and whether or not he or she is a smoker.

Generally speaking, when you apply for life assurance you will be asked for details of your medical history, including certain details of medical facts relating to close relatives which may have some bearing on your own potential medical health. You will also be asked for the name of your General Practitioner and in many cases a medical report will be sought from that source. Provided the amount of cover you require is low and there is no evidence of recurrent or serious illness or injury, you will not be asked to attend for an independent medical examination. However, if a recurrent or life-threatening condition is discovered, you could be asked to pay a higher premium or, in particularly serious circumstances, refused a policy altogether. The rapid spread of AIDS has had a major impact on the life assurance industry. For this reason, you may be asked to confirm that you are not a member of a 'high risk' group. Single male applicants are always required to fill in a questionnaire, as are people requiring regular injections or blood transfusions – diabetics and haemophiliacs, for example.

Most life assurance policies can be assigned. This means that they can be used as security for a loan or a mortgage. In effect, what you are doing is allowing your policy to be used to pay off a debt should you die during the term of the loan. Such loans and mortgages must be repaid before, or at the expiry of, the policy's term.

Term assurance

This is probably the cheapest form of life assurance available. It is also the least flexible and has no investment value whatsoever. As its name suggests, a policy of this type runs for a specified period of time. If you die within the specified term, the payment received from the life assurance company will be the amount you specified at the outset – no more, no less. If you survive the term, the policy simply ceases – you pay no more premiums, you no longer have a life policy, and you get nothing back.

A term assurance policy can be a useful policy to have in addition to others, particularly if you have dependants who would suffer financial hardship in the event of your unexpectedly premature death. It may be that your mortgage will be repaid by another insurance policy but, if your spouse is left with a couple of young children to feed, clothe and educate, where will the money come from? A lump sum from this type of policy can be invested to provide an income, avoiding the need to find a job immediately, and providing a cushion of security in the early years.

As an alternative to term assurance, and in order to provide an income for your dependants, you might choose to have what is known as a Family Protection Plan but what is, in effect, a variation of a term assurance policy. These also run for a specific term at a specific premium, but instead of paying out a lump sum they are capable of paying a regular specified income for the remainder of the original term stated.

A further application for term assurance policies is to provide funds to complete the repayments on a repayment mortgage, should you die before the end of the mortgage term. These are frequently effected on a 'decreasing' basis, so that, as time goes by and you owe less on the mortgage, the amount of cover also reduces; at the end of the term of the mortgage, the policy simply ceases. By using, instead, an ordinary term assurance, equal to the amount of your original loan, alongside a repayment mortgage, there will come a time when the amount that would be paid out in the event of your death would be far greater than the amount owed on the mortgage. In that way, you are more likely to provide a surplus fund which could be used by your dependants.

Endowment assurance

In the past, these policies have been commonly used as the security for mortgage borrowing. Their popularity has waned in recent years as different methods of repaying mortgages have been developed, and also as a result of uncertainty regarding their ability to meet the need for a specific amount of capital at the end of the term – about which there has been much press comment.

Endowment policies are more expensive than term assurance. This is because part of the premium is invested with the object of achieving a 'target' amount to be paid out as a lump sum at the end of the investment term. Like term assurance, an endowment policy has a specified number of years and a specified sum assured. In many cases, the sum assured can be increased. Should you die within the term of the policy, the sum assured will be paid out by the insurance company. If you survive the term, then the current value of the policy, including any profits or growth that the investment has achieved, will be paid to you. This is known as the maturity value. At maturity, the policy ceases, you stop paying the premiums, you receive a lump sum of money (with which you may repay your mortgage), and you cease to have any life cover under that policy.

An endowment policy will gradually develop a value over the years and, should you no longer require it, it can be surrendered within the term stipulated at the outset. Generally, it is not wise to take this option. You will receive only what is known as a 'surrender value', and this could be substantially less than you have paid in premiums, and will almost certainly be less than the actual value of the fund. Nowadays, it is also possible to sell an endowment policy. The buyer will usually buy the policy at a higher price than the surrender value in the hope that, by continuing the premiums, he will make a profit on the investment by the time the maturity date is reached. There are specialist companies who advise on this, and arrange for the purchase and sale of endowment policies.

Whole of life assurance

Again, the name gives a clue to the type of policy. In this case, you specify the amount of the sum assured but you do not specify the number of years you require the policy to run. Whether you live one more year or until you are 120, the policy will provide your specified sum when you die, provided you continue to pay the required premiums. Should your need for life cover cease, you can stop paying for the policy but it is unlikely to have any substantial cash value, particularly in the early years. Alternatively, in many cases you can 'adjust' the policy, so that instead of paying for a large sum assured, you pay for a minimum sum assured and have a larger part of the premium directed towards investment.

This type of policy is commonly used simply to provide a lump sum to dependants or beneficiaries when you die. It should not be viewed as a means of saving – there are better ways to save.

Whole of life policies are frequently used to provide for inheritance tax. Written into a trust with named beneficiaries, they will provide a sum of money which is free of tax – the life company will have paid any taxes due on its life funds – and which can be used to pay all or part of the inheritance tax arising on your estate when you die. By providing funds in this way, you can avoid the necessity for your beneficiaries to borrow funds to pay the tax, which must be paid before probate can be granted. This, in turn, can avoid the forced sale of assets in order to repay borrowings, following grant of probate.

Before putting any life policy in trust, you should always obtain advice. Trusts can be useful tools if used correctly, but if they are not used correctly they can create insurmountable problems.

Waiver of premium and premium protection

Supposing you are ill or disabled and unable to work, and cannot pay the premiums on your life or pension policy. Most companies offer the facility, at very little extra cost, for waiver of premium or premium protection to be incorporated into a policy. This means that if you are unable to pay the premiums because of long-term illness or disability which prevents you from working, you can still retain the benefits of the policy, but at no further cost to you while the illness or disability continues and, if necessary, until your normal retirement age.

General guidance

(a) Obviously, if your life assurance policy is intended to provide funds for the repayment of your mortgage, it should equal your borrowing at all times.

(b) The younger you are, the less expensive the premiums will be, whatever the term, assuming you are in good health. Don't delay – if life assurance is a requirement, take out your policy as soon as you can and for as much as you can afford. There are some individuals, however, for whom life assurance would not be a necessary requirement – for example, a single male with no dependants would have no need of life assurance, except for mortgage cover.

(c) Excluding policies used in conjunction with a mortgage, the general rule of thumb is that a breadwinner's total life cover should be capable of paying out ten times his or her annual income. Therefore, an individual earning £30,000 per annum should have policies totalling £300,000 of sum assured.

(d) Review your life cover regularly – increase it to stay in line with your income and your family's needs should you die. If an indexation option is available, use it.

(e) If you have policies which were effected prior to March 1984, do not be easily persuaded to cease them or surrender them within the term – you may be receiving tax relief on the premiums. Policies taken out after that date do not qualify for tax relief.

(f) Take advice on putting policies in trust – it is possible to avoid inheritance tax and probate delays by doing so, but it needs to be done with great care.

(g) Get the right kind of policy – make sure it meets your needs now, and that there is sufficient flexibility for it to adapt to changes in your needs.

(h) Ask for waiver of premium – the extra cost is usually negligible, and the protection it affords is extremely valuable and reassuring.

INCOME PROTECTION

Why is it necessary?

I wonder how many of us bury our heads in the sand on this point. 'It will never happen to me' is a phrase which many long-term incapacitated people bitterly regret applying to themselves, as they recover slowly from illness or injury and wonder how to pay next month's bills. The bills continue, indeed they often increase, when you are ill and cannot work.

The long-term sick or disabled breadwinner is a huge financial burden when he or she can no longer earn but still has to be fed and cared for. Recent reductions in benefits paid by the Department of Social Security have rendered the provision of income protection a vital part of financial planning. Self-employed individuals in particular can obtain very little assistance from the state nowadays, and in point of fact they are the most vulnerable at times of incapacity – their income stops immediately they are unable to work. An employee often, but not always, has the security of knowing that income will continue for a few weeks or months.

In recent years, the protection of income has become more readily available from an increasing number of companies. The terms and conditions of policies may vary from company to company, but the basic concept is the same – to provide enough money to replace lost income and to enable survival through a potential financial disaster.

How does it work?

In some respects income protection is similar to term assurance: you pay a premium to provide an income in case you cannot work at some point within a specified term – just as with term assurance you are paying a premium to provide a benefit in case you die within a specified term. In both cases, you hope you won't need the benefit, and in both cases you get nothing back if you survive the term without needing to use it.

Income protection policies pay a regular income based on your earnings at the time you become unable to work – or on the income you have insured. You are not allowed to receive more than 75% of your pre-disability income, less any state benefit entitlement. For that reason, it is a waste of money to insure for more than you are earning. However, you should choose a policy which allows for premiums and cover to increase annually, so that your plan continues to stay in line with your income and with inflation.

Premiums are based on several factors which are additional to those applying to life assurances:
  (a) the amount of income required per week,
  (b) your age and sex,
  (c) your retirement age,
  (d) the deferred period you select,
  (e) whether or not you require the plan to be index-linked, and
  (f) your occupation and your state of health.

(a), (b) and (c) are self-explanatory, but (d) and (e) perhaps require some clarification.

Deferred period: The longer you can defer receiving your benefit following your incapacity the cheaper the premiums become. If you feel you could survive financially for, say, six months or more, it will cost you less to provide your required weekly income than if you wish the plan to begin paying you after only four weeks.

Indexation: If you want your chosen income to be index-linked, either when it begins to pay you, or from the time when you effect the policy, the premiums will be higher than if you simply ask for a set amount which will never change.

The additional provisions of policies such as these are not standard. There are those which will continue to provide you with an income after you go back to work if your incapacity is such that you cannot return to the profession for which you were trained and are forced into working for a lower income. There are those which will pay an income while you make a gradual return to work and are not yet able to earn your former income. Hospitalisation benefit can be provided, so that if you become an in-patient for a certain period your plan begins to pay you immediately, irrespective of the deferred period you have chosen. Important features to look for are how frequently the premiums are reviewed and whether they are likely to be increased in the future, and what changes, if any, might be imposed if you were to change your occupation, or became ill and then returned to a different occupation. It is possible to obtain cover which is guaranteed to remain in place without any increase in premiums, regardless of these factors, but many companies will impose an increase in premiums at specified regular reviews of the policy or on a change of occupation.

Income protection benefit ceases at normal retirement age and, even if you have made no claim during the policy's life, the policy also ceases at that time. It is rare for there to be any cash value at the end of the policy term.

CRITICAL ILLNESS PROTECTION

There has always been a great emphasis put upon the need to protect dependants in the event of an individual's death, and it is only in recent years that the need for capital at the time of serious illness or disability has been viewed as an important financial provision. Often referred to as 'dread disease' insurance, the objective of this type of policy is to provide a capital sum in the event that you contract one of a number of specified illnesses, such as cancer, kidney failure, or stroke. As a result of progress in medical science, people no longer necessarily die as a result of illnesses which were formerly fatal; many live for a number of years, but their illness may require major changes in lifestyle: perhaps stopping work altogether, reduced working hours, or changes in occupation. The result can be financially catastrophic. Even if an illness is diagnosed as terminal, there may be things for which money is required before death – the long-awaited holiday, perhaps. If the condition is not terminal, would it not be reassuring to know that the mortgage can be repaid and household outgoings reduced by that expense, at least?

A critical illness policy is designed to provide money while you are alive. It is a provision of a life assurance policy and is designed to pay out the sum assured 'early', on diagnosis of illnesses or conditions which the insurance company will define very specifically.

The amount of the sum assured should be determined by the anticipated need for capital, but many people choose to link it to their mortgage borrowing, on the basis that the mortgage will be repaid if they die – but what if they don't?

There is no restriction placed upon the way in which you use the capital.

MEDICAL INSURANCE

For many people, medical insurance is a valuable part of their protection. The advantages have been mentioned earlier in this chapter, and I believe few would argue against the convenience of choosing when and where you are treated, and the security of being able to have a non-urgent but extremely distressing condition dealt with quickly.

Depending upon the company you choose, medical insurance will provide a range of plans offering a variety of benefits. Costs will be determined according to the range of choice you require. The more facilities you want to cover – such as out-patient treatment, central London hospitals, dental or optical treatment and alternative medicine – the more expensive the cover becomes. Tax relief on premiums is available to those over the age of 60.

You may find that your policy is restricted if you have a pre-existing condition which could recur or which needs continual treatment. Alternatively, there are companies which will accept the pre-existing condition but will impose a higher premium.

It is normal to be able to include your entire family on one policy but, generally, children will be taken off the policy when they reach the age of twenty-one, usually with an offer of favourable terms by the provider if they maintain cover in their own right.

Medical insurance is frequently put at the bottom of the list of priorities, but it is certainly worth raising its status if a medical condition requiring surgery or regular treatment is likely to affect your career or earnings, or simply your availability for work at a particular time. What happens, for instance, if you are booked to appear in a concert and, two days beforehand, you receive your NHS letter saying 'A bed is available for you ... '? You have probably waited quite a long time for that operation. Do you choose the concert, the bed, or private medical care?

PENSIONS AND MORTGAGES

CHRISTINE NORMAN

Note: You should bear in mind that any reference to taxation is based on current legislation, and is subject to change in the future.

PENSIONS

Most people neglect pension planning until it is too late to provide themselves with a level of income which will maintain their pre-retirement standard of living. If financial commitments are such that only a very small monthly contribution can be made, it is still important to begin planning as early as possible. Even a very modest £20 per month then has many years in which to achieve investment growth from which an income can be derived to supplement the state pension to which you may be entitled.

It is quite likely that your financial needs will change when you retire, and a common excuse heard by most financial advisers is 'Oh well, I'll have paid off the mortgage by then, and the children will be grown up and self-sufficient'. But, even allowing for these factors, if you were to retire tomorrow, could you live on the current basic state pension and still maintain your present lifestyle? If you are employed, rather than self-employed, an additional pension, linked to previous earnings, would normally be payable by the state, but this will be steadily reduced if you are retiring after the year 2000, and you would still experience a significant drop in your income.

There are several types of pension scheme available, but the paragraphs which follow will only deal with those most commonly encountered – Final Salary Occupational Schemes and Personal Pension Plans. This chapter is intended to give an outline of the provisions of each, and further advice should be obtained before embarking on either.

Occupational pension schemes

Occupational schemes are provided by many employers for the benefit of their employees. Employees may be required to contribute a percentage of their annual salary to the scheme, but in some cases such contributions are made on a voluntary basis. They are not available to self-employed individuals. However, self-employed people who have salaried employees – and this can include their spouse – can effect such a scheme for those employees. The benefits of doing this are explained later in this chapter.

If you are an employee and have the opportunity to join an occupational scheme, it is almost certain that you should do so. It is only in rare and very exceptional circumstances that you should decline the opportunity. Occupational schemes make a 'promise' to provide a pension based on a fraction (often one-sixtieth or one-eightieth) of the employee's final remuneration for each year of service in that employment, up to a maximum of forty years. This is in contrast to a personal pension plan, where the benefits available at retirement age are based on the value of the fund which has accumulated as a result of your contributions.

The benefits which emerge from an occupational pension scheme at retirement age are restricted to a maximum of two-thirds of the employee's final pensionable salary. 'Pensionable salary' is not necessarily the actual salary paid in the final year of employment, but is usually based on an average of the salary paid in the last three years. As a result, the pension which becomes payable can be less than two-thirds of the actual salary paid in the last year of employment. Furthermore, if you change jobs frequently and accrue a 'basket' at retirement age, each of those pensions will be related to the salary you were earning when you left that scheme. Your total pension could, therefore, be substantially lower than two-thirds of your final salary. However, you are at least guaranteed to receive a pension when you reach retirement age, and recent legislation ensures that, even if you change jobs and leave an occupational scheme, the benefits must be 'revalued' by a certain percentage each year until retirement. A personal pension plan does not provide any guarantees, nor does it have to be revalued if you cease payments into it.

As an employee belonging to an occupational scheme, you are entitled to contribute money of your own, either to the main scheme, or to an Additional Voluntary Contribution Scheme operated by the employer, or to a separate Freestanding Additional Voluntary Scheme operated by a provider of your own choice. Contributions which you make will be eligible for tax relief at your highest rate of income tax, provided you do not exceed the Inland Revenue's contribution limits.

Contractual contributions Frequently, the scheme requires a contribution from the employee – commonly 5% or 6% of salary – which is deducted from monthly pay. The maximum contribution which can be paid into the scheme is 15% of your total remuneration, inclusive of any contractual contribution. Total remuneration is not just your salary; it includes any benefits to which you are entitled as part of your 'salary package' and on which you pay income tax (that is, your P11D benefits). However, you may not pay so much to the scheme that when you reach retirement age you would obtain more than the maximum two-thirds of salary as a pension.

Additional Voluntary Contributions (AVCs) Your employer must operate an additional voluntary contribution scheme into which you can pay money, by choice. Again, your contributions must not exceed 15% of your total remuneration, inclusive of any contractual contribution, and must not lead to a situation where you could provide for a greater pension than you are entitled to receive. The great advantage of using your employer's AVC scheme is that your employer is usually paying the charges made by the pension provider, and your contributions are thus used entirely for your pension. Investment choice may be restricted, however, and provisions for indexation in payments during retirement are not always the same as for the main scheme. You should investigate the scheme thoroughly before embarking upon it, particularly since joining the employer's AVC scheme means that you cannot also join a free-standing AVC scheme.

Freestanding Additional Voluntary Contributions (FSAVCs) These are offered by most pension providers, and enable you to choose where you invest your additional contributions. The same monetary restrictions apply. The main advantages of these are that you can remain with the same provider through-out your career and do not need to 'leave pensions behind' or constantly change providers as you change your job. You retain choices as to where your money is invested, how much you invest, the provision of indexation, and widow(er)'s pensions where appropriate. However, you also pay the charges imposed by the pension provider.

At retirement age, the main scheme will provide you with a retirement pension, as referred to above. You will also have the option to take a lower pension and have part of your fund paid to you as a tax-free lump sum. Again, this is restricted to 1½ x your final pensionable remuneration with a maximum limit (in 1995) of £150,000. AVC schemes, however, can only provide an income, and that income forms part of the calculation to reach the maximum two-thirds of final remuneration. It therefore follows that, if you are in employment where you are likely to obtain the maximum pension to which you are entitled, AVCs will not be a necessary part of your pension planning. However, if you change jobs from time to time, or there have been periods of time when you were not a member of a pension scheme, AVCs of one kind or another will be vital to you if you are to obtain a retirement pension which truly reflects the income you received prior to retirement.

Personal pension plans

These are available to anybody who has earnings from employment or self-em-ployment, and who is not a member of an occupational scheme in respect of those earnings. Whereas an occupational scheme restricts the amount of pension which may emerge at retirement, a personal pension plan restricts the amount which can be contributed and, at a certain level, also restricts the amount of income on which the contribution can be based.

In selecting your pension plan, you should be aware that, within the limits set by law, you may be offered a number of optional extras. Your plan must be capable of adapting to changes in your circumstances, and should therefore be flexible. Even if you do not need all the extras now, your plan should be capable of providing such things as a widow(er)'s pension on your death during retirement and, on your death prior to retirement, either a dependant's pension or a return of the value of the fund. You should be able to obtain an index-linked pension when you reach retirement. An Open Market Option should be avail-able. This will enable you to remove your accumulated fund from the provider with whom you have been saving and buy the pension (the 'compulsory annuity') from a provider who is, perhaps, offering a more favourable annuity rate. You should have the option to increase, decrease, stop and re-start contributions without penalty during the contribution period.

Prior to legislation which took effect in 1988, pension plans were referred to as Retirement Annuities or Section 226 Schemes. These older plans are now known as Section 620 Schemes and are no longer available to new members. The restrictions and provisions attaching to these schemes are substantially different from the newer personal pension plans and, on the basis that people who have an old scheme will be aware of its provisions, I outline below only the provisions relating to the newer schemes. I would, however, suggest that before changing from an old scheme to a new one you examine carefully the implications of each, and that you consult a professional adviser. The old schemes have many good points which are worth holding on to, even if circumstances suggest that an additional new scheme would be to your advantage.

Contributions The maximum percentage of taxable income which can be contributed in any one tax year to a personal pension plan depends upon the age of the individual. Until the age of thirty-six, up to 17½% of taxable earnings (referred to as net relevant earnings) can be paid, and this rises by degrees to a maximum of 40% of taxable earnings from the age of sixty-one. However, you may not take into account earnings in excess of £78,600 (1995-96), the 'earnings cap', which changes from time to time at the discretion of the Chancellor of the Exchequer.

Taxation Contributions attract tax relief at your highest rate of income tax. Self-employed individuals pay their contributions gross and reclaim the income tax against their personal tax bill at the end of the year. Employees, however, pay their contributions net of basic rate income tax, and the pension provider collects the tax relief from the Inland Revenue, crediting it to the pension. Any higher-rate tax relief is awarded through their tax coding.

Pension funds, except in very rare circumstances, are not subject to any UK taxation. Unlike the income and capital taxes imposed on other investments, the growth on pension contributions and any underlying dividend income which arises does not attract tax. This makes a pension an extremely tax-efficient method of saving for retirement because (a) the contributions attract tax relief, (b) part of the emerging fund can be tax free, and (c) all growth achieved is exempt from tax.

Apart from the tax-free cash sum, the pension benefit at retirement is taxed as earned income. It is added to any other taxable income, and tax is paid if that total income exceeds your personal allowances.

Benefits When you reach retirement age, the fund which your contributions and their investment growth have created must be used to provide an income, but up to 25% of the fund can be taken as a tax-free cash sum. Other benefits can be included in your policy, such as indexation and a widow(er)'s pension, but these will reduce still further the amount of income which you draw from the scheme initially.

Retirement Age Normally, retirement benefits from a personal pension plan can be taken at any age from fifty, but must be taken by age seventy-five. There are some professions, such as ballet dancing, where benefits can be taken considerably earlier. It is not necessary actually to retire in order to start drawing your benefits, and this can be a useful feature of personal pension plans, because it enables you to supplement your income as you grow older and, perhaps, are inclined to work fewer hours and earn less. Also, of course, and provided the total contributions do not exceed the Inland Revenue limits, it is possible to have more than one scheme, each with a different retirement age, so that your retirement can be phased over a period of time.

Spouse's pensions

Many self-employed individuals neglect this highly tax-efficient method of planning for retirement. It is well-known that a wife often undertakes work for her husband (or, of course, vice versa), typing, filing, answering the telephone, and generally assisting him in the development of his business or career. Part of a self-employed individual's income can therefore be paid to a spouse as salary. The popular way of calculating such part-time earnings is to ensure that they are below the level at which national insurance and income tax become payable, although this is not always the sensible route. In this way, a spouse earning £3,000 (at present rates) will have that income paid gross, with no tax liability and no national insurance contributions. Additionally, the payment of the salary is an allowable business expense, and so reduces the taxable income of the self-employed spouse.

Though some may have grasped the advantage of this and taken steps to implement it, many fail to take the exercise one stage further by providing their spouse with a pension. While there may be no real tax advantage for a husband or wife with no taxable earnings to contribute personally to a pension scheme, his or her spouse can gain a further advantage by making a contribution as an employer. There is thus another allowable business expense to set against gross earnings which, again, reduces taxable income. A further advantage is the fact that the spouse will receive a pension in their own right at retirement age, free of taxation if it is below the level of their personal allowance, and joint net income in retirement is substantially improved, in addition to tax efficiency during their working lives.

MORTGAGES

There are numerous sources for borrowing money to purchase your home, and several different methods of repaying the resulting loan. Few of us are in the happy position, when we first enter the property market, of being able to buy our homes outright and, if we ultimately want to own our homes, borrowing is the only solution.

When you borrow money, a lender requires interest to be paid on the loan.

The interest rate will fluctuate according to economic conditions but, in recent years, has been relatively low, with loans available at as low an interest rate as 4%. However, it is not so long ago that interest rates rose to 16% – and they could do so again.

Most lending sources offer a variety of 'packages'. For example, your interest rate could be fixed at a certain percentage for a specific period of time or it could be variable, rising and falling in line with rates generally.

A fixed interest rate is a good idea when interest rates are low: you know what your outgoings will be for a certain period of time and you also know that, even if interest rates generally rise, yours will not. Furthermore, most lenders will offer you their 'newest' fixed rate when your own reaches the end of its fixed term, so there is a good chance that you will always be paying slightly less than the variable rate. Fixed interest rates are not so good, though, when interest rates are high. It can be quite depressing if you have an interest rate fixed at 12% to watch the variable rate falling to 8% or, as happened to many people in recent years, as low as 6%.

A variable rate will, as its name suggests, vary up or down, probably several times during the period of your loan. You need to be fairly certain that, even if it rises, you will still be able to afford it.

'Low Start' rates were introduced a few years ago. They have a major advantage in that you begin paying your mortgage at a rate substantially lower than the norm and, over perhaps a five-year period, the rate increases annually, bringing it eventually into line with normal rates. These have been found to be a problem to many borrowers because the 'unpaid' interest in the early years is added to the mortgage loan and, in the short to medium term, you can find that you owe more on your property than it can be sold for. This problem has been seriously compounded by the fall in house values, and has added to the already serious 'negative equity' position in which many people have found themselves.

The interest you pay on up to £30,000 (1995) of your loan attracts income tax relief. This has been steadily reduced over the years and only 15% tax relief is given in the 1995-96 tax year. If your mortgage qualifies for the Mortgage Interest Relief at Source (MIRAS) Scheme, you will pay the interest net of basic-rate tax. Otherwise, tax relief will be allowed through your PAYE code number if your are employed, or as a deduction from your regular tax payments if you are self- employed.

Endowment mortgages

These are designed to provide funds to repay the amount of your loan at the end of a specified term – commonly 25 years. Throughout the term of the loan, interest is paid on the loan to the lender – and you always owe what you originally borrowed. In addition to the loan, an endowment life assurance policy is taken out for which you pay a monthly premium. The premium is calculated so that, at the end of the term of the loan, there should be enough money in the fund to repay the lender – and, if you die during the term, the mortgage is repaid by the endowment policy. In the recent past, this method of repaying a mortgage has been extremely popular.

Of late, there has been great concern that endowment policies are not always meeting their 'target fund' at the end of the mortgage term and, as a result, people have had to contribute more in premiums, or risk having a shortfall in the fund at the end of the term. Most companies now have in place a system whereby endowment policies are reviewed on a regular basis, and policyholders are advised immediately if the investment is not meeting the growth target required. Reviews are not that frequent in the early years, but policies are given far more intense examination in the later years. This is all very reassuring, but do bear in mind that there could come a time when you will have to increase your provisions for the repayment of the loan through additional savings of one kind or another. The final outcome can never be guaranteed, although it is always guaranteed that the sum assured will pay out if you die whilst the policy remains in force – provided, of course, that the premiums are up to date.

Should you find that your endowment policy is not meeting the required growth rate and that there could be a shortfall in the amount of money available at the maturity date, you should address the problem immediately. Try to identify how much extra is required to meet the loan. You are not obliged to increase and use the same endowment policy – with which, understandably, you may be a little disappointed. But from your own point of view it is important to put in place either another endowment policy, or a savings plan geared to producing the necessary sum of money. Remember that, should you die before the end of the mortgage term, the original endowment will pay out the sum assured – it is only the capital sum at maturity that needs to concern you.

Pension mortgages

The majority of mortgage lenders will accept part of your pension as security for a loan. As was explained above, some of your pension fund can be taken as tax-free cash, and that tax-free cash can be used for any purpose you choose, including repaying your mortgage (although the plan cannot be formally assigned to your lender). The lender will require you to maintain your pension contribution at a level which will provide enough tax-free cash to repay the loan. Often, they will require the loan to be no more than 80% of the anticipated tax-free cash, and will take into account only the lowest growth rate illustrated by the pension provider.

Because your pension will grow gradually during the period in which you are making contributions, it will not be capable of repaying the loan if you die in the early years. Therefore, you need life assurance in addition to the pension. This can be incorporated into the pension, or can be an entirely separate policy, but usually a term assurance policy is sufficient – and is the cheapest method of providing the protection required.

Occupational pension schemes cannot always be used in the same way as personal pension plans in conjunction with mortgages. Sometimes the rules of the scheme will not allow the life cover to be assigned to the lender, and details of the pension's tax-free cash element may be refused if the employer has designed the scheme in this way. This is understandable, in view of the fact that an employer who sets up a pension scheme is doing so in order to provide for his employees' retirements, not to buy their homes.

Pension mortgages have been popular, and can have their place in the overall scheme of things, but when considering this option do remember that you are compromising your retirement income, in that part of your pension fund will be used to repay the mortgage. For older people, the implications of this are much more serious because they have less time to replace that income.

A pension mortgage can be a useful and extremely tax-efficient method for younger people who wish to provide for a pension and buy a house, but cannot immediately afford to do both. As soon as possible, however, you should aim to change to a different method which will release your pension for the purpose it should be intended – your own use at retirement.

PEP (Personal Equity Plan) mortgages

The advent of Personal Equity Plans has opened up a new and extremely tax-efficient and flexible way of providing for the repayment of your mortgage.

As discussed in an earlier chapter, PEPs attract no tax liability whatsoever, either on the growth during the investment period or on the total fund when it is withdrawn. Most lenders will accept the undertaking of an individual to save into a PEP for the duration of their mortgage, gradually building a fund of money from which the mortgage will eventually be repaid. There are many advantages and possibilities arising from this method:

(a) The amount that you save *can* be varied to suit your budget. However, the amount that *needs* to be saved in order to meet the loan at the end of the mortgage period will be calculated for you, and will usually be based on a pre-determined assumed rate of growth. Most lenders will not allow you to assume that your PEP will grow at more than an average of 8% or 9% per annum. For example, if you are borrowing, say, £50,000, and require a mortgage term of twenty-five years, you must accumulate that amount in your PEP. At an annual growth rate of 8.5%, this would require a minimum regular payment of £63.20 per month into your PEP.

(b) The PEP remains your own and, should your circumstances allow it, there is nothing to stop you contributing more than the minimum to the plan or, indeed, adding single lump sums to it from time to time – provided you do not exceed the maximum limit in any one year. Because all or part of a PEP can be encashed at any time, it is possible to repay the mortgage – or part of it – earlier than planned, thus reducing your monthly interest payments. Look carefully at the provisions of the scheme, however, because some PEP providers have no initial charge, but impose charges on encashment within a specified period.

(c) Provided you do not have more than one PEP with any one provider in any one year, there is no reason why you should not spread your investment around a number of companies, giving you some diversity of investment.

With a PEP mortgage, interest is still paid to the mortgage lender, of course. You must also provide some protection in case you die before repaying the loan. In this case, you would require only a simple term assurance policy for the amount of the loan. In time, of course, the PEP will build up in value and eventually, when combined with the life assurance policy, will repay the mortgage on your death, leaving some capital available to your dependants.

Repayment mortgages

With this type of mortgage, the loan is actually repaid by the time you reach the end of the term. The payments you make to the lender are partly interest and partly repayment of capital. In the early years, practically all of your monthly payment will be interest but, as the capital loan is slowly reduced, so the interest element of your monthly payment reduces until, in the latter years, the capital being repaid is far greater than the interest.

Nowadays, when negative equity is a very real danger to many borrowers, a repayment loan could be viewed as the most appropriate. Even if, when you come to sell your property, you obtain a price which is lower than you paid, there is a greater chance that you will have built up a little equity in the property, and can handle the loss in value a little more easily, particularly if you have owned the property for a number of years.

Again, you will be required to have a life assurance policy of some kind in order to repay the borrowing if you die before the end of the term. This can be done either with a decreasing term assurance policy, a term assurance policy, or an endowment policy.

A decreasing term assurance policy will carry the same premium throughout the term and will be quite inexpensive. However, the sum assured will, as the name suggests, decrease during the period, so that if you die the amount paid out will always be roughly what you owe to the lender – very little near the end of the mortgage.

Term assurance will carry the same premium throughout the term and the sum assured will also be maintained. After a few years, therefore, you are also building in a little added protection for your dependants, because not all the sum assured will be required to repay the lender.

An endowment policy will guarantee to pay the sum assured (the amount originally borrowed) if you die during the term, and will also aim to match the borrowing by the end of the term, as described above. This could be viewed as a way of protecting your mortgage and also of saving a capital sum in the hope that you survive the term and can take the maturity value of the endowment. But, as commented earlier, there are better ways of saving.

Second homes and holiday homes

Some people are fortunate enough to be able to buy a second home – perhaps with a view to retiring to it, perhaps simply for holidays or for convenience.

If you have sufficient equity in your first home, or are earning enough to qualify for more borrowing than you currently have, it is possible to purchase more than one property on a mortgage. You will not be granted tax relief on your additional borrowing, even if the total amount remains below the £30,000 threshold and, if you sell the property, you may be liable to pay capital gains tax on any profit you make.

MAKING A WILL

CHRISTINE NORMAN

Whatever your financial circumstances, however little you own, it is vitally important that you make a will. If you die without a will, all your possessions will be distributed according to strict, inflexible laws, and will quite probably not be distributed in accordance with your wishes.

Without a will, the granting of probate can take months, sometimes years, resulting in trauma and hardship to your dependants.

Financial implications

Look at the financial implications of your death. Will there be an inheritance tax liability? Can you mitigate or provide for it in any way – perhaps by making use of the tax exempt 'nil rate band' on the first death, if you are married.

The 'nil rate band' is a portion of an individual's estate which is exempt from inheritance tax. If all assets are passed to a surviving spouse at the time of the first death, there is no inheritance tax liability but, equally, that exempt portion has not been used. By ensuring that assets up to the value of the nil rate band are *not* passed directly to the surviving spouse, but pass either to others or into a trust, the exemption is used at the first death and again at the second death. On 1995-96 tax rates, this can save as much as £61,600 in inheritance tax. Solicitors and financial advisers alike will be able to advise on this, and there are various trusts which can be created advantageously.

What should you include in a will?

If you wish to leave specific gifts to individuals, or amounts of money, shares or property, describe clearly and/or quantify the gifts, and name the individual(s).

List your insurance policies, bank accounts, and the names and addresses of anyone referred to in the will – this will help your executors deal with things quickly and efficiently.

If you have children under the age of eighteen, you should select a guardian.

Consider your funeral arrangements and stipulate things you particularly prefer – such burial or cremation.

Finally, and most importantly, sign the will and have it witnessed. It is not a legal document, and can be contested very easily, if it is unsigned.

Using a solicitor

A solicitor is clearly well qualified to help you. He is a professionally-trained individual who, simply by talking to you, can often identify a potential problem which needs to be overcome. He will know how to create a trust where necessary and, should you need him, he will usually act as a trustee or executor. Charges will vary according to the complexity of the will, and hence the amount of work involved, and also according to the status of the solicitor: a partner's charges, for example, will be higher than those for a junior member of his staff. Whatever the fee, it should be within the guidelines of the Law Society, to whom you can refer if you feel that charge is excessive.

Will-writing agencies

Professional will-writing agencies have emerged in recent years. Many have been started by solicitors who wish to concentrate on this element of their expertise; most have a qualified individual on the staff. They can do a similar job to that of a solicitor, but will often limit their work to estates with a maximum value. They will usually arrange for one of their representatives to take from you the details of what you wish to happen to your estate when you die. The representative will not necessarily be a qualified solicitor, however. He will then take your details away and they will be converted to a formal will. Efforts are now made to use as little legal jargon as possible, making the will simple to understand.

Do-it-yourself wills

It is possible to obtain a will form from various stationers, and to write your own will. This is not ideal, but it is better than nothing at all. The danger of a do-it-yourself will is that you will write it ambiguously, simply because you know what you mean and you assume that anyone reading it will interpret it in the same way. This is not always the case and, if there is any danger of your wishes being disputed (perhaps by an ex-wife or an estranged relative), it is even more important to have a will professionally drafted.

A note about witnesses

Finally, do remember that the witnesses to your will cannot also be beneficiaries under the terms of the will. They do not need to read the will, or to know its contents. They are required simply to witness your signature on each page of the document. They have no legal liability or rights whatsoever in witnessing your will.

FINANCIAL ADVICE, ADVISERS – AND YOU

CHRISTINE NORMAN

In a book of this nature, it is impossible to cover every aspect of the legislation surrounding the provision of financial advice and the manner in which financial advisers can operate. However, it is important that you understand the basic rules, which are there to protect you, and that you are aware of the steps that you can take to ensure that you are advised competently and in accordance with the regulations, and that you know your rights as an investor.

Regulations

Many years ago, it was possible for anybody to set up in business as an insurance broker. There were few, if any, rules governing their training, their ethics or their proven competence to provide advice to their clients. This led to a great deal of concern and, over a period of almost twenty years, a vast number of rules have been brought in which now attempt to protect individuals from 'bad advice', and to ensure that any advice they receive is appropriate. The background to the legislation is extremely complex, but it is now a criminal offence to offer investment advice unless the adviser has been properly authorised to do so under the terms of the Financial Services Act 1986 (FSA). Most investments, long-term insurance and pension contracts are regulated by the FSA, although there are a few exceptions. The Securities and Investment Board (SIB) oversees the operation of the FSA's requirements, and delegates its powers to various regulatory bodies which have to be approved. Those regulatory bodies then oversee the way in which their members operate in the investment market, carrying out regular checks to ensure that rules are not breached, and that certain minimum standards are met.

Authorisation

The authorisation of individuals who sell life assurance, pensions and investments depends on whether they are company representatives, tied agents or independent intermediaries, but in all cases they will have to have proved that they are competent, or 'fit and proper', to carry out their business.

Company representatives and tied agents will be authorised to sell only the products of one company. The company is authorised, and takes responsibility for the actions of the adviser, but must also take steps to ensure that the adviser is competent. Most advisers are self-employed people who are paid a commission on the products they sell, but there are some who are salaried employees, possibly receiving bonuses linked to the amount of business they do, but not necessarily relying totally on commission for their income.

An independent intermediary can sell the products of any company, but must obtain his own authorisation, thus, the individual companies whose products he sells are not responsible for his competence or his actions. An independent intermediary will either receive a commission from the companies whose product he sells, or he will charge a fee for the advice he provides.

All financial advisers are now required to offer what is referred to as 'best advice'. This means that they must recommend to you the most suitable type of product or contract for your needs. In the case of a company representative or tied agent, this must be a product from the range offered by the company for whom they work and, if the company does not have a suitable product, they must tell you that. An independent intermediary must offer you the most suitable product and the most suitable insurance company from which it can be obtained. He must also demonstrate that he does not place all his business with a very small number of providers, and must show the range of providers used and the percentages of business placed with them.

Dealing with the financial adviser's approach

We all receive mail and telephone calls from various individuals and financial institutions wanting to influence our choice of product or company, singing the praises of their own wares, asking us how we will survive in old age, how our dependants will survive if we die, whether our savings are really in the right place, and so on.

Telephone calls out of the blue are known as 'cold-calling'. There are very strict rules which govern how and when such calls should be made, and the information which must be given before any discussion takes place or an appointment is made. They must not be made at 'unsocial' hours, for example, unless invited. The caller must announce his name and the name of the company on whose behalf he is calling.

Unless the call happens to come at a time when you want to speak to an adviser, it can be irritating but, believe me, most advisers hate making those calls. They are performing what is only one aspect of their job – trying to obtain more clients for their company, and more business.

It is your *right* to reject them, or to listen to what they have to say. It is their *obligation* to terminate the call politely if you reject them. They are not allowed to sell you anything over the telephone – although they are allowed to explain why they want to visit you.

Insurance companies often have 'special offers' which run for a limited period, and a representative will use these as a means of gaining your interest. Don't discount them out of hand. They may be relevant to you and, even if they are not, they are rarely tricks, unlike the fabulous holidays or cars we find we have won but can only collect if we witness a demonstration of a particular product or attend a presentation evening. Even a special offer cannot be sold to you unless it can be demonstrated that you need it, want it, and can afford it.

Direct mail and advertising must also comply with strict rules concerning information which is provided or implied, the status of the company or representative, and an indication of the body which regulates them. In certain cases, such as unit trusts, it must make clear the fact that fluctuations up or down can occur in prices and income. If you respond to such advertising, it is likely that a call from a representative will follow unless you specify that you do not want one.

Choosing an adviser

Having concluded that you may have some gaps in your financial planning, it is always better to meet an adviser and sort out your problems properly, rather than to try to do it yourself and without any specialist help. Although insurance salesmen have had a great deal of bad publicity in recent years, a good adviser can be an extremely valuable contact. Despite the bad publicity, there are a vast number of people in the financial services industry who carry out an ethical and professional job, and who make every possible effort to give good, sound advice for the benefit of their clients. While you should be cautious in your choice of adviser, you should not necessarily assume that they are all driven by self-interest and greed. Most are not, and those who are are unlikely to survive for long in the current, highly-regulated environment in which they work.

So, how do you choose a good one? Often, the adviser will have been recommended to you by a friend or relative who has been impressed with the service they have received. You may simply choose a well-known company name and ask to see a local representative. Perhaps, as noted above, somebody happens to contact you at the right time.

The attitude and behaviour of the adviser will usually give a clue to their integrity and ability. If, on the first occasion that you meet them, they launch into a sales pitch without even trying to identify your needs, you can be fairly certain that they are not the person you want to deal with. Having arranged a meeting with you, a good adviser will usually confirm that meeting in writing, giving you a telephone number and address where he can be contacted if you wish to cancel the arrangement. When he arrives, he should offer you his business card and a note of the Terms of Business under which he works. This will explain to you whether he is a company representative, in which case he can advise on only the products of one company, or an independent intermediary, the parameters within which he and his company can operate, and the regulatory body under which they operate. If these things are not offered, ask for them.

You have every right to ask the adviser questions concerning his level of competence. Advisers are trained in a very structured way, learning and working with relatively easy contracts for a while, before moving on to the next level. It takes a considerable time to complete the training and, during that time, it is almost inevitable that a new or inexperienced adviser will stumble across a client with needs upon which he is not yet fully competent or licensed to advise. This does not mean that he is not a good adviser. What it should mean is that, when he next visits you to discuss your affairs, he will be accompanied by an adviser who is competent and qualified at that level, and who can make sure the advice is appropriate and that your questions are answered properly. There will be occasions when even a highly-experienced adviser will be accompanied by a senior manager. This is part of the way in which continuing competence is assessed, and does not mean that the adviser 'not good'. These are further built-in safeguards for you, and a product of the industry's determination to protect the consumer.

The meetings

The adviser's job involves a 'duty of care', and he needs to find out as much as possible about you, your aims and objectives, your existing financial situation, your needs and your investment philosophy. You have the right to refuse to provide that information but, if you do, you cannot blame the adviser if he gets it wrong! The process is effected by completion of a comprehensive questionnaire known as the 'fact find'. A good adviser will not usually make a recommendation at your first meeting, although he may offer some indication of what the advice might be. At the end of the meeting, the adviser will usually make an appointment to visit you again to present any recommendations he has to offer.

Apart from any shortfalls which you are aware of and which you may indicate as areas that you particularly want to deal with – your priorities – he will also make recommendations regarding other matters, if this seems appropriate.

By the time of your next meeting, the adviser will have examined the information given by you, and will have looked at the various ways of meeting your needs. He must then follow very strict guidelines in presenting the solutions:

(a) He must make sure that you understand the recommendations he is making and the type of contract he is suggesting.

(b) He must be able to explain the product, the costs and the risks, and must ensure that you are aware of the implication of cancelling, encashing or surrendering a long-term plan. These will also be available to you, in written form, in a brochure or 'product particulars' leaflet.

(c) He must give you what is known as a 'key features' document, which is a synopsis of the product, written in non-jargon terms. It must include details of the effect of the company's charges on your policy, and the cost of the advice you are receiving.

(d) Commission paid to an independent intermediary or the remuneration paid to a company representative must be disclosed. However, the costs shown for a company representative will also include the costs incurred by the company in providing their services, and the representative will not normally be receiving all that cost as a commission or salary.

Until you have seen the correct documents, you should not sign a proposal form or an application form.

Once you have agreed to proceed, and have completed the various application forms and any other relevant documents, the adviser will pass these to his company and, assuming that the company accepts that 'best advice' has been provided and the papers are in order, you will receive a 'reasons why' letter. This will explain why you have been sold that particular product or products, and will in effect summarise the recommendations which have been made to you. You will also be issued with a 'cancellation notice' explaining your statutory rights to cancel your application within the cooling off period, normally fourteen days.

Depending upon the status of your adviser – whether they are independent or not – and the type of business you are placing with them, some of the documentation may be slightly different but, in essence, they are all designed to achieve the same objective, that of ensuring that you, the client, are made fully aware of what you are undertaking, the risks and the costs involved.

If there is any aspect of the procedure about which you are unsure you must *ask questions.*

What do you do if it all goes wrong?

In simple terms, you complain. But before making a complaint you should consider exactly what you are complaining about. While it may be disappointing that an investment has not performed as well as you hoped, you do not really have a justifiable complaint unless you were made specific promises which have not materialised, or unless you believe you were wrongly advised.

You have every right to complain to the company's regulatory body, but it is better if, in the first instance, you complain to the company itself, preferably in writing. Your complaint will be investigated: every authorised company must have in place proper procedures for dealing with complaints, and they must offer prompt action to remedy the situation if your complaint is found to be justified. If they cannot provide a satisfactory remedy, they must advise you how to take your complaint further.

Compensation

Procedures which are now in place render it unlikely that investors will lose money as a result of negligence or fraud on the part of an adviser. An Investors' Compensation Scheme exists to protect people who suffer financial loss as a result of an authorised company's insolvency. Investors may claim specified amounts in such cases and, if the company has breached the rules and regulations of the regulatory body, damages can also be claimed.

This chapter can, of course, offer only the briefest outline of the legislative measures and codes of practice applying to the provision of financial advice. It is hoped, however, that sufficient guidance has been given to make you aware of how professional advisers should operate, and how you can recognise and avoid things that should not happen when you seek their advice.

INDEX

ALPAHABETICAL INDEX
OF ADVERTISERS